A Texas Ranger

A Texas Ranger, c. 1880

Courtesy Western History Collections,
University of Oklahoma, Norman

The Lakeside Classics

A TEXAS RANGER

By
N. A. Jennings

EDITED BY
BEN PROCTER

The Lakeside Press

R. R. DONNELLEY & SONS COMPANY

CHICAGO

Christmas, 1992

PUBLISHERS' PREFACE

THIS YEAR represents an anniversary of sorts for the *Lakeside Classics*. It is the ninetieth selection in what we believe to be the longest uninterrupted series of Americana.

The idea for a holiday book came in 1902 from T. E. Donnelley, son of the founder and president of the company, when he received a gift of straight-edge razors from a supplier of cutting instruments. The special appeal of the gift came from the fact that the blades were a product directly associated with the donor's business. T. E. thought it would be a fine thing if his company could provide something of similar character. He had for some time been advancing the thought that machine-made books could be produced at the same quality level and much more economically than the handmade books then preferred.

The project took root quickly and by December, 1903, the first *Lakeside Classic* had been produced and was ready to be distributed without charge to an ever-growing group that has always been known as "friends and employees of the company."

It seems appropriate at this milestone to reprint part of the 1903 Publishers' Preface:

> This little volume goes forth as a modest protest against the craze for so-called "Editions de Luxe"— books printed in unreadable type, on handmade

paper, on hand presses, and sold at prices prohibitory to all except the rich. Such books may have their places in the collection of the dilettante, or on the shelves of those who affect a love for fine books, and thus attempt to convey an impression of literary culture. But to fulfill its grand mission of giving and preserving to the world the great thoughts of men and women, a book must be within reach of that world. To return in the name of art to the costly and elaborate antique methods of performing by hand what can be cheaply and better performed by machines seems a crime against progress.

In opposition to these attempts, this volume stands for the machine-made book. Its paper, its typesetting, its presswork, and its binding all are the product of the very latest labor-saving machines. It aims to be readable rather than eccentric, plain rather than decorative, tasteful rather than unique, useful rather than useless; withal, to hold to all the essence of the art of the old masters of bookmaking, and not to copy the mechanical shortcomings which they themselves strove so hard to overcome.

If, in a modest way, this volume conveys the idea that machine-made books are not a crime against art; that books may be plain but good, and good though not costly, its mission has been accomplished.

Ninety years later, the machine-made book has won worldwide acceptance from publishers in every market. And, the *Lakeside Classics* series has grown in popularity as it has in longevity. With only a few exceptions this series highlights firsthand accounts by individuals who were in some way involved in important events associated with the building of the United States.

Our selection this year is *A Texas Ranger*, the story of a famous Texas Ranger company under the leadership of the legendary Captain Lee McNelly, who did so much to bring peace to south Texas in the decades of the 1870s and '80s. The author, Napoleon Augustus Jennings, was a well-educated son of a well-to-do Philadelphia family who became obsessed with the prospect of finding his fortune in Texas, but ended up as a Ranger private under McNelly during this most difficult period in the histories of Texas and Mexico.

To serve as editor for our reprinting of Jennings' story we called upon Ben Procter, Ph.D., long-time professor of history at Texas Christian University in Fort Worth. Dr. Procter is an expert on history of the southwest, and has recently won acclaim for his book, *Just One Riot, Episodes of the Texas Rangers in the 20th Century*, published in 1991 by Eakin Press in Austin.

His Prologue begins by describing the dire conditions that prevailed in Texas following the capitulation of the Confederacy, and the similar conditions that existed in northern Mexico, which could be traced back to the war with America, the loss of Texas, and the rash of revolutionary governments. Lawlessness was rampant on both sides of the Rio Grande, and settlers and ranchers suffered incredible depredations. When Texans were finally able to return to self-government, Ranger forces were organized and given the mission to defeat the outlaws of three cultures—the American desperado, the Indian rogue warrior, and the Mexican bandit.

Jennings' text relates events as seen through the eyes of a private, while Procter's work takes us behind the scenes for the larger picture. We believe you will enjoy his insights and we warmly welcome him to our list of distinguished editors.

Again, it was our good fortune to find a sizable number of illustrations to enhance the story. Many historical repositories in Texas and Oklahoma allowed us to use pictorial material from their archives. These, plus photographs from the Library of Congress and the National Archives, are most appreciated. We also wish to point out that we have replaced the "outline titles" used in the first edition with single-thought chapter titles, and have made modest text editing without changing the meaning or the author's style.

Traditionally, this series showcases our ability to produce a top-quality book using latest equipment and technology. Text is generated electronically by Donnelley Database Technology Services in Willowbrook, Illinois, and sent on disk to our book manufacturing plant in Crawfordsville, Indiana. There the digital information is electronically imposed in page format and paginated sequence on film that is pre-sized to actual press forms. From this single piece of film, press plates are prepared. Crawfordsville's new pre-press center also electronically scans the furnished illustrative materials. Printed signatures from high-speed, narrow web offset presses are gathered and Smythe sewn. After trimming and gilding, the case is affixed and the finished books pass through a final quality check before automatic cartoning, labeling, and shipping.

This year's map is an excellent example of our customized cartographic capabilities. Please note the south Texas counties reflect the geographical boundaries of the 1870s. The county names shown in boldface type are those mentioned in the text.

Last year we converted to recycled paper stock that possesses the same color shading and manufacturing characteristics as in the stock previously used.

This second portion of the preface is usually reserved for an informal updating of the company's progress in the year just ending. Unfortunately, we begin on a note of sadness by repeating the news so many of you already know: On Easter Sunday, April 19, Gaylord Donnelley, the eldest member of the R. R. Donnelley family, died in his sleep at his South Carolina vacation home. As President and later as Chairman of the Board (1952–75), Gay was a key member of the visionary management team that prepared us to face the challenges of the late twentieth century. He left us with a legacy of quality and a tradition of service. He had an uncompromising commitment to the highest standards and devoted his energy to company business and to lifelong interests in conservation and philanthropy.

Those values will long continue to guide us as we strengthen our business relationships.

One measure of our success is demonstrated by our financial performance in 1992. Both sales and net income set new records, despite a difficult economy. Cash flow from operations—the lifeblood of all business—also continued to grow and was used, in part, to fund a large, ongoing capital investment program. We again increased our dividend to shareholders, something we've done each year since 1971, and, in September, we split our outstanding stock two-for-one, our sixth stock split since we became a public company in 1956. Reflecting our strong performance in 1992, the price of our common stock achieved several all-time highs.

Earlier this year, a pair of important events— one on this continent, one in Europe—initiated a time of change and growth. We acquired Laboratorio Lito Color, S.A. de C.V., an established printer of catalogs, promotional materials and magazines, with operations in Mexico City and San Juan del Rio, ninety miles to the northwest. This represents our first operation devoted solely to serving Mexico's domestic publishing and merchandising businesses.

Also, in March, R. R. Donnelley (UK) Ltd., our London-based financial printing subsidiary, entered into a joint venture with Pindar Graphics London to provide desktop publishing, multilingual digital composition, and printing. This alliance adds to our ability to serve financial customers globally.

Our computer documentation business continues to show impressive growth. In May, we purchased Professional Lithographers, Inc. (PROLITHO), of Provo, Utah, a provider of prepress, web and sheetfed printing, quality finishing and distribution services. As U.S. software publishers "go global," we are committed to meeting their needs from start to finish in the publishing cycle. Last July, for example, we opened a full-service facility at Apeldoorn, The Netherlands, our first in continental Europe, and in September another operation was opened in Cumbernauld, Scotland, to serve multinational computer and consumer electronics companies located in Scotland. Many specialty services like kitting and assembly, diskette replication and labeling, multicurrency transaction processing, a European toll-free telephone network, multilingual telephone fulfillment, procurement management of computer accessories, computerized inventory management, and warehousing will be offered in both locations. In addition, to serve this growing business we opened two new sales offices—one in The Hague and one in Livingston, Scotland.

Our other businesses were equally active this past year. In October, we increased our presence in trade magazines with the acquisition of Combined Communication Services (CCS) of Lisle, Illinois, one of the ten largest trade magazine printers in the United States. We also signed a long-term contract with Gannett for its West Coast version of

USA Weekend. Our Casa Grande Division will produce more than three million copies of the publication weekly starting January 1993. Other new titles in 1992 include *Golf Magazine* and *Bon Appetit.*

We continued to expand our relationships in the telecommunication area. This year, as part of a ten-year contract extension, NYNEX, the regional Bell operating company in the Northeast and a longstanding customer, awarded us all their directory printing starting in January 1994.

For Mediatel, a partnership between NYNEX and the Czechoslovakian national phone company, we printed more than 600,000 Prague directories, in our Ben Johnson/U.K. plants. Our Ben Johnson facilities also manufactured directories for Dutch PTT, The Netherlands' national telephone company, covering Curaçao, Netherlands Antilles.

Many telephone companies outside the United States are exploring ways to add value to their directories for both the advertiser and the consumer. This year, TelMex, Mexico's national telephone company, added special two-color advertising in three major markets. Under an agreement signed this year, our Norwest/Greeley plant will print those directories.

In still another business segment, we were awarded a major long-term contract to produce free-standing inserts for News America, the American operating unit of Rupert Murdoch's News Corp.

1992 was also noteworthy because we produced

the largest financial printing order ever. It was a five-million copy, 350-page policyholder documentation for Equitable Life Assurance Society. Five of our financial printing divisions combined their skills to complete this project.

One of our new business units produced another high-profile job. Intervisual Communications, Inc., designed an unusual dimensional insert for Major League Baseball's All-Star Game program. It featured a pop-up catcher's mitt holding a collector's baseball card and a musical chip that played "Take Me Out to the Ballgame," a good example of an added value to give our customer a competitive edge.

Late in the year, we announced the formation of ViewPoint Information Systems, an organization to provide important component information to the semiconductor and electronic design industries, major customer segments for us. VIS electronically transfers component information from suppliers to product design engineers in machine-readable format, saving time and increasing productivity.

Compact disc technology continues to manifest itself in an ever widening variety of applications. By utilizing its memory in "read only" format— known familiarly as CD-ROM—a growing number of customers have used our experience to find new business extensions with this medium.

For example, our Database Technology Services (DTS) unit has formed an alliance with Compton's NewMedia to produce Compton's SmarTrieve®

Publishing Toolkit software using CD-ROM. The Toolkit includes indexing and text search software to create interactive books and reference sources in multiple media: print, on-line, and magnetic and optical disk formats. DTS also prepared data and produced an electronic CD-ROM catalog for SunSoft, a subsidiary of Sun Microsystems.

We participated in two CD-ROM applications with NYNEX during the year. First, we helped create a consumer electronic directory on CD-ROM that integrates the Boston-area NYNEX White and Yellow Pages with maps to provide consumer travel information. Also, through a strategic alliance between our Metromail subsidiary and NYNEX Information Technologies we have jointly introduced a national search directory on CD-ROM. This new product is MetroSearch®, a comprehensive, nine-volume set of CD-ROMs with more than 77 million national listings—an up-to-date database for looking up phone numbers via a personal computer.

Our subsidiary, R. R. Donnelley Japan, K.K., signed an agreement with Nippon Shinpan Co., Japan's largest issuer of credit cards, to market our American Showcase™/Japan program, the direct mail "catalog of catalogs" that features American products. The agreement gives us access to Nippon Shinpan's database of credit card holders, affording us the highest-quality demographic information available for targeting information to consumers.

Our GeoSystems unit acquired the map data and

software assets of GeoSoft Corporation. We can now provide our customers with sophisticated map databases used in touch-screen travel directions, the so-called address-to-address routing. GeoLocate Plus™, a PC-based electronic directory and locator system available on CD-ROM, recently came on stream. It features unique locating, routing, and digital mapping capabilities. Now in operation at *Official Airline Guide* is our electronic version of GeoLocate™ for travel publishers. In this application, *OAG* uses our proprietary map data to create and keep up-to-date travel directories.

We joined with Apple Computer in a strategic business relationship to provide digital publishing services for Apple's Personal Interactive Electronics (PIE) division. Initially, GeoSystems will provide travel-based applications for Apple's handheld computers that will allow users to locate restaurants, sights to see and other travel information on a map and get accurate directions from any starting point.

Over the past year, we said farewell to valued friends. Jack Schwemm retired from our Board of Directors after a distinguished career with the company: President, 1981–87, Chairman of the Board, 1983–89, and as a Director since his retirement in 1989. During his 24 years of service, Jack encouraged the company's shift to a long-term strategy of acquisitions and diversification into new printing and information-processing technologies, reinforcing our position as an industry leader. Also retiring from the board is G. Morris Dorrance, Jr., who has served us well as a Director since 1967, especially as the long time chairman of the finance committee of the board.

In June, the company was forced from its corporate headquarters on Chicago's near South Side to make room for an expansion of McCormick Place. Our new address is 77 W. Wacker Drive in downtown Chicago. And, because we are a major tenant, the building is known as the R. R. Donnelley Building. Included in our new headquarters is the Gaylord Donnelley Library, a two-story, wood-paneled repository of products produced by our company. Included are nineteenth century hand-bound books and directories, early twentieth century catalogs and magazines, and late twentieth century examples of our newest digital and electronic products.

As 1993 comes into view, it is appropriate to reaffirm the standards that have guided us for the past 128 years. Quality, service, innovation, and industry leadership have always been best exemplified through our dedicated employees. To them, and to our valued customers, trusted suppliers, friends, and neighbors, we express our gratitude for a year of solid accomplishment. We extend to all of you our best wishes for the Season and the New Year.

THE PUBLISHERS

Christmas, 1992

CONTENTS

List of Illustrations xxi
Prologue. xxiii
   I. I Arrive in Texas 3
  II. Down to the Border 15
 III. From Clerk to Deputy Marshal . . . 35
 IV. An Unpopular Chief of Police . . . 49
  V. I Join the Revolutionists 67
 VI. I Meet McNelly and Join Up . . . 81
 VII. Ranger Work 95
VIII. My Fellow Rangers 113
 IX. Our Fight with Espiñoso 133
  X. Jesus Sandobal Becomes a Ranger . . 151
 XI. Across the Rio Grande. 169
 XII. McNelly's Ultimatum 195
XIII. A Quiet Border 217
XIV. The Capture of King Fisher 227
 XV. Lieutenant Hall Arrives 243
XVI. The Fight at Lake Espantoso . . . 255
XVII. A Threatened Ambush 267
XVIII. The Sutton-Taylor Feud 281
XIX. Catching Famous Desperadoes . . . 301
 XX. Proud to Have Been a Ranger . . . 319
Epilogue 331
Index 335
List of The Lakeside Classics 349

ILLUSTRATIONS

A Texas Ranger, c. 1880 . . . . . *Frontispiece*

Richard King xxix

Mifflin Kenedy xxix

Governor Richard Coke xxxix

Lieutenant Governor R. B. Hubbard . . xxxix

Secretary of State William H. Seward . . liii

General John M. Schofield liii

Secretary of State Hamilton Fish lvii

General William Tecumseh Sherman . . lvii

Colonel Ranald S. Mackenzie lvii

President Benito Juarez lxiii

Map: *Where Al Jennings Rode
    with the Texas Rangers* lxix

San Antonio, Eastside Main Plaza, c. 1870 . . 7

Laredo, Main Street, c. 1870 27

Laredo Transfer Company Office 27

General Porfirio Diaz 55

President Sebastian Lerdo 55

Major Henry C. Merriam 59

Ranger Captain Leander H. McNelly . . 83

Ranger Camp, c. 1878 97

Ranger Major John B. Jones 103

Governor Edmund J. Davis 107

Brigadier General Thomas Green . . . 115

McNelly's Ranger Company 123

Ranger Sergeant John B. Armstrong . . . 129

Martin S. Culver 137

Cattle Raid on the Texas-Mexico Border . . 141

General Juan N. Cortina 147

Brownsville, Texas Riverfront and Ferryboat
to Matamoros, Mexico, c. 1880 153

Ringgold Barracks, c. 1870 161

President Ulysses S. Grant 177

Secretary of War William W. Belknap . . . 177

Corrals at Rancho de Las Cuevas 187

Restored Home of Juan Flores at
Rancho de Las Cuevas 187

Mexican Rurales 191

Captain S. B. M. Young 197

Colonel Joseph H. Potter 197

Fort Brown on the Rio Grande 201

John King Fisher 229

Ranger Lieutenant Jesse Lee Hall 247

A Mexican *Jacal* 269

Pitkin Taylor and Wife Susan 287

Judge Henry Clay Pleasants 291

John Wesley Hardin 311

PROLOGUE

IN MID-JUNE, 1865, although the Confederacy had capitulated two months earlier and organized military resistance had ended, not one Union soldier was on Texas soil. Yet the ravages of war and the humiliation of defeat were readily apparent. The state government was bankrupt, the economy in ruins, and more than one-fourth of the male population dead or conspicuously absent. Confederate leaders, such as Governor Pendleton Murrah and Generals John Magruder, Joseph Shelby, and Kirby Smith, were seeking refuge with Emperor Maximilian in Mexico. Everywhere, it seemed, lawlessness prevailed. Confederate deserters pillaged government commissary depots and arsenals; mobs of civilians decided to "get theirs" by doing the same to privately owned stores and warehouses; and a band of renegades looted the state treasury in Austin. Then on June 19, Union General Gordon Granger arrived in Galveston with eighteen hundred troops, while soon thereafter two additional detachments marched overland from Louisiana. Texas was now under military rule.[1]

[1] See C. W. Ramsdell, *Reconstruction in Texas* (New York: Columbia University Press, 1910); T. R. Fehrenbach, *Lone Star: A History of Texas and the Texans* (New York: The MacMillan Company, 1968), pp. 393–408; Robert A. Calvert and Arnoldo De Leon, *The History of Texas* (Arlington Heights, IL.: Harlan Davidson, Inc., 1990), pp. 127–29.

But a majority of Texans, residing mainly in east Texas, along the Gulf Coast, and as far west as San Antonio, were concerned about conducting their government in a lawful and orderly manner—and therein lay the problem. Texas was a land—always there was the land—of huge proportions. Over half of the state was a frontier, with few trees and a scarcity of water, a desert of cactus and tumbleweed or a brush-country area of mesquite and chaparral. Even in the more habitable sections of the state, mainly east of the Balcones Escarpment,[2] much of the populace had little or no connection with the outside world. In other words, nearly all Texans were isolated and living in an agrarian setting of double log cabins with dirt floors and stick-and-mud fireplaces, with fields of cotton and corn all around. Transportation and communication were abysmal. Although steamboats linked a few inland towns to the Gulf Coast, railroads had not as yet progressed, except near Houston; only a few stage lines were in operation; rivers oftentimes had to be forded because of the few bridges; and roads were, at best, "rutted washboards in dry weather and boggy mires when it rained."[3]

[2]The Balcones Escarpment is a geologic fault zone which divides west Texas from south and east Texas. In postbellum Texas the westernmost line of settlement stretched along the escarpment from Fort Worth to Austin to San Antonio to Del Rio.

[3]Seymour V. Connor, *Texas: A History* (Arlington Heights, IL.: AHM Publishing Corporation, 1971), pp. 176, 178–82.

To regain control of their way of life, Texans worked to rid themselves of the military. But during the next eighteen months they negated such a possibility by their actions. In July, 1865, Andrew Jackson Hamilton, a former congressman from Texas and a Unionist, arrived as provisional governor, his express instructions being those of restoring the state to the Union. Most Texans, although declaring secession null and void, repudiating the Confederate war debt, and confirming that slavery and involuntary servitude were illegal, stubbornly resisted the many attempts at reconciliation. For governor, in the summer of 1866, they selected James W. Throckmorton over the Hamilton nominee, ex-Governor Elisha M. Pease, while at the same time returning former Confederates to Congress. The legislature then enacted "black codes," which seriously hampered the rights of the freedmen. And, at every turn, they resisted the army of occupation, with townspeople ostracizing the soldiers in blue and armed bands of men in the surrounding countryside waging guerrilla warfare against Union supply trains and military details. Nor did the freedmen escape Texan wrath. Racial hatred and bigotry bred violence. Typical of the times was an occurrence in Grayson County (near the Red River), where a racist white mob arbitrarily murdered three blacks.

The Radical Republicans in Washington, headed by Speaker of the House Thaddeus Stevens of

Pennsylvania and Senate Majority Leader Charles Sumner of Massachusetts, were not about to allow such conduct to continue in Texas or, for that matter, in any Confederate state. Hence, on March 2, 1867, Congress began "reconstructing" the South by replacing the popularly elected governments with military commanders, requiring the establishment of new state constitutions which guaranteed black suffrage, and demanding the passage of the Fourteenth Amendment which disfranchised any person who had engaged in "insurrection or rebellion against the United States." The Radicals both in Washington and Austin, and at times with the help of the military, thus controlled the political destiny of Texas. Earlier in 1869 state Republicans adopted a new constitution and in the ensuing election (November 30 to December 3) chose Edmund J. Davis as governor.

During the next four years many Anglo-Texans, who had fought for the Confederacy, suffered under "carpetbag rule." Governor Davis, with the legislature reflecting his program, sustained his position against the majority with a series of pertinent laws. To enforce his authority, two acts were passed—one created a state police and the other a militia, both of which were under the governor's direct control. At his discretion, Davis could also declare martial law, thereby sending armed troops anywhere in the state to restore order as well as to deal with opponents. To allow his administration time to solidify its posi-

tion, another act empowered the governor to post-
pone congressional elections for two years (as late
as November, 1872), while still another authorized
him to fill all vacancies, which amounted to more
than eight thousand appointments during his four-
year term. And to present a favorable picture to the
public, the governor could designate any newspaper as the state printer and have it publish "the official record" of events.

Texans reacted defiantly to such arbitrary powers. Lawlessness was rampant, with the State Police
partly to blame. Governor Davis's men, although
both necessary as well as effective on any number of
occasions, aroused fierce indignation and flagrant
disrespect for the law. At times, various members
of the force disrupted Democratic Party meetings,
altered elections by stuffing ballot boxes, entered
private homes without search warrants, and falsely
arrested opponents, while allowing personal friends
to escape from prison. Whether to their credit or
not, they also enforced martial law on four separate
occasions and quelled riots in several communities.
In fact, during their brief three-year tenure, they arrested more than seven thousand outlaws, of which
thirteen hundred were charged with murder or attempted murder.

Yet this rise of violence did not rest solely on the
State Police; other factors were also responsible. As
early as 1867, an Illinois cattle buyer named Joseph
G. McCoy decided to extend a branch of the Union

Pacific Railroad to the small Kansas village of Abilene. Thus, for the next twenty years, the "long drive" north from the Rio Grande and Nueces River took place. Cowboys and their lieges—respected cattlemen like Richard King and Mifflin Kenedy, as well as dangerous, flamboyant rogues like King Fisher and Shanghai Pierce—drove "ornery" Longhorns nine hundred miles along the Chisholm Trail (and later the Goodnight-Loving and Western trails) so that beef-loving Easterners could be fed.[4] This era of the last Cattle Kingdom not only attracted men who realized the possibility of great wealth, but also sycophants who wished to profit therefrom. As a result, a kind of cultural feudalism emerged, composed of hardy, independent, free-spirited individuals, imbued with a certain lawlessness and often bereft of many societal norms. These cowboys, in turn, encountered another culture in driving their herds through the Indian Territory to Kansas. The Comanche and Kiowa, "lords of the Plains," also had to be reckoned with. Texans were forever encroaching upon their tribal haunts and hunting grounds. The cattlemen caused some alarm by such "invasions," but they were merely crossing the land. More threatening were the land-hungry Americans—unromantic, sod-busting farmers—who

[4]See E. C. "Teddy Blue" Abbott and Helena Huntington Smith, *We Pointed Them North: Recollections of a Cowpuncher*, ed. by Ron Tyler (Chicago: The Lakeside Press, 1991), for an excellent account of the "long drive" and life on the trail.

Richard King

Courtesy Archives Division,
Texas State Library, Austin

Mifflin Kenedy

Courtesy Barker Texas History Center,
The University of Texas at Austin

began arriving in increasing numbers early in the 1870s because of generous homestead exemptions, tenacious in their goal to change the land and tame it for cultivation. Hence, on the northwestern Texas frontier, violence was a growing, seemingly natural commodity, with horse-stealing and depredations on one side and equally brutal retaliation on the other. Added to all these ingredients were the Texans themselves, provincial by circumstance and violent by nature because of a frontier environment, where the use of pistols defended individual honor and settled personal differences. Consequently, in many areas of the state, bloody feuds—the Sutton-Taylor Feud in DeWitt County being the most prominent—periodically occurred, terrorizing the populace and often rendering helpless the existing law enforcement agencies. Not surprisingly, lone gunfighters, the likes of John Wesley Hardin, Bill Longley, Ben Thompson, King Fisher, and Sam Bass, emerged as folk heroes, admired and eulogized, even though ruthless killers.

But in south Texas, from Corpus Christi to the Rio Grande and then up the river to Laredo and Eagle Pass, violence took on a different hue, one of ethnicity and hatred and discrimination. In the years following the Texas Revolution (1836) and the Mexican War (1846-1848) Texans reviled their former rulers, continually remembering the cruel circumstances surrounding the battle of the Alamo and the ruthless execution of 350 men at Goliad.

Nor would their bitterness subside throughout the decades. Texans would not distinguish between Mexican nationals and Tejanos (Texans of Hispanic origin). They thus used the courts against them as an instrument of property dispossession, as an exaction for misdeeds by their ancestors. And if protests or resistance occurred, the "man who might shoot an Indian or Mexican," author T. R. Fehrenbach noted, "even on dubious grounds, was not a criminal"—at least in the eyes of Anglo-Texans.[5]

Hence, on the Mexican side of the Rio Grande all the way from Matamoros (opposite Brownsville) to Piedras Negras (opposite Eagle Pass) lived an unsettled population that nurtured an enduring hatred for Texans, that needed little or no excuse to inflict physical hurt or monetary loss upon them—and they surely did. Their leader was Juan Nepomuceno "Cheno" Cortina, whose bitterness toward Texans stemmed partly from the fact that Texas courts had refused to recognize some of his family's ancient Spanish land titles, thereby depriving him of his inheritance. Then, at Brownsville in July, 1859, he had confronted the town bully, City Marshal Robert Shears, for brutally beating a defenseless Mexican laborer and, in the ensuing quarrel, had shot him in the shoulder. In September he returned to Brownsville with one hundred armed men, released all prisoners from jail, hoisted the Mexican flag over the federal post at Fort Brown, and executed three

[5]Fehrenbach, *Lone Star*, pp. 562–64.

Americans who were "notorious for their misdeeds among the [Mexican] people." Over the next year, in the so-called Cortina War, he became a hero to his people, but an infamous brigand—"the red robber of the Rio Grande"—to Texans. During the Civil War his legend continued to grow; by 1864, in the eastern state of Tamaulipas, he proclaimed himself governor and commandant general, which positions he maintained until March, 1866. Then Cortina, together with General Juan Flores of the Mexican army, encouraged rustlers and brigands to continue their illegal activities with impunity for the next decade. Consequently, the business of contraband goods and stolen property flourished in a protected zone from Matamoros to Vera Cruz.

Because of such blatant lawlessness, Texans suffered terrible losses in the Rio Grande-Nueces River region (the so-called Nueces Strip). From 1869 to 1874 Mexican bandits, together with ex-Confederate cohorts, stole an estimated nine hundred thousand head of cattle, a minimum of five thousand a month. The King Ranch alone, although protected by numerous armed vaqueros, claimed that 33,827 cattle were rustled during a three-year period. From such activities involving hides and stolen cattle, "Cheno" Cortina reportedly had deposited three hundred thousand dollars in an English bank and still had enough Texas cattle to stock four large ranchos. To add to this epidemic of lawlessness, the raiders slaughtered anyone who opposed them, murdering an estimated two thousand ranchers and citizens, both Anglo and Tejano. Towns became isolated outposts in this sea of violence, with citizens venturing into the country only under armed escort. And the marauders, if faced by U.S. troops or state lawmen, crossed the Rio Grande to the protective sanctuary of Mexico.

Because of state protests and innumerable individual complaints, the United States Congress was finally prompted to act. On May 7, 1872, it appropriated six thousand dollars for a three-man commission, composed of Richard H. Savage, Thomas P. Robb and J. J. Mead, to investigate the Texas-Mexico border problems. Armed with instructions to interrogate witnesses and interview state officials, then recommend appropriate action, the Robb Commission proceeded immediately to the Rio Grande, where for some two months it toured the Nueces Strip, from Corpus Christi to Port Isabel and Brownsville to Del Rio. It received 132 petitions for punitive damages and 354 supporting depositions. In all, Texans estimated their losses at an inflated figure of $25,049,722, which included both damages and interest.[6]

[6]See U.S. Congress, House of Representatives, *Depredations on the Frontiers of Texas*, 42d Cong., 3d Sess., House Exec. Doc. No. 39, Serial 1565 (Washington, 1872), for Robb Commission findings. See Michael Gordon Webster, "Texan Manifest Destiny and the Mexican Border Conflict, 1865–1880," Ph.D. dissertation, Indiana University, Bloomington, IN, 1972.

The Robb Commission, by accepting testimony without any questions, reflected the prejudices of Texans. In fact, the three commissioners agreed that the preponderance of evidence was not just over-whelming, but damning and reprehensible. They thus presented a distressing picture of banditry as well as a stinging indictment against the Mexican government. With increasing frequency and "aston-ishing boldness," the report stated, armed banditti had attacked south Texas communities and ranches, probing as far north as Corpus Christi. These raids went unpunished because the invaders, upon en-countering opposition, quickly fled back across the Rio Grande, where the "corrupt" officials of Tamau-lipas, under the iron-fisted control of General Juan Cortina, not only protected them but shared in their profits. The commissioners therefore recom-mended that the United States should deploy suf-ficient cavalry into frontier forts "to enforce law and protect life and property on the Rio Grande"—but they stopped short of suggesting punitive mili-tary incursions.[7]

The Mexican government officials, however, were not about to let such charges go unanswered; there-fore, in 1873, they established a probe of their own concerning border disturbances. Not too surprising-ly, their conclusions completely refuted the Robb

[7]U.S. Congress, House, *Depredations on the Frontiers of Texas*, Serial 1565, p. 40; Webster, "Texan Manifest Desti-ny," p. 84.

Commission findings. They found no proof of the charges leveled at Cortina. They flatly rejected the assertion that large-scale cattle rustling had taken place; instead, they pointed out that Texas stock-raisers—for example, in Cameron County—had assessed their losses four to five times greater so they could avoid state taxes; hence, the commissioners determined: "Either they [the stockraisers] have cheated the state, or committed perjury by complaining of the loss of property they never owned, which is probable." However, the all encompassing reason for such complaints, the Mexican commissioners concluded, was a "pretext" aimed at acquisition and conquest, indeed a diabolical plot that would expand the Texas boundaries southward to the Sierra Madres.[8]

Thus the matter stood in 1874—but not for long. The "carpetbag" administration of E. J. Davis, beleaguered by multiple problems and under constant Democratic assault, was losing power. In January, 1873, the Thirteenth Legislature, which was ruled by Democrats, repealed all of the most objectionable acts passed earlier by the state Republicans; it thus stripped the governor partially of his extraordinary powers, such as the disbanding of the State Police (April 23). Then, in September, Democrats

[8]The Sierra Madres are two parallel mountain chains in Mexico bordering the Central Plateau on the east and west. Some Texans hoped to annex Mexican territory from the Rio Grande to the Mexican state of San Luis Potosi.

from all over Texas converged upon Austin, where they enthusiastically nominated, in convention, Richard Coke for governor and R. B. Hubbard for lieutenant governor. In the ensuing fall election Coke defeated Davis by a two-to-one margin. And on January 19, 1874, after a brief armed confrontation at the capitol, Davis quietly withdrew.

One of the most urgent problems confronting the new Coke Administration was that of protecting the citizenry, their lives and property, but more specifically that of curbing the statewide epidemic of violence. It soon became apparent the members of the Fourteenth Legislature would call upon the Texas Rangers, a frontier fighting force that had been established informally as early as 1823 in the Stephen F. Austin colony and officially under the revolutionary government in November, 1835.

From their inception the Rangers were effective. In this raw land of Texas they pooled past knowledge and experience. Out of necessity they used whatever means at hand to survive. From the Mexican they learned horsemanship, the importance of a good mount on the open prairies, the spirit of the vaquero. From the Indian they acquired an understanding of plainscraft, of tracking and relentless pursuit, of savagery in fighting. And from their own background they inherited a rugged stubbornness for frontier living and an ability to adapt to a new environment. In fact, through this combination of cultures, they became an awesome force of men, prompting John Salmon "Rip" Ford, a surgeon with the American army during the Mexican War (and later a senior Texas Ranger captain), admiringly to remark: "They ride like Mexicans; trail like Indians; shoot like Tennesseans; and fight like the devil."

In looks and manner the Rangers were quite distinguishable from such fighting units as the militia or regular army. Recruited at first from the craftiest frontier fighters, and later from leather-faced cowboys and hard-bitten lawmen, they were not concerned with clothes and personal appearance, but rather with performance and achievement. During the Mexican War—and, for that matter, during most of the nineteenth century—they had a "ferocious and outlaw look" about them, usually "dressed in every variety of garment" and "armed to the teeth" with knives, rifles, and at least a brace of pistols. In fact, the only well-groomed "critters" among them were their horses—truly magnificent animals that the Rangers cared for meticulously. Nowhere was there evidence of the military—no flags or pennants, no insignias or indications of rank, no furnishing of equipment or medical supplies, no formality between officers and enlisted men.

Yet no one—either in the nineteenth century or in 1992—would mistake a Ranger captain. He had a charismatic quality that set him apart from his men. Although not necessarily large or powerful physically, he exuded a quiet confidence. In a time of

Governor Richard Coke

Lieutenant Governor Richard B. Hubbard

Courtesy Archives Division,
Texas State Library, Austin

xxxix

crisis he knew almost instinctively what to do, possessing that rare combination of boldness and judgment that allowed him, as historian Walter Prescott Webb perceived, "to lead rather than direct his men." For him retreat was unpardonable, defeat unbearable; his reputation and prestige demanded success, for in any situation he still had to prove himself capable of leadership before his men.

Since 1823, the Rangers had protected Anglo settlers in an almost personal manner. Along the Rio Grande or on the northern and western frontiers they had conducted investigations in man-to-man confrontations, relentless in their performance of duty and oftentimes pitiless in their administration of the law. After all, nothing about frontier justice was complex. The only criteria for law enforcement officers seemed to be: Could they ride? Could they shoot? Did they have the guts and skills to enforce Anglo-American law?

Because of their special aptitude for survival, the Rangers achieved an awesome reputation as frontier fighters. In the Mexican War—with Captains John Coffee "Jack" Hays, Ben McCulloch, and Samuel Walker as leaders—they were "the eyes and ears" for General Zachary Taylor, as well as "the cutting edge" for the American army that conquered Mexico City in September, 1847. And because of their exploits both on the battlefield and against the civilian populace, they achieved the notorious reputation as *diablos Tejanos*—the Texas devils. Then during the late 1850s, under the leadership of Senior Captain "Rip" Ford, they fought the formidable Comanches to a standstill.[9]

Thus in the spring of 1874, the Fourteenth Legislature, knowledgeable of Ranger exploits and traditions, created two distinct military forces, whose purposes were to protect the frontier and to curb lawlessness. One of these units was the Frontier Battalion, which was composed of six Ranger companies of seventy-five men each and was under the sterling leadership of Major John B. Jones. It had the enormous responsibility of protecting Texas frontier settlements against Indians and outlaws all the way from the Red River and Texas Panhandle to the Rio Grande. The other, known as the Special Force of Rangers, had an equally challenging assignment, that of suppressing bandit activities along the Mexican border.

The commander of the Special Force was Captain Leander H. McNelly. Although unimpressive in appearance and demeanor, he was notwithstanding a formidable opponent. Rather small and slender, carrying only 130 to 135 pounds on a 5'6" frame, McNelly had brown hair and a beard that framed a face with regular but undistinguished features. His voice was reedy, almost wispy at times, perhaps be-

[9]See Walter Prescott Webb, *The Texas Rangers: A Century of Frontier Defense* (2d ed.; Austin: University of Texas Press, 1965), pp. 11–15; Ben Procter, *Just One Riot: Episodes of Texas Rangers in the Twentieth Century* (Austin: Eakin Press, 1991), pp. 1–3.

cause he was tubercular—and slowly dying. Yet his calmness and courage in a dangerous situation, his intensity in achieving objectives, and his tenacity to succeed, set McNelly apart from other men. On the border, or for that matter wherever the assignment, he was deadly in purpose and lethal in action. In other words, he seldom took prisoners, unless deciding to extract information from them before their execution by knife or by "stretching hemp." He reputedly coined the phrase: "You just can't lick a man who just keeps on a comin' on." And his actions in battle without any doubt epitomized the Ranger tradition of "charging hell with a bucket of water."

McNelly became head of the Special Force—and, as far as Governor Richard Coke was concerned, for very good reason. Born in Brooke County, Virginia on March 12, 1844, McNelly migrated in 1860 to Washington County, Texas, where he herded sheep for rancher T. J. Burton. On September 13, 1861, although only seventeen years old, he enlisted in the Texas Mounted Volunteers of General Henry H. Sibley's Confederate brigade. During the following two years he won distinction at Val Verde in the New Mexico campaign, then at Galveston, and in Louisiana soon thereafter. On December 19, 1863, he was promoted to captain of scouts, with express orders to recruit his own company. He immediately proceeded to Washington County, Texas, and, during the next few months, enlisted a tough group of mounted troopers, before returning to Louisiana in time for a Confederate offensive. In the capture of Brashear City (March, 1864) he "played a spectacular role" by capturing a number of Federal soldiers. Soon thereafter he continued such heroics at the Battle of Mansfield,[10] until being wounded on April 8. Then, after a brief recuperative period, he again led his unit, late in May, against Federal troops, who were known as the "Texas Traitors" and commanded by E. J. Davis. Upon his discharge in 1865, McNelly took up farming in an area west of Brenham (in Washington County), married a teenager named Carrie Cheek, and had two children—a son, Rivel, and a daughter, Irene. Then in 1870, for some inexplicable reason, he accepted Governor Davis's offer to be one of the four captains in the State Police, during which time he distinguished himself as a fearless law officer, forthright and audacious and incorruptible.

Late in the spring of 1874, after being appointed as captain of the Special Force of Rangers, McNelly and his men were assigned to DeWitt County to curb lawlessness, which was caused by the Sutton-Taylor Feud. For the remainder of the year they were partially effective. They found it impossible to diminish the bitterness and hatred between the two

[10]On April 8, 1864, the Battle of Mansfield occurred just south of Shreveport, Louisiana, on the Red River. Confederate forces inflicted a stunning defeat upon the Union forces led by General Nathaniel P. Banks, thus halting the final attempt by the Union army to invade Texas.

factions. But they did dampen certain terroristic activities during the remainder of 1874 by protecting prisoners, serving writs for court appearances, and intimidating others by their ominous presence or forcefully arresting the more violently inclined.[11]

Early in 1875, however, lawlessness in the Nueces Strip began to command their attention. On January 26, in Starr County, bandits killed five troopers of the U.S. Ninth Cavalry, stripping their bodies of boots and weapons. And then on February 27, near Edinburg, marauders swooped down on a general store, killed a Tejano clerk, and riddled with bullets the body of the proprietor, who was also the local justice of the peace. And again in March, on two separate occasions, heavily armed raiders assailed small country towns near Corpus Christi—150 miles north of Brownsville—committing murder and mayhem in their path. The situation became so bad that Governor Coke wrote to General E. O. C. Ord, Commander of the Department of Texas, headquartered in San Antonio, that the counties in the Nueces Strip were rapidly being depopulated, that both ranchers and farmers were abandoning their homes for safer areas.

Governor Coke, however, wanted further corroboration for his statements. He therefore sent Texas

[11] In the spring of 1874, when McNelly's Special Force of Rangers first went to stop the violent Sutton-Taylor feud in DeWitt County, Jennings was not a Ranger. Nor was he with Lee Hall in 1877 when the Rangers were again assigned that task.

Adjutant General William Steele and State Senator Joseph E. Dwyer on a fact-finding journey into the Nueces Strip. The evidence uncovered by their investigation was alarming, if not grievously appalling. In essence, they verified most of the Robb Commission conclusions. But they also noted that local Anglo vigilante committees and other self-appointed seekers of justice had engaged in a large-scale "private killing." Indeed, in their quest for vengeance (or justice), they had committed vicious atrocities against both Tejanos and Mexicans on both sides of the Rio Grande. And the slaughter would continue, they concluded, without disciplined law enforcement, which, of course, meant the Special Force of Rangers under McNelly.

*   *   *

Into this dangerous scenario along the Texas-Mexican border, a young man with the unlikely name of Napoleon Augustus Jennings would thrust himself. On this Texas frontier he surely seemed to be a misfit, especially due to his background and training. Born in Philadelphia on January 11, 1858, the son of Caroline and Napoleon Augustus Jennings, Sr., he was the youngest of seven children (two brothers and four sisters). His father had profited handsomely in business, listing his occupation in the U.S. censuses as an "auctioneer." For a brief time in the 1830s the senior Jennings found work in Mississippi, before returning to Philadelphia early in the 1840s, where his father and uncle had become prominent civic leaders. He provided well for his family, by 1870 acquiring a home and real estate worth about $130,000 and amassing a personal fortune of $150,000. Young Jennings, who became known to his friends as "Al," thus realized the opportunities that came from wealth. He received an expensive education at St. Paul's School, an exclusive academy in Concord, New Hampshire. He had money for books and journals, which he obviously put to good use. And upon returning home for holidays and vacation, he had four female Irish immigrants who cared for him and the family.[12]

In September, 1874, however, when he was eighteen, Jennings sought to escape the confines of his environment, to experience a completely different kind of world. And why? For posterity he testified that "some copies of *The Texas New Yorker*" had

[12] 1850 U.S. Census, Schedule I: Population, Philadelphia County, Pennsylvania, p. 566; 1860 U.S. Census, Schedule I: p. 56; 1870 U.S. Census, Schedule I: p. 182; Dora Neill Raymond, *Captain Lee Hall of Texas* (Norman: University of Oklahoma Press, 1962), pp. 49–50, 301; J. Frank Dobie, *Prefaces* (Austin: University of Texas Press, 1982), p. 15.

In 1842 and again in 1844 Jennings' great-uncle, Morton McMichael was elected sheriff of Philadelphia. In 1865 he became mayor of the city. He was also editor of the *United States Gazette* and the *Saturday Evening Post*. See Michael Feldberg, *The Philadelphia Riots of 1844: A Study of Ethnic Conflict* (Westport, Conn.: Greenwood Press, 1975), p. 117; Adrienne Siegel, *Philadelphia: A Chronological and Documentary History, 1615–1970* (Dobbs Ferry, N.Y.: Oceana Publications, Inc., 1975), p. 40.

"inflamed" his mind and that he became enthralled with "the highly colored accounts of life in the Lone Star State." But Jennings may not have been entirely candid in this explanation. While he was at St. Paul's, older brother John (four years his senior) was apprenticing as an auctioneer with his father, eventually preparing to take over the family business. Yet possibly even more disconcerting to young Al, if not emotionally more disruptive, was the death of his mother, together with his father's subsequent remarriage to a twenty-eight-year-old Missouri woman.[13]

Hence, Al Jennings left his seemingly comfortable life and traveled to Texas in September, 1874. That a young "Yankee" lad, who was practically penniless, survived in that violent land was a testimony either to his foolhardy endurance or his incredible luck—or possibly both. However, he did so remarkably well, with a flare for the dramatic as well as a "nose" for adventure. After a brief stay in San Antonio, he became acquainted with the cattle culture in the brush country that flourished in the mesquite and cactus to the south and west of the city. Then he moved on toward the Rio Grande— into the desert lands of chaparral and baked soil around the border town of Laredo. After almost unbelievable adventures with U.S. Commissioner Hamilton C. Peterson and a brief, hazardous tenure as sheriff of Laredo, followed by a more tenuous

[13] 1870 U.S. Census, Philadelphia, p. 182.

experience as a Mexican revolutionist, Jennings met Captain McNelly, who allowed him to join the rugged Special Force of Texas Rangers.

Jennings then described the dramatic Ranger episodes of the next several months of 1875—the "fire fight" with Mexican raiders, in which Ranger Berry Smith was killed, the McNelly decision to stack twelve bodies in the Brownsville square, McNelly's invasion of Mexico, and the Ranger attack on Las Cuevas. But Jennings, in his interesting and well-told account, took some journalist liberties, which would later cause minor historical controversies. As an example, he made the Las Cuevas incident appear as if that action took place in one day even though it extended over a three-day period. He also seemed to be, as Ranger George Durham caustically commented, the "Captain's right-hand man." Yet Jennings did not participate in any of these events, although presenting the reader with an eyewitness account. McNelly did recruit him, but Ranger records clearly show that Jennings did not enter the service until May 26, 1876, and was discharged on February 1, 1877, a tour of a little more than eight months. Both William Callicott and Durham, who were Rangers in McNelly's Special Force on the Mexican border in 1875, testified that Jennings was not with them. And in 1899, shortly after the publication of *A Texas Ranger*, Jennings corroborated their statements by providing this explanation to McNelly's widow: "In the book I made myself a member of the company a year before I actually joined. I did this to add interest to the recital and to avoid too much of a hearsay character. Told in the first person, adventures hold the attention of the reader." Without question, Jennings knew, as well as interviewed, a number of the participants. And even though Ranger George Durham remembered him as a mere "field clerk to do the writing" and had stated that Jennings' book "was pretty awful," J. Frank Dobie, the renowned Texas folklorist, concluded: "If his own eyes did not see every act he has described, we may yet be sure that the stuff of his book, which is only incidentally autobiography, came to him from eyewitnesses."[14]

Jennings also raised another point, which historians have since addressed. He asserted that McNelly "had been in direct communication with President Grant regarding the Mexican outrages, and I, in common with many others, obtained the impression that Grant would welcome the chance to invade the Republic directly to the south of us." Although no extant information corroborates the McNelly claims, Jennings may have arrived at such postulations because of certain historical evidence that may or may not have been available to him. For instance, General of the Army Ulysses S. Grant had been concerned about the Texas-Mexican frontier at the end of the Civil War because of the possible threat to peace by the seating of Maximilian, the self-

[14]Dobie, *Preface*, p. 18.

proclaimed and French-backed emperor of Mexico. During the summer of 1865, Grant transferred fifty-two thousand troops into Texas, with a reportedly forty thousand stationed along the Rio Grande. And then, with the support of General Philip H. Sheridan, commander of the Military District of the Southwest, he contrived to drive the French out of Mexico. Since President Andrew Johnson was extremely reluctant to commit United States forces, Grant supported arrangements late in 1865 for a volunteer expedition to invade Mexico. But Secretary of State William H. Seward skillfully undermined this scheme by offering its proposed leader, General John M. Schofield, a prestigious diplomatic position in France. In 1867, the rise of Benito Juarez, the withdrawal of French forces, and the execution of Maximilian soon eased border tensions. As one historian put it, "direct military intervention seemed to be out of the question."[15]

By 1872, however, Grant, now as president, again focused on the Rio Grande because of the mounting turbulence and violence. In March, Texas congressmen and "many concerned citizens" of Brownsville spoke with the president who, according to newspaper reports, was "in complete sympathy with the Texans and concurred in their opinion that annexation [as far as the Sierra Madres] was the inevitable solution."[16] Soon thereafter (May, 1872) the Robb

[15]Webster, "Texan Manifest Destiny," p. 49.
[16]Ibid., p. 81.

Commission was on its way to investigate. And, accordingly, its findings and recommendations, together with another strong appeal from Brownsville citizens, found their way to Grant and Secretary of War William W. Belknap along with the annual report of General C. C. Augur, commander of the Department of Texas, which specifically called for extra troops plus an "offensive" policy to protect lives and property along the Texas-Mexican border.

Jennings most likely was referring to the United States' policy toward the Kickapoo Indians, which was not only well-known but reported widely in the press. At the end of the Civil War, they were the "scourge of the Texan frontier," raiding continually from Laredo to Eagle Pass (and 100 miles into the interior). State leaders, individual citizens, and American military commanders all verified the extent and intensity of such depredations. On two separate occasions in 1870 and 1871, the Texas legislature passed resolutions imploring Congress to put an end to these bloody incursions. In fact, the situation became so bad that Secretary of State Hamilton Fish urged the Mexican government to renew an 1866 treaty agreement, which would allow American troops to cross the Rio Grande in pursuit of "hostiles"—and on more than one occasion he threatened an invasion by the United States to rectify repeated injustices. Nor was President Grant ambivalent regarding this matter. Since the Mexican government seemed to be incapable of deterring,

Secretary of State William H. Seward

General John M. Schofield
Courtesy Prints and Photographs Division,
Library of Congress

much less preventing these raids, he instructed his old comrade-in-arms, General William Tecumseh Sherman, to dispatch the irascible and somewhat headstrong Colonel Ranald S. Mackenzie and the Fourth U.S. Cavalry to the Texas border, because he would "impart to his Regiment his own active character."[17] Then on May 18, 1873, with Grant wanting results and with Secretary of War Belknap standing "firm" in support, Colonel Mackenzie attacked a Kickapoo encampment in the Mexican state of Coahuila, approximately thirty miles from Santa Rosa, killing nineteen and taking prisoner forty women and children as well as an old Lipan chief. A year later, on May 25, 1874, Mackenzie led a hundred troopers across the Rio Grande above Piedras Negras, stalking—what he believed to be—Indian cattle thieves. But upon learning that the rustlers were Mexicans, he broke off pursuit and returned to the American side of the river.

The Mexican attitude regarding the Mackenzie raids, both officially and in the press, was guarded, restrained, almost to the point of being indecisive. Whereas "invasion" threats by American forces on the lower Rio Grande to chastise Mexican raiders "touched the sensitive subjects of race and national honor," pursuit and punishment of the Kickapoos or other Indians was something else.[18] After all, the Mexicans—through long tradition—detested these

[17] Ibid., p. 110.
[18] See ibid., pp. 111-20.

"savages" as much as the Texans did. And although the government in Mexico City did announce that an immediate investigation would be called, actions were slow in happening and lackadaisical in application, especially since American troops, and not Texas Rangers, were the invaders.

But from Laredo to Brownsville and northward into the Nueces Strip, the governments of the United States and Mexico looked upon the boundary situation and the resulting endemic lawlessness quite differently; neither wanted to be drawn into a diplomatic brouhaha of any magnitude. But others surely did. Texas Democratic governor Richard Coke, unlike his predecessor E. J. Davis, was not about to pull back the pressure on the Republican administration of Grant, especially since the frontier defense was one of his foremost state programs. Coke, together with other Texas leaders, not only wanted these deadly incursions to end, but also demanded the incarceration, if not execution, of "the recognized leader and protector of all the cattle thieves"—that "evil genius," Juan Cortina.[19] Military Commander of the Southwest General E. O. C. Ord was also embarrassed, if not humiliated, by the Mexican raids near Corpus Christi in March, 1875. Accordingly, on June 9 he convinced his superiors

---

[19]Ibid., p. 140. See also Michael Collins, "Los Diablos Tejanos: McNelly's Texas Rangers and the Las Cuevas War," paper delivered at the annual meeting of the Texas State Historical Association, Dallas, Texas, March, 1991.

Secretary of State Hamilton Fish

neral William Tecumseh Sherman   *Colonel Ranald S. Mackenzie*

*Courtesy Prints and Photographs Division,
Library of Congress*

to initiate "gunboat diplomacy" all along the Rio
Grande by placing at hand two heavily armed steam
launches—U.S.S. *Plymouth* and U.S.S. *Rio Bravo*—
to assist the military. Then, in anticipation of a possible confrontation, he transferred three troops of
cavalry and one infantry company to Fort Brown.

Although Mexican President Sebastian Lerdo de
Tejada tried to alleviate border tensions with the
United States by ordering the arrest and subsequent
imprisonment of General Cortina on July 11, 1875,
new intrigues to nullify his efforts and to promote
military confrontation soon arose. Early in October,
with the arrival at Brownsville of the U.S.S. *Rio
Bravo*—a twenty-two-year-old Alabama steamboat,
formerly named the *Planter* but now appropriately
rechristened because of its mission—its captain,
Lieutenant Commander DeWitt C. Kells plotted
to rid the area of all adversaries. Even though his
express orders were to patrol the Rio Grande, to
deter incursions, and to "avoid any act which might
be made a just . . . complaint on the part of the Mexican government," he schemed, imaginatively and
Machiavellian-like, with Captain McNelly and John
L. Haynes, the United States customs collector at
Brownsville.[20] Somehow they must provoke an international incident. Of course, ideally, they hoped

---

[20]Robert L. Robinson, "U.S. Navy vs. Cattle Rustlers:
The U.S.S. *Rio Bravo* on the Rio Grande, 1875–1879,"
Military History of Texas and the Southwest, Vol XV, No. 2,
pp. 44–45; Webster, "Texan Manifest Destiny," p. 142.

that Mexican raiders would attack the *Rio Bravo*.
But if such action did not occur, Kells suggested
that a group of Brownsville citizens fire upon the
Rio Bravo from the Mexican side, thereby giving
him "an excuse to return the fire, destroy the adja-
cent Mexican ranches, and occupy Mexican soil,
ostensibly to avenge the insult to the United States
flag." Still other scenarios involved McNelly Rangers. Either they should pose as Mexicans and attack the gunboat or drive a herd of cattle across the
Rio Grande to the raiders' infamous refuge, which
was known to all as Las Cuevas. In either case,
Kells would be forced to commence hostile action.
But no matter which plot was chosen, McNelly and
Kells were ready to strike the enemy, to deal the
Mexican raiders a withering, devastating blow.

All such machinations were proceeding according to plan during the fall of 1875, until Thomas
Wilson intervened. As the United States consul at
Matamoros, he soon "got wind" of Kells' activities.
Thus, on October 14, he cabled his limited information to Secretary of State Hamilton Fish, asking
him to send an observer to Brownsville—and with
all due haste. Three weeks later Washington re-
sponded affirmatively to this request, at the same
time instructing Kells not to leave Brownsville. But
two days later Wilson found Captain McNelly and
Kells "aboard one of the steam launches," ready
to depart, except that the pilot failed to appear.
And when Wilson cabled once again to Secretary

Fish that a joint expedition, composed of U.S. Navy personnel and Texas Rangers—and supported by a cavalry unit under the command of Colonel J. H. Potter, the commander at Fort Brown—was about to depart (under the semblance of preventing a "suspected cattle crossing"), Kells received orders that grounded him forthwith. Then, on November 15, Commander George Remey arrived in Brownsville to relieve him as captain of the *Rio Bravo*.

The Grant administration quickly put a quietus on all military activities along the Rio Grande. So on November 19, when McNelly, rashly but fearlessly, led his Special Force of thirty-one Texas Rangers across the Rio Grande in a dawn attack on Las Cuevas, he did so without help from the *Rio Bravo* or the United States cavalry. Major David R. Clendenin "positively forebade any crossing by the U.S. soldiers," even though McNelly later asserted that Clendenin "promised me that in case I was cut off in my attack . . . he would come to my assistance." Captain James F. Randlett of the Eighth Cavalry, fearing that McNelly might be annihilated by a Mexican force of three hundred men, at first violated his orders by crossing the Rio Grande with forty troopers to aid the Rangers, then returned to the Texas side upon learning that a truce had been established. And Major A. J. Alexander, the senior cavalry officer at Fort Brown, had also pledged McNelly his support, only to have his word countermanded by orders from General Ord.

After the Las Cuevas incident, raids continued to occur in the Nueces Strip, but with less frequency. But the problems between the United States and Mexico would persist during the next several years. Then Porfirio Diaz, a *mestizo*[21] who had elevated his position in life through the military, would emerge upon the Mexican scene. Late in 1871 he had made the mistake of trying to seize power from "his life-long tutor, friend, and fellow-Liberal, Benito Juarez." But his timing was wrong. After more than a year of fighting, his forces suffered severe defeats and he sought refuge in the mountains, sometimes dressed as a priest. Unexpectedly, on July 18, 1872, President Juarez died of a heart attack, and Vice President Sebastian Lerdo de Tejada succeeded him. But in December, 1875, Diaz arrived in Brownsville to organize his forces, then, within a month, raised the standard of revolt, and by 1877 defeated the Lerdo forces and assumed the presidency.

Diaz, now in power, changed significantly the situation along the Rio Grande. To maintain his position he soon realized the importance of American recognition, and that meant the removal of the most serious problem between the two countries, "the Texas border trouble." He therefore worked to that end. First of all, he dealt with Juan Cortina, the "villain extraordinaire," the "culprit" most hated by Texans. In April, 1877, Diaz ordered Cortina,

[21] In Spanish America, a *mestizo* is a person of mixed Spanish and Indian blood.

President Benito Juarez

Courtesy Archives Division,
Texas State Library, Austin

who had ineffectually supported him, to be escorted to Mexico City and "established in a private residence"—actually house arrest—as his "guest." At the same time he sent to the Rio Grande his most reliable general, "with adequate forces to subdue unruly elements and hostile Indians." Those who persisted against this policy of peace were to be "adobe-walled"—stood up against an adobe wall and shot. Hence, late in the 1870s, an uneasy calm returned to the Nueces Strip and the United States recognized the Diaz government.

For that matter Texans across the state would begin to realize the effects of civilizing forces. Surely the epidemic of violence and lawlessness was gradually diminishing. By 1876 the United States cavalry and the Frontier Battalion of Texas Rangers had broken the power of the nomadic Comanches and Kiowas, forcing them onto reservations in the Indian Territory of Oklahoma. Cowboys still participated in the "long drive" north along the several trails, visiting lively frontier towns like Fort Worth, but by the mid-1880s this way of life would evolve into fenced pastures and registered cattle and stationary bunkhouses. In January, 1877, McNelly's Special Force was reorganized. Under the effective leadership of Lee Hall and John B. Armstrong, the Rangers helped end the Sutton-Taylor feud in DeWitt County as well as curb the activities of thieves and cutthroats along the Rio Grande, especially in the Eagle Pass area. Then the Special Force, together

with the Frontier Battalion, effectively winnowed
out the Texas "bad men," either jailing or "putting
to final rest" the likes of such notorious gunmen as
King Fisher, John Wesley Hardin, and Sam Bass.
And by the mid-1880s railroads had come to Texas,
bringing emigrants by the hundreds of thousands
and thereby pushing back the frontier.

*   *   *

Yet no matter what the significant changes in the
state, no matter what new traditions, the story of
McNelly would remain a part of Texas history. His
tour of duty in the Nueces Strip in 1875, including
his "invasion" of Mexico and the Ranger attack on
Las Cuevas, was his "last great scout." Within fourteen months he retired from the service and nine
months later, at age thirty-three, he died of consumption. But his actions and deeds would continue to be remembered, either inspiring admiration
and adulation or incurring hatred and denuncia-
tion. For example, prominent rancher Richard
King, who provided McNelly and his men with
fresh mounts, later gave them five hundred dollars
(a considerable amount in 1875) for their valiant
service in defending Texans, their lives and property. The Texas Rangers, as an organization, now had
a role model, a legend in action and deed. Although
outnumbered ten-to-one at Las Cuevas, McNelly
stubbornly refused to retreat to safety north of the
Rio Grande; instead, he forced the Mexican bandits

to parley, then to return stolen cattle as the stipulation for his withdrawal. And with the publication of N. A. Jennings' *A Texas Ranger* (1898) and Walter Prescott Webb's *The Texas Rangers: A Century of Frontier Defense* (1935) the McNelly legend would pass along to new generations. At the same time, however, such torture and brutality, such reckless disregard for international as well as individual rights, would be anathema to many, particularly to those south of the Rio Grande, who looked upon McNelly as an apparition of death on horseback. In reviewing the dramatic episodes and controversial actions of McNelly, historian Michael Collins was given to conclude: "Were the Rangers keeping the peace, or provoking a war? Were McNelly and his men heroic Rangers, or riders from hell? Well, maybe it all depends upon which side of the river you are on."[22]

BEN PROCTER

Texas Christian University
Fort Worth, Texas
July, 1992

[22]Collins, "Los Diablos Tejanos," p.32.

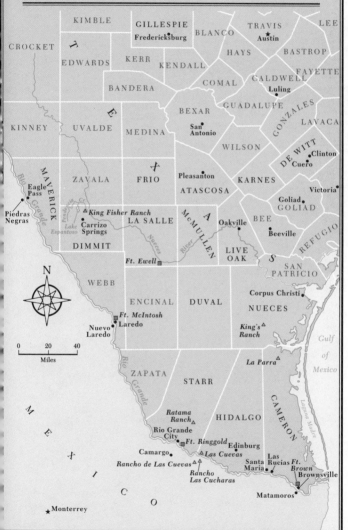

WHERE AL JENNINGS RODE
WITH THE TEXAS RANGERS IN THE 1870'S

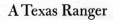

A Texas Ranger

I

I Arrive in Texas

IN THE following story of those years of my life which were passed on the broad tablelands of Texas, I have endeavored to set down, plainly and truthfully, events as they actually occurred. I have always given the correct names of places, but in some instances have thought it proper to change the names of persons. During a recent visit to Texas, for the purpose of going over the scenes of the adventures of earlier days, I found a number of highly respected citizens, living exemplary lives, who had at one time been eagerly hunted by the officers of the law. It would be manifestly unfair to give their real names in this history, and so expose them to the criticism of their fellow citizens at this time. In other instances, however, where the malefactors are notorious, I have used their real names.

In justice to the great State of Texas, I wish to say that the conditions which existed in the period embraced in this narrative have undergone a complete change, and that in no state in the Union is the law more respected than it is in Texas today.

It was in September, 1874, that I first visited Texas. I was eighteen years old, and had only a short time before left the famous New Hampshire school where I had been a pupil for a number of years.[1] My father, a Philadelphia merchant, was very indulgent to me, and I had never been obliged to contribute a penny toward my own support. The reading of many books of travel and adventure had roused in me a spirit of wanting to see the world.

Some copies of *The Texas New Yorker*,[2] a paper published in the interests of some of the southwestern railroads, came into my hands, and my mind was inflamed by the highly-colored accounts of life in the Lone Star State. I read every word in the papers, and believed all I read. Since then I have learned that Colonel J. Armoy Knox,[3] later of *Texas*

[1] Jennings attended the exclusive St. Paul's School in Concord, New Hampshire. See J. Frank Dobie, *Prefaces* (Austin: University of Texas Press, 1975), p. 15.

[2] *The Texas New Yorker*, published by George H. Sweet in New York City from 1870 to 1874, was a monthly journal specifically "devoted to making known to the capitalist, merchant, mechanic, and emigrant the agricultural, horticultural, stock-raising and other latent wealth of the state of Texas." E. W. Winkler, "Some Historical Activities of the Texas Library and Historical Commission," *Texas Historical Association Quarterly*, XIV (April, 1911), 302.

[3] John Armoy Knox (1850–1906) immigrated from Armoy, Ireland to Texas in search of better health. While in Austin, he was a sewing machine agent and then a journalist. In 1881 he and Alexander E. Sweet established a weekly humor magazine, *Texas Siftings*. In 1885 they transferred it to New York City, where Knox was business manager until leaving in 1892 to become the editor of the Atlanta *Herald*. Two years later he returned to New York, where he began writing articles for several magazines and newspapers. See Frank Luther Mott, *A History of American Magazines* (Cambridge: Harvard University Press, 1938), III, 269–70.

Siftings, was one of the men who wrote the most lurid articles for *The Texas New Yorker*. I was a callow youth at the time, however, and had never met the genial Colonel. I should know better now than to take him so seriously, but his humor was all sober fact to me then.

After reading of the wild, free life of the Texas cowboy, I made up my mind that life would not be worth living outside of Texas. In a few years—or was it months?—I had the assurance of Colonel Knox's paper that, so surely as I went to Texas, I should be a cattle king, and the owner of countless herds of beeves on unlimited acres of land. I forget now just how I was going to acquire these without money or experience, but I know the Colonel made it all as plain as daylight to me then. As a "boomer," he was a glorious success.

About the first of September, then, I told my father that I had decided to try life in Texas, if he would give his permission. I said that I knew a fortune awaited me there, and I wanted to go and get it before someone else gobbled it up. To my vast astonishment, my father gave his consent, but said that if I went, I must depend on my own exertions for a living. He suggested that my enthusiasm had obtained the upper hand of my judgment, but said that he would not stand in the way of my following my inclination to try a little outdoor life and shifting for myself. He gave me his blessing and one hundred dollars.

I started for Texas at once, my objective point being San Antonio. From there I intended to go farther West and find the site for my cattle ranch. Of course, this sounds ridiculous, but it seemed quite feasible to me at that time. Many and many a young man has gone out into the West with such ideas in his head; just as many and many an immigrant has come to America with the expectation of finding money lying loose in the streets for him to pick up as he pleased.

At that time, the railroad ran only to Austin, the capital of Texas, and about eighty miles from San Antonio. I went from Austin to San Antonio on top of a stagecoach. I had lived well on my journey, and when I came to pay my stage fare I found that my supply of ready money was getting dangerously low. I had bought a six-shooter and felt that I was a real Texan, which made me happy, but when I arrived in San Antonio, I had only $3.25. I went to the Baker House, a second-class hotel on the Main Plaza of the quaint old town. I was well dressed, and I had a sole-leather trunk filled with clothing, so, fortunately for me, I was not asked to pay for my board in advance.

My first week in San Antonio was one of real misery. I knew that I could not pay my hotel bill when it should fall due, but farther than that I did not know. For the first time I wondered how I was going to get out on the plains to start my cattle ranch. How was I to get away? How could I pay my bill

East Side of Main Plaza, San Antonio, c. 1870
Courtesy The Institute of Texan Cultures, San Antonio

without money? What was I to do? What would become of me?

I was in my first serious predicament, and as unhappy a youth as could well be imagined. I thought with longing of the safety of my father's house in Philadelphia, and heartily wished myself to be back there again. Further, my mind was not one bit relieved by an incident which occurred at the hotel, three or four days following my arrival.

I was sitting in the hotel office, wondering what I should do to get out of my trouble, when the proprietor, Baker—a large, heavy, broad-shouldered man with a long, gray beard which gave him a patriarchal appearance—walked in. He was extremely excited. He walked straight up to a young man who was sitting close to me and caught him roughly by the collar.

"Here, you rascal!" he exclaimed, "I've found you out. You thought you could beat me, did you? Take that!"

Old Baker emphasized his words by hitting the young man over the head with a heavy cane. The blood ran down the man's face, and he struggled to get away. He finally succeeded in escaping from Baker and ran out of the hotel.

"I guess he won't try to beat a hotel out o' board and lodging in a hurry again," said old Baker, looking after him, with a grin.

Naturally, this assault made a deep impression upon me. I looked upon Baker with distrust every time he came near me, and felt like throwing up my arm to ward off a blow whenever he greeted me.

The end of my first week came all too soon, and the clerk handed me my bill; it amounted to $10.25. The extra quarter was for bringing my trunk from the stage office to the hotel. I had seventy-five cents in my pocket when I received the bill. I thought it over, and then made up my mind to go to Baker and make a clean breast of the whole matter to him. It was not without many misgivings that I decided to take this course, but it turned out to be the best thing I could have done. Mr. Baker listened with patience to my rather lame explanation of why I could not pay the bill. I was so nervous that I was almost crying with mortification.

"Well, my boy," said the old man, kindly, when I had finished, "we must find something for you to do. How would you like to work on a ranch?"

I told him that I had come to Texas to work on a ranch. I was willing to do so for a short time, I said, until I learned something about the business, then I proposed to start a ranch of my own. He asked me if I had any capital in prospect, and I told him I had not. I was very young, indeed, in those days.

The upshot of our conversation was that he then introduced me to one of his guests, a cattleman named Reynolds, who owned a ranch in Atascosa County, south of San Antonio. Reynolds asked me if I had ever worked in Texas before, and when I told him I had not, he hesitated about employing me. I assured him that, although I had not worked in Texas, I was not a bit afraid of any kind of work, and only longed for the chance to show what I could do. This did not seem to impress him greatly, but he finally said he would give me a trial.

Mr. Baker said I could leave my trunk at his hotel until I was able to pay him what I owed. I thought this was very kind of him. My trunk, by the way, with its contents, was worth about ten times the amount of his bill.

I was so elated over my good fortune that I started out that evening to "see the town," a thing I had not attempted before. The first place I went to was a Mexican gambling room. There were several games of *monte*[4] in progress. I had never seen *monte* played, nor any gambling for that matter, and I became greatly interested. At last I grew so fascinated that I ventured to bet seventy-five cents—my entire fortune—on the turn of a card. I regret to say, I won. I bet again and again, until I had won over twenty dollars. I kept on playing, with the inevitable result that I left the place penniless. For the first time in my life I was "flat broke."

Early the next morning I started with Reynolds for his ranch. He brought two little Texas ponies around to the front of the hotel about sunrise, and

---

[4] *Monte* was a popular game played with a forty-card pack in which players bet that one of two layouts, each consisting of two cards drawn from the top or bottom of the deck will be matched in suit by the next card turned up.

told me I was to ride one of them. I was delighted. I had ridden a horse perhaps a dozen times in my life and I thought I was an expert rider. But I had never ridden very far at a time, and when Reynolds said we should have to go thirty-five miles that day, I had some misgivings as to how I was going to stand it, but I kept them quiet. Upon starting, Reynolds set the pace at that easy "lope" which the tough, wiry little Texas ponies can keep up for hour after hour without showing fatigue. The easy motion was like that of a rocking chair, and I thought I should never tire of it. I did, though.

Long before we had covered the thirty-five miles I began to suffer. I had often heard the common expression about every bone in one's body aching; I had probably used it, carelessly, myself; but before that ride was over I knew precisely what it meant. Not only did every bone ache, but every muscle, and joint, and nerve in my body—from the crown of my head to the ends of my toes—was giving me excruciating pain.

We stopped at noon to rest and eat and let the horses graze. After about three hours, Reynolds said it was time for us to be going on, and it took real courage for me to get on that little mustang again. It was after dark when we at last reached Reynolds' ranch. I tumbled from the pony's back more dead than alive, and I then and there resolved never again to ride a horse. I was far too tired and in too much pain to sleep that night.

Before I left Texas, I practically lived on a horse for three years. I have ridden for three weeks at a time in pouring rain, and have slept every night during that period on wet ground, covered with a wet blanket. I have ridden "bucking broncos," and horses that trotted with the gait of an animated pile driver. I have raced for my life in front of a herd of stampeded cattle. I have been chased forty miles at night by desperadoes, anxious to make a sieve of my body with bullets. But never have I experienced anything like that first Texas ride.

Long before daylight the next morning, I was called by Reynolds, who said that he wanted me to go to Pleasanton with him to a "stock meeting."[5] I didn't know what a "stock meeting" was, but I was quite sure I didn't want to go to that one. I simply wanted to lie quiet and die, but pride came to my aid and, stiff and sore as I was, I struggled to my feet, ate a breakfast of black coffee and cornbread, and again mounted my mustang. We started just as the first faint streak of dawn showed in the sky and reached Pleasanton about an hour after the sun had risen. Reynolds probably came to the conclusion

[5] Pleasanton, thirty miles south of San Antonio, was founded in 1856. It replaced Navatasco as the county seat of Atascosa County in 1858. By the 1860s its citizens claimed it as the cattleman's capital of Texas; and in the spring of 1873, cowboys "drove 43,000 Atascosa County cattle up the trail." See A. J. Sowell, *Early Settlers and Indian Fighters of Southwest Texas* (New York: Argosy-antiquarian LTD, 1964), pp. 249–50; *Atascosa County History*, pp. 26–27.

that I was too much of a "tenderfoot" or "short-horn" for his use, for he deserted me in Pleasanton, and left me there to shift for myself. He calmly told me he had changed his mind about employing me, and went away and left me, taking with him the horse I had so painfully ridden.

II

Down to the Border

I HAD been in a sad predicament in San Antonio, but now my situation was, indeed, desperate. I was not only penniless, but hungry and friendless. The town was full of cattlemen and cowboys, who had come to attend the stock meeting. They were a good-natured, jolly set of fellows, but through my inexperienced, young, Eastern eyes I saw in them only a lot of rough, loud-talking, swearing ruffians.

At that time, Texas had but few fences in it, and cattle roamed at will all over the State. The only way a cattle owner had of keeping his property was by branding the calves and cutting their ears in some fanciful way. These brands and ear markings were duly registered in the county clerk's office and determined the ownership of the cattle. All un-branded cattle were known as "Mavericks."[1] They were usually only a year or two old and belonged to nobody in particular, but if a cattleman came across

---

[1]In August, 1856, the term "maverick" became a part of cowboy "lingo" when Samuel A. Maverick rounded up and sold four hundred Longhorns, many of which were unbranded yearlings. The name "maverick" soon identified these strays. See Rena Maverick Green, ed., *Samuel Maverick, Texan, 1803–1870: A Collection of Letters, Journals, and Memoirs* (San Antonio: H. Wolff, 1952), pp. 411–12.

one, he would "rope" it, throw it down, and brand it.

The principal market for Texas cattle was in Kansas, and the cattlemen would gather great herds and drive them up through the Indian Territory to Kansas, where they would sell them. The cattlemen did not necessarily confine themselves to driving their own cattle, but would take those belonging to others as well. They were supposed to keep a careful record of all such cattle they had taken up and sold, and to make a settlement at a stock meeting every three months. As a rule, the cattlemen were not any too honest in keeping their records, and the stock meetings were in the nature of a farce. Very little money ever changed hands. The owner of a brand would meet the owner of another and say to him:

"Jim, I took up twenty-one o' your cows an' sold 'em. I'll give ye an order to take up twenty-five o' mine if ye ain't took up any lately."

"Yah well, I did round up sixteen o' your 'BT' brand," the other would reply, "so I reckon we can fix up the difference all right."

The chances were that both men were lying outrageously as to the number of cattle each had sold belonging to the other, but as all were doing the same thing, it was pretty thoroughly understood that the smartest man in gathering stock was the one to come out ahead.

Under no circumstances would a cattleman ever kill any of his own stock for beef. He invariably hunted up for that purpose some brand which did not belong to him, and it was an unwritten law that cattle killed for beef should not be accounted for at the stock meetings. Some of the large cattle owners actually advertised in the little county newspapers the brands which they wished other ranchmen to use for beef.

I am not exaggerating when I say that at that time in Texas ten times more cattle were stolen every year than were bought and sold.[2] A man would acquire possession of a few cattle of a certain brand and would forthwith gather all cows and steers of all brands he could round up, drive them to Kansas, and sell them. Very often there were fights about

---

[2] Jennings may not have exaggerated that about "ten times more cattle were stolen every year than were bought and sold." From 1869 to 1872, Richard King (of the King Ranch in South Texas) claimed that thieves stole 33,827 cattle, almost thirty-eight percent of his herd. Consequently in May, 1872, Congress appropriated six thousand dollars to send a United States Commission to Texas specifically to investigate border problems. After holding formal sessions from Point Isabel to Rio Grande City (July 30–October 3), the Commission submitted a "strong report" to Congress, detailing hundreds of cases in which American citizens along the Rio Grande suffered "outrages and losses." In fact, the Commission estimated that Texas ranchers—between 1865 and 1872—lost an average of five thousand head every month. Tom Lea, *The King Ranch* (Boston: Little, Brown and Company, 1957), I, 266–76; House Executive Document No. 39, 42d Congress, 3d Session, p. 20. See also Walter Prescott Webb, *The Texas Rangers: A Century of Frontier Defense* (Boston: Houghton Mifflin Company, 1935), pp. 238–42.

the cattle and, as every man carried a six-shooter in that country, "killings" were of somewhat frequent occurrence. Still, there was a difference between a regular cattleman and a common cattle thief. The former always was the legal owner of at least one brand; the latter owned none at all.

My predicament at being thrown on my own re-sources among these rough-and-ready frontiersmen was, as may be imagined, a serious one. I was des-perate. I hung around the stable where a good many of the stockmen put up their horses, and asked one after the other if he did not wish to employ me. I was not the sort they wanted, however, and I met with no success. I had about given up hope when the proprietor of the stable came to me and asked if I didn't want to go out into the yard and draw water from the well for the horses. He said he would give me a dollar if I would draw water for two hours.

I had never done any hard work in my life, but I jumped at the opportunity that time. The yard was filled with horses, and close to the well was a trough for their use. They crowded around the trough and fought to get the water I drew from the well in buckets. My position was dangerous and I fully re-alized it; in fact, I probably magnified it, for I was not used to being with horses.

I worked hard, however, and to such good pur-pose that in half an hour I had exhausted the well. The stableman acted handsomely. He paid me the dollar, although I had worked but half an hour. Later in the day I worked again for him, and that night he let me sleep in his hayloft.

For two weeks I worked around the stable and at other odd jobs in the little town, chopping wood and doing anything I could get to do, and I managed to make a bare living, but no more.

It was there that I first met John Ross.[3] He was a big-hearted, bluff Scotchman, with a bright red beard and the broadest of Scotch accents. He had come to Texas from Glasgow and had married a young San Antonio girl of good family, the granddaughter of José Antonio Navarro,[4] a hero of the

[3] John C. Ross and William F. Ross were brothers who were born in northern Scotland and arrived in Texas in 1867. They established Rossville in 1873, the first Scottish community in southwest Texas. See Atascosa County Records, Texas Historical Commission, Austin, Texas.

[4] José Antonio Navarro was born in San Antonio de Bexar on February 27, 1795. He formed a friendship with Stephen F. Austin and, following the creation of Texas as a Mexican state in 1824, was elected to represent Texas. He was a signer of the Texas Declaration of Independence and helped draft its constitution. He served in the Congress of the Republic (1838–39), participated in the ill-fated Santa Fe Expedition (1841) after which he was jailed for three years. He attended the Texas Annexation Convention in July, 1845; was elected a state senator in 1846–49, at which time the legislature created Navarro County in his honor. In 1857 he donated land for the county seat in Atascosa County but plans for the township of Navatasco never materialized. On January 13, 1871, he died in San Antonio. See Louis Wiltz Kemp, *The Signers of the Texas Declaration of Independence* (Salado: The Anson Jones Press, 1959), pp. 235–43; Frederick C. Chabot, *With the Makers of San Antonio* (San Antonio: Artes Graficas, 1937), pp. 203–05.

Texas revolution. To this day, I look back with feelings of deepest affection and gratitude to these good people, for they were father and mother to me when I was alone in Texas and friendless.

Ross spoke with me in Pleasanton and said he would take me to his ranch on the Atascosa Creek, about eighteen miles from Pleasanton, and give me work. He said he could not afford to pay much at first, but would give me board and lodging and pay enough to keep me in tobacco. He took me to the ranch in his wagon.

The first day he set me to work digging postholes for a new fence he was building; but he was not a hard master, and when he saw I was getting tired he sent me to the creek to catch some catfish, a form of labor which was much more to my taste.

I helped Ross on his farm for three months, and gradually became used to harder work than I had ever supposed I could stand. It even became easy for me to get up before daylight and to go to bed with the chickens. My muscles had hardened, and I learned how to use them to the best advantage, not easy knowledge to acquire when one is city bred and has lived an idle life.

At the end of three months Ross told me he had decided to go to Laredo,[5] a town on the Rio Grande

[5]Laredo, established in 1755, was one of the chief ports of entry on the United States-Mexican border. In 1870 its population was 2,046. Gilberto Miguel Hinojosa, *A Borderlands Town in Transition: Laredo, 1755–1870* (College Station: Texas A&M University Press, 1983), p. 83.

about one hundred and twenty miles south of his ranch. He said that he was going to cultivate a market garden there, and that if I could raise about three hundred dollars he would take me in as a partner. I wrote to my father that I had a fine chance to go into business and he kindly sent me the three hundred dollars by return mail, together with a letter filled with loving advice. I fear I did not appreciate the advice nearly so much then as I do now, looking back from the standpoint of experience. This is a veracious tale, however, and I am in duty bound to tell exactly what became of that money.

We started for Laredo early one morning in January, 1875. In the big, covered farm wagon were Mrs. Ross and "Tommy," the baby, the same who lately won distinction in a Texas Ranger company by hunting down desperate characters near Corpus Christi.[6] Will Ross, John's brother, rode on horseback, as did I. I had about all the money in the outfit. We were fairly well armed, for the country was not free from Indians at that time and their raids from Mexico were quite frequent.

Never shall I forget that first trip to Laredo, for I suffered much, both physically and mentally. The weather was very trying for one so new to the country as I. The days were extremely warm and the nights uncomfortably cool. During the day the sun

[6]The reader is reminded that the story dates back nearly 100 years. It was first published in 1899.

blazed in the heavens and its rays beat down on our heads with tropical force, but no sooner did the shades of night come on than the air grew icy cold, and before morning it was freezing. Two hours after the sun arose the next day, the terrible heat began again. To add to the discomfort of these extreme changes in temperature, water was very scarce and rattlesnakes extremely plentiful.

It was on this journey that I first experienced a Texas "norther." It came upon us early one afternoon. Will Ross and I were riding about a mile ahead of the wagon. We were coatless and our shirts were open at the throats, for the heat was stifling. All at once, without the slightest warning, an icy wind swept across the prairie from the north. It chilled us, through and through, in a few seconds.

"Hello! a 'norther's' coming," said Will Ross. "We'd better go back and get our coats."

We turned back to the wagon, but when we attempted to ride into the teeth of that terribly cold wind, we suffered so that we gave up the attempt. We dismounted and stood in the lee of our horses until the wagon came lumbering up. Then we bundled into our coats and overcoats and rode on to a creek, a mile or so ahead. There, under the shelter of one of the banks, we built a great fire and went into camp, to remain until the "norther" should blow itself out. This, Ross knew from experience, would be in two days.

A "norther" invariably blows from the north for

twenty-four hours. Then it comes back, almost as cold, from the south for twenty-four hours more. The third day there is no wind, but the cold continues, gradually abating until, on the fourth day, the temperature is what it was before the "norther" blew in. I have been in New Hampshire when the thermometer marked forty degrees below zero; I have passed a night, lost in a snowstorm, in the Rocky Mountains in Colorado; but never have I suffered so from the cold as I have in a Texas "norther." One's blood gets thin in a warm climate, and it is not so easy to resist cold as in Northern latitudes. Not infrequently thousands of cattle will die, frozen to death, in a Texas "norther." During the winter months the "northers" sweep over Texas about once in every two or three weeks.

Lawrence Christopher Criss, an old Texas guide and buffalo hunter is responsible for the following tale of a "norther." Criss vouched for the absolute truth of it, and even offered to take me to the spot where it happened and show me the ashes of the campfire to prove it.

"It was along in the winter of '69 that I was out huntin' buffalo with a little hunchback we called 'Twisted Charley,'" said Criss, relating the yarn one night, sitting by a campfire near El Paso, Texas. "We were up in the Panhandle, and had run across a herd in the afternoon, and killed nineteen between us. 'Twisted Charley' and I were skinnin' them, and were takin' off the hides of four or five when the worst 'norther' I ever remember struck us.

"We piled all the wood we could find on the fire, but we couldn't begin to keep warm, and when night come on it got colder, and colder, and colder, till the coffee, boilin' in the pot on the fire, had a skim of ice on it that we had to break before we could pour the coffee out.

"Well, a bright idea struck me, and I took one of the green buffalo hides and wrapped myself up in it, and in a minute I was as warm and comfortable as a man could wish to be anywhere. You know there's nothin' warmer than a buffalo hide, and this one was extry thick. 'Charley' saw what I had done, and he went and got a hide, too, and wrapped himself up in it. We were not long in fallin' asleep after that, and I was peacefully dreamin' about skinnin' deer and antelope to make moccasins out of, when, all of a sudden I was awakened by the most awful howlin' I ever heard.

"I was sure the Injuns were down on us, and I jumped up and grabbed my rifle in a hurry. Then I saw that it was 'Twisted Charley' who was doing the yellin'. I went over to where he lay, wrapped up in the green buffalo hide, and I gave him a kick to wake him up, for I thought he had a nightmare."

"Help me out, help me out!" he yelled.

"What's the matter with you?" I asked.

"Don't you see I'm froze up in this hide and can't get out?" he howled.

"I took hold of the hide and tried to unroll it, but

it was froze 'round him as hard as boiler iron. He was warm enough, for he had wrapped himself in it with the hairy side next to him, but he wanted to get out bad.

"I can't unwrap that hide any way," I said, after I'd made a trial at it.

"Cut it open," he said.

I took my skinning knife and tried to cut it, but the hide was so hard it turned the knife edge.

"I'll have to give it up," I said, at last.

"What?" yelled Charley. "Man, I can't stay in this hide forever."

"You won't have to," I said, "this 'norther' will blow itself out in three days, and then you'll thaw out naturally."

"Thaw me out at the fire," said Charley.

That seemed reasonable, and I rolled him over by the fire and began toastin' first one side and then the other. I thought I'd never get him out; but after a while, when the hide was actually roasted, I managed to unroll it enough for him to get out. He sat up by the fire the rest of the night, swearin'. He was a beautiful swearer, and the air moderated a whole lot while he was sittin' there inventin' new oaths and lettin' 'em out.

There was one other thing which I did not particularly fancy on that trip to Laredo, and that was the howling of the coyote wolves around our camp at night. Any Texan will tell you that a coyote is the most cowardly and harmless of animals, but his howl is bloodthirsty and horrible at night. It is a shrill, wild, piercing yelp, tapering off to a long, dismal howl. There is something very human about it, and yet it is weird and uncanny and creepy, especially when the one listening to it is a young and inexperienced man, fresh from the quiet of Philadelphia streets. Even when one becomes quite used to it, the howling is anything but soothing to the nerves.

Many a night on that trip I was kept awake for hours by the little wolves around the camp, for I could believe they would attack us, there seemed such a menace in their howling. However, the others in the camp, including Mrs. Ross and her baby, paid no attention to the coyotes.

We arrived in Laredo at night, about ten days after we had started, and found the little town in gala attire. The annual *fiesta*, or fair, was in progress in Nuevo Laredo, just across the Rio Grande, in Mexico.[7] The Mexicans of both towns had entered into the activities and enjoyment of the holiday season, and only *monte*, *mescal*, *fandangos*, bullfights, and general hilarity were in order. *Mescal*, by the way, is a liquor made from the century plant, and is about

[7]Nuevo Laredo was established in 1848, a direct result of the Mexican War. In other words, American newcomers in Laredo drove the previous Hispanic settlers south of the Rio Grande. See Hinojosa, *Borderlands Town*, p. 59; M. L. Crimmins, ed., "W. G. Freeman's Report on the Eighth Military Department," *Southwestern Historical Quarterly*, LII (1948–49), p. 351.

Main Street, Laredo, Texas, c. 1870

Laredo Transfer Company Office

as strong as "moonshine" corn whiskey. It has a smoky taste which, to the American palate, is not particularly agreeable.

When we entered the town that night, the inhabitants were all out of doors and enjoying life to the utmost. At that time, Laredo—now an important railroad terminus of twelve or fifteen thousand inhabitants—had about three thousand Mexicans and about forty Americans for its population. Of course, it was "run" by Mexicans. It was on American soil, but in its make-up and system of government there was little or no difference between it and Nuevo Laredo, on the Mexican side of the river. We arrived in town about seven o'clock in the evening and, after a supper of *chile con carne* and *tamales*, we crossed the Rio Grande to see what we could of the *fiesta*.

The market plaza in the Mexican town was given up to the fair. It was filled with booths, and there were enough games of chance and wheels of fortune in operation to stock a dozen county fair racetracks in this country. In a big adobe building on one side of the plaza a great game of *monte* was in progress. On a long table extending down the middle of the main room in this building were many stacks of Mexican silver dollars. Smaller heaps of half-dollars and quarters were scattered here and there on the table. There were about five thousand silver dollars on the table, and I was told the bank was good for any amount up to fifty thousand dollars.

The dealers sat at intervals around the table, and between them were the players, who were bunched around three or four deep. The players wore gayly striped blankets thrown gracefully over their left shoulders. Nearly all wore enormous *sombreros*, wide of brim, and with high peaked crowns, and covered, in many instances, with a wealth of silver or gold lace and embroidery.

Every man in the room was smoking a cornhusk *cigarito*. I was impressed by the cold-blooded way in which they played the game. Win or lose, they displayed absolutely no emotion. They watched the dealer closely with keen eyes from under their wide-brimmed hats; but, no matter whether they became richer or poorer by the turn of the cards, they gave no sign of excitement.

I watched one old fellow lose steadily for almost half an hour. He calmly smoked his *cigaritos* as he continued to stack up his silver dollars, fifty at a time, and he seemed to regard the outcome with utter indifference. He had a well-filled wallet, and time after time he took bills from it, and had them changed by an attendant into silver to bet on the game. Only silver was allowed on the table. After a time, this old man began to win as rapidly as he had lost, but there was no change in his demeanor. He seemed devoid of nerves. He was an ideal gambler, but he was only a type of all the others.

From the fascination of watching others to the excitement of playing was a very little step, and I took it. I came out of the room about fifty dollars poorer than I entered it. I had become separated from the Ross brothers, and I started around the plaza to hunt for them.

I had not gone far before I found myself surrounded by a crowd of Mexicans. I attempted to pass on, but one of them caught me by the coat-sleeve and detained me. I now have no doubt whatever that he merely wanted to invite me to take a drink from his bottle of *mescal*, but at that time I did not understand the language, and I feared I was about to be assaulted and robbed.

I still had over $200 of the $300 which I had intended to put into the vegetable gardening business with Ross, and when that Mexican caught hold of me and held me, I was frightened. I was so frightened, indeed, that I did something very foolish. I roughly broke away from him, and when he reached to catch me again, I turned and hit him in the face. Then I ran.

How I escaped from that crowd and away from the plaza has always been a puzzle to me, but I know that I found myself running as fast as I could down the long street which led to the little ferry-boat which connected the two republics. Behind me, I knew there was a crowd of irate Mexicans bent on capturing me, and wreaking vengeance for the insult I had put upon their companion and countryman. I flew on the wings of fear, for I doubted not that my fate would be sealed if they caught me. Suddenly, to my great horror, I felt myself caught around one arm by such a powerful hand that my progress was instantly arrested, and I was swung about as though I were on a pivot. Before I realized what had happened I heard a drawling voice say:

"You seem to be in a hurry, friend; where are you bound for?"

My captor was a superb looking fellow. He was over six feet in height, and built like an athlete. His handsome, manly face was smiling good-naturedly. His mouth was hidden by an enormous drooping light moustache, but his blue eyes twinkled in evident enjoyment of my discomfiture.

He wore a big, wide-brimmed white felt hat and a richly embroidered buckskin Mexican jacket, and he was puffing a *cigarito*.

"Let me go! Let me go!" I cried. "A crowd of Mexicans are after me, and if they catch me, they'll kill me."

"What do they want you for?" he asked, in his drawling, amused tone.

"I hit one of them; and ——"

"Oh, well, I reckon we can stand 'em off," he said. "Here, take this gun, an' use it."

As he spoke he handed me a six-shooter. By this time the advance runners of my pursuers had nearly reached the spot where we stood, under the flaring lamp in front of a saloon. My new friend whipped out the mate to the revolver he had given me, and fired straight at the rapidly approaching men. They turned, instantly, and ran the other way. I think they went a little faster than they had come. Then the big man, who had so strangely come to my rescue, smiled again, in his quiet way, and, putting up his six-shooters, said:

"Come in and have a drink; it'll do you good."

"Hadn't I better get over to Texas?" I inquired, anxiously; "those Mexicans may come back here at any moment."

"Oh, I guess they ain't in any hurry to come back for awhile," he answered. "If they do, we can have some more fun with 'em."

So I went into the saloon with him and took a drink of the vilest whiskey that ever passed my lips. I got away as soon as I could, and reached the ferry and the Texas side of the river without any further adventure. Not, however, until I saw Ross' wagon, which he had put in a wagon yard, did I feel safe.

The name of my friend in need was Thompson— Bill Thompson.[8] He was a brother of the notorious Ben Thompson, the desperado marshal of Austin, Texas, who, with King Fisher, another desperado,

[8]Prior to coming to Texas, Bill Thompson was a confirmed drunkard. At Ellsworth, Kansas, he and his brother, Ben Thompson, opened a saloon and gambling establishment, which apparently caused problems with the local law. While drinking heavily, Bill quarreled with and killed the Ellsworth sheriff. He fled to Texas, while Ben sought refuge in the mining camp at Leadville, Colorado. See Charles Askins, *Texans, Guns & History* (New York: Winchester Press, 1970), pp. 76–86.

was killed in San Antonio one night by William H. Simms, whom they attacked. But I shall tell their story further on. Bill Thompson, at the time he helped me, was a fugitive from justice, charged with killing a man in Kansas. There was a $500 reward on his head. In another place I shall also tell how, as a Texas Ranger, I was able to repay Bill Thompson for what he did for me that night.

III

From Clerk to Deputy Marshal

JOHN ROSS met with many disappointments in Laredo in his attempt to start a market garden, and in the end gave it up. In the meantime my money was soon used up and when, at last, we found the scheme was a failure, I was down to my last ten dollars. I saw that I should have to look about for some way in which to make a living, and the outlook was not bright.

I made the acquaintance of many of the men in town, and among others, I came to know a certain lieutenant of the Twenty-fourth Infantry Regiment, two companies of which were stationed at Fort McIntosh,[1] about a mile above Laredo on the Rio Grande. The lieutenant was the Quartermaster of

[1] Fort McIntosh was built on a bluff overlooking the Rio Grande soon after the Mexican War when United States soldiers entered Laredo on March 3, 1849. Although at first named Camp Crawford, it was renamed Fort McIntosh in honor of Colonel J. B. McIntosh on January 7, 1850. It would remain an army post until May 31, 1946. See Robert B. Roberts, *Encyclopedia of Historic Forts: The Military, Pioneer, and Trading Posts of the United States* (New York: Macmillan Publishing Company, 1988), p. 768; Hinojosa, *Borderlands Town*, p. 60. See also an original diagram of Fort McIntosh in "Colonel J. K. F. Mansfield's Report of the Inspection of Texas," *Southwestern Historical Quarterly*, XLII (1938–39), p. 239.

the post and had an office in Laredo. He came to it from the post every morning. I heard he was in need of a clerk and I applied for the position. I was probably the only applicant he had, since he took me immediately.

I soon learned the routine of the office and found the work easy. But I did not keep the job long. The Quartermaster, like many other officers stationed at remote frontier posts, was not quite so abstemious as he might have been. In the mornings he was always quite sober, but upon his return from lunch, he wasn't. One afternoon he signed several reports which I had prepared, and instructed me to send them off. He did not so much as glance through the reports when he signed them, in an unsteady hand, and I was not certain they were correctly made out. I was new to the business and did not want to get into trouble myself nor to get him into trouble, so I held the reports until the following morning, with the idea that he would look them over when he was fresh and clear-headed. That was where I made a mistake. He was furiously angry when I delicately hinted, the next morning, that he had been slightly under the influence of intoxicants the day before.

"Make out a voucher for your pay to date, at once, sir," he said, gruffly. "You are grossly impertinent, sir."

I did not think I had been impertinent in trying to avoid trouble for him, but he would listen to no explanation, and I had to go.

There was one curious thing which happened while I was a Quartermaster's clerk and which may be worthy of brief mention. In the same building with the Quartermaster's office was the storeroom of the commissary department. It was filled with all sorts of canned goods and glass jars containing preserves, jams, pickles, butter, and fancy groceries of many kinds. One day, word came that the Inspector General was about to make a call on the office. The Quartermaster received the letter and gave it to me to file. He told the Commissary Sergeant about it.

About an hour later there was a great crash in the storeroom adjoining the Quartermaster's office. We ran in to see what was the matter, and found that all the shelves on one side of the room had broken down, carrying with them the glass jars. Butter, pickles, preserved fruits, jams, olives, and the like lay in a heap on the floor, mixed up with broken glass. When the Inspector General arrived the next day, he looked long and earnestly at the wreck and then condemned the whole lot to be thrown into the Rio Grande. The accident seemed a most timely one, for the Commissary Sergeant had been doing a thriving retail grocery business among his acquaintances before the Inspector General's visit.

After leaving the Quartermaster's service, I was again thrown on my own resources, and it was at this time that I met Hamilton C. Peterson, United States Commissioner at Laredo. Peterson had formerly been a captain in the army. He was a good lawyer and an expert civil engineer. He was the best revolver shot I had ever seen, and was always ready to bet anything, from a drink of whiskey to a basket of champagne, on his marksmanship.[2]

Physically, Peterson was a fine looking man. His face was handsome, and his big, fierce, black moustache gave the impression that he was a daredevil of the most pronounced type, shading, as it did, a resolute, well-modeled chin. His appearance did not belie his character. His principal occupation, at the time I made his acquaintance, was challenging men to fight duels. He was a hard drinker, and very quarrelsome when into liquor. Every time he had a dispute with a man, he would, as soon as possible thereafter, challenge him to fight a duel. Sometimes he would get me to write a challenge at his dictation. But since the fame of his marksmanship had spread all over the state, his challenges for a duel were never accepted.

Upon my leaving the Quartermaster, I went to Peterson and asked him if he could get me something to do. He said he could and would. He was going on a surveying trip in a few days, and would take me with him to carry a surveyor's chain and to

---

[2]Hamilton C. Peterson has been difficult to trace. The Official Register of the United States (Washington: Government Printing Office, 1875, 1877) shows that he was the U.S. Commissioner in Laredo, and was reappointed in 1875 and in 1877; it also mentions that he was from Ohio. The power of a U.S. Commissioner ranged between that of a U.S. District Judge and a U.S. Deputy Marshal.

assist him in other ways. Having decided this important matter for me, he proposed that we go and play a game of billiards. We did so, and it was not until midnight that we started for Peterson's little adobe, one-roomed house, to which he had invited me as his guest until he was ready to leave on the surveying trip.

On the way to the room, a cat ran across the street in front of us. It was too good a chance for Peterson to miss trying his marksmanship, and he pulled his six-shooter and blazed away at the cat. The animal gave a yowl and disappeared in the darkness. We continued up the street, but had not proceeded far before we found ourselves surrounded. In command was the city marshal, a stalwart young man named Gregorio Gonzales. His companions were Mexican policemen. They at once put us under arrest for shooting in the street, but Peterson managed to throw his pistol away in the dark before they could search him.

I had a sword cane in my hand, but they did not know it was anything but a plain, ordinary walking stick. Despite Peterson's protests, they took us to the house of a magistrate named Sixto Navarro,[3] an

[3]In 1870, Sixto Navarro was listed as a thirty-seven-year-old Tejano rancher, living at Pleasanton in Atascosa County. He was the son of José Antonio Navarro. He apparently had moved to Laredo by 1874. Ninth U.S. Census, 1870, Schedule I: Population, Atascosa County, Texas, p. 192; *Atascosa County Centennial, 1856–1956* (Pleasanton: Atascosa County Centennial Association, 1956).

uncle of Mrs. John Ross. It was nearly one o'clock in the morning when we reached Señor Navarro's house. The magistrate said he was willing to let us go on our own recognizances until morning, but City Marshal Gonzales insisted that we be made to give bonds for our appearance, or else spend the rest of the night in the "calaboose."

"But I am the United States commissioner, and you surely know I am not going to run away," said Peterson. "Let this young man and me go for the night and I give you my word of honor that we will be on hand whenever you say in the morning."

Señor Navarro was willing, but Gonzales was obdurate, and at last Peterson had to send for a friend and give the required bail. It was fixed at $300 each.

As soon as we were liberated, we went at once to Peterson's room. He was as mad as a hornet. He lighted a lamp and began to rummage over a lot of papers which he took from his desk. At last he selected one and, turning to me, he said:

"Here, my boy, I want to swear you in as a special deputy United States marshal. I have work which must be done tonight, and you must do it."

"What kind of work?"

"Why, I want you to execute *capiases*[4] on Gregorio Gonzales and Sixto Navarro. Navarro could easily have let us go if he had really wanted to do it. I have affidavits here that both of them have been

[4] A *capias* is a writ authorizing a law officer to arrest the person specified therein.

smuggling goods across the Rio Grande from Mexico. I will make out the *capiases* for them, and I want you to arrest them. You have the right to summon as big a posse as you think you need in making the arrests, and the *capiases* call for their bodies, dead or alive. When you have arrested them, bring them here and I'll show you some fun."

It looked as though I would have some "fun" in the execution of those *capiases*, and so I consented to be sworn in as a special deputy marshal.

"Now," said Peterson, when he had administered the oath, "you go directly across the street and awaken St. Clair and his partner and take them along with you to help make the arrests."

St. Clair and his partner were sign painters who had wandered into Laredo looking for work, and had been kept busy repainting the sacred figures in the church. The shop was usually half full of saints in all stages of dilapidation. St. Clair, whose bump of reverence was not very strongly developed, used one of the figures for a hatrack, and the effect was quite startling.

I went across the street and aroused the painters, who at once entered into the spirit of the thing. As soon as they were dressed, we started off to find the city marshal.

We didn't have far to go. We found Gonzales in a barroom, surrounded by a large crowd, graphically describing the way he had arrested Peterson and me and taken us before Navarro. He seemed surprised to see me walk in with St. Clair and his partner, but he was still more astonished when I walked up to him and, touching him on the arm, said:

"I have a *capias* for your arrest. My orders from the United States commissioner are to take you before him, dead or alive. You'd better come quietly and avoid trouble."

"Wha— what do you want me for?" he gasped, while his companions looked on in wonder.

"You are wanted for violating the revenue laws of the United States," I answered in as harsh a voice as I could assume. "The *capias* will explain that, if you care to read it."

"But you are not an officer."

"I am a United States deputy marshal. Come, I haven't time to stand here talking to you. I arrest you, and if you don't come quietly, I will use force to make you."

He saw that I was in dead earnest, and he had too much respect for the law to think of disobeying the mandate of an officer armed with a *capias* and backed by a posse with six-shooters. He hesitated no longer, but came at once, followed by the men who had been listening only a few minutes before to the story of Peterson's arrest. Peterson's office was close by, and in a very few minutes we were there. The Commissioner was seated at his desk. He wore an expression of great solemnity. Entirely ignoring the presence of the city marshal, he turned to me and said:

"Mr. Marshal, you will please open my court."

I stepped to the door, and called out loudly:

"Oyez, oyez, oyez. The Honorable United States Commissioner's Court for the Western District of Texas is now open. All persons having business with said court draw near and ye shall be heard."

I had never opened a court before, but I thought that was about the right thing to say. Having startled the night air of the sleeping town, I went back to Peterson's desk.

"Mr. Marshal," said he, "you have brought a prisoner into court."

"Here he is, your Honor."

"That man? Why, he is armed! Disarm him."

Gonzales handed me his pistol and cartridge belt with an exceeding bad grace.

"Mr. Gonzales," said Peterson, turning for the first time to the city marshal, "you are here, charged with a very serious offense against the revenue laws of the United States of America. A very serious offense, indeed, sir. It is, of course, impossible for me to give you a hearing now, at two o'clock in the morning, but I can put you under bonds at this time to appear before me later. As your offense is such a serious one, I shall have to fix the amount of your bail at twenty thousand dollars. If you are not able to give that amount of bail, you must pass the night in the military guardhouse at Fort McIntosh."

Poor Gonzales could only stand and stare helplessly at the Commissioner. He knew Peterson was in earnest, and that he would do as he said. He also knew he was guilty of smuggling. Peterson kept a desk full of affidavits against hundreds of men. The affidavits were usually sworn by anyone having a grudge against the offenders. Peterson seldom did anything in these cases, but he carefully kept the affidavits. He thought they might be useful sometime. This was one of the times.

"Mr. Marshal," said Peterson to me, after amazing Gonzales with the twenty-thousand-dollar bail proposition, "you will now go and execute the other *capias*. I will be responsible for this prisoner until your return."

Taking my posse with me, I went at once to the house of Don Sixto Navarro. He had gone to bed, and we had some difficulty in arousing him. When we at last succeeded, and I showed him the warrant for his arrest, he was greatly excited. There was nothing to do but come with me, however, and he accordingly dressed himself and came.

At Peterson's office the same action was taken as in the case of Gonzales. Navarro was told he must produce twenty-thousand dollars bail or go to the guardhouse for the night. He started to protest that the amount was excessive, but Peterson said he was the best judge of that, and would not consider reducing it.

"You may send for bondsmen, if you wish," said the Commissioner, "but you must hurry, as I do not propose to stay up much longer on this matter."

In ten minutes a dozen henchmen were scurrying all over the town, waking up the wealthy men and explaining what was wanted of them. In half an hour Peterson's office was crowded with the richest merchants in Laredo. He was exceedingly particular as to who went on the bonds of Gonzales and Navarro, and it was not until after four o'clock that the prisoners were allowed to depart. They were to appear for a hearing before Peterson at ten o'clock that morning. The hour set for our appearance in the court of Magistrate Navarro was nine o'clock.

After the last person had gone, Peterson told me to go to the door and adjourn court. I did so, and when I turned back to him, he was roaring with laughter.

"I'll turn the old town upside down," he said, as he began to sort over a big quantity of affidavits on his desk. "These affidavits will stir things up. I couldn't convict on them, but I can do a lot of scaring. Some of them are two years old, but I guess they are fresh enough for my purpose."

Soon we lay down and went to sleep, but arose in time for our appearance in Navarro's court at nine o'clock, and hurried to the office. The little room was crowded to suffocation. The mayor, the sheriff, the county judge, and nearly all the most prominent citizens and merchants were there. Our arrival was the signal for a cessation of the buzz of excited voices and the crowd made way for us to pass.

We took seats near Señor Navarro's desk. That

gentleman looked as though he had not slept since we had last seen him, and he seemed worried. He cleared his throat nervously and asked in a low tone if any of the witnesses against us were present. There was no answer, and the magistrate seemed much relieved. He braced up wonderfully and, smiling at Peterson and me, said pleasantly:

"Gentlemen, as you see there are no witnesses against you, so I shall have to dismiss the case."

All this had evidently been arranged beforehand, so as to appease the Commissioner, but they knew little about the man with whom they had to deal. Peterson merely shrugged his shoulders and asked me to go to breakfast with him. He took not the slightest notice of the numerous greetings of *"Buenos dias, Señor; cómo está V.?"* which met his ears continually. We had breakfast in a little restaurant and then went to Peterson's office.

A large crowd had congregated in the street in front of the office, awaiting our arrival. As soon as the office was opened, it was completely filled with men, and many were unable to get in for want of room. I opened court, and Gonzales and Navarro were told to stand up. Peterson looked at them very seriously and then said in a stern voice:

"I am not prepared, at this time, to give you a hearing and will delay each case for two weeks more. In the meantime, I shall require you to renew your bonds in the sum of twenty thousand dollars each, or you may go to the guardhouse, as you please."

Then immediately after saying this, the Commissioner turned to me, and in a very loud and distinct voice said:

"Mr. Marshal, you will find a number of warrants on my desk. Select those for the mayor, the sheriff, and the most prominent merchants and execute them at once. I propose to put a stop to this smuggling, and the best way to do it is to begin at the top and take the big men first."

This bombshell had an immediate effect. The crowd in the office began to thin out rapidly. The mayor and the sheriff disappeared; so did the prominent merchants. The others were not long in following, and in a few minutes Peterson and I were alone. I was looking over the *capiases* and selecting some of them, according to the Commissioner's instructions, when he said:

"Oh, don't bother with those things. I only wanted to frighten them a little and teach them not to interfere with me."

He had done so very effectually. The accused men went over into Mexico as quickly as they could get there. When Peterson learned of this, he was so tickled that he immediately sent a telegram to the *Galveston News*, which read this way:

"Laredo set on fire. The mayor, sheriff, and big merchants have skipped to Mexico to avoid arrest. Particulars later."

Unfortunately, he was not in a condition to send the later particulars, and so the *Galveston News* came out the next morning with a startling article based on the brief telegram. The headlines of the article read:

LAREDO ON FIRE

———

TERRIBLE CONFLAGRATION ON THE RIO GRANDE

———

THE SHERIFF AND MAYOR OF THE CITY SUPPOSED TO BE THE INCENDIARIES

———

THEY AND THEIR PALS HAVE FLED TO MEXICO

———

EXCITEMENT ON THE BORDER

———

IV

An Unpopular Chief of Police

Peterson and I left town early the next morning
to go on the surveying trip. He was to lay out
some homestead sections on the Nueces River,
about sixty miles from Laredo. It seemed to me a
queer country for anyone to select for a home. The
only trees were a few live oaks and mesquite, the
latter being completely useless except for firewood.
Prickly pears and rattlesnakes were everywhere. We
were three weeks on the trip; part of the time I carried a chain and the rest a red flag.

It was hard work and very exciting. The excitement consisted of killing rattlesnakes. We killed, on
an average, three snakes to the mile. We saved their
rattles, and when we went back to Laredo, Peterson
put them in a cuff-box. They completely filled the
box. It was on this trip that I learned what a wonderful shot Peterson was with the revolver. One day
he killed five "cottontail" rabbits without reloading
his six-shooter, and he was riding a fractious horse
at the time. Never before or since have I seen such
marvelous shooting, and in my ten years of Western
life I have met some splendid marksmen.

When we returned to Laredo I continued to act
as deputy United States marshal. I did not serve any

more *capiases* on prominent citizens, but I did capture some smugglers in the act of bringing dutiable articles across the Rio Grande. I took as "prizes" a cartload of Mexican sugar and three barrels of *mescal*. And since one can usually depend on five fighting drunks in a quart bottle of *mescal* and soon thereafter five splitting headaches, my capture was of direct benefit to humanity.

Seizing contraband goods was a precarious way to make a living, however, and I soon saw that I should have to obtain some steadier and more remunerative employment. The unpopularity of the work was another drawback. As seven-tenths of the people were smugglers, either chronic or occasional, I was not exactly a favorite with many, and so I went to Peterson and resigned.

"How would you like to be on the police force?" he asked. "If you want to try it, I will get the appointment from the mayor for you."

I said I would try it, and he sent me with a note to the mayor. Peterson's influence with the authorities since his threat to put a stop to the smuggling would have made a Tammany leader in New York turn pale with envy.

The mayor read the note and at once appointed me chief of police!

To do this he had to depose the current chief, but he would have turned out his own brother if he had thought he could please Peterson by so doing. I assumed my new duties at once. I hadn't a very clear idea of what they were, but I knew I had them to perform and that there was money to be made in doing it. I received $2.50 from the town for every arrest that I made, and $1 a day was allowed me for every prisoner in the "calaboose," as the jail was called. As it cost me but forty cents a day to board each prisoner, there was a clear profit of sixty cents a day. This system was certainly open to criticism, since it encouraged the policemen to make as many arrests as possible.

I had ten Mexicans under me on the police force. They detested me from the beginning, partly because I had been the cause of the ousting of their former chief, but mainly because I was a "gringo." The Mexicans on the border called all Americans "gringos." The origin of the term "gringo" is curious. There is a legend that, in the early days of the Mexican border, an American made himself unpopular there by overreaching the natives, and it is said that this man was in the constant habit of singing:

"Green grow the rushes, O."

The Mexicans couldn't call him "green grow," but they came as near to it as their tongues would allow and made it "gringo." From then on the nickname gradually was used to identify all Americans.

I had not been at the head of the Laredo police force two days before stories of vague threats having been made by some of the policemen under me began to reach my ears. I was young and did not pay much attention to the threats. I reasoned that if the men should become openly hostile I could easily dismiss them from the force. There was no civil service reform nonsense about the city government of Laredo.

The third day after my appointment I made my first arrest. The mayor had given me a silver badge, which I pinned on my coat. I had a .45 calibre six-shooter in a holster slung to a cartridge belt about my waist, and I was impressed with the sense of my own dignity and appearance. On the day of my first arrest, I was walking quietly down the street when I saw a man standing on the corner giving a series of wild yells. As I approached, I saw that he was very, very drunk. I went up to him and grasped his arm to lead him to the "calaboose." He looked at me in blank amazement for a moment and then jerked his arm away. Before I could get hold of him again, he reached down to his bootleg and, drawing a big knife, made a savage pass at me with it, and I retreated a couple of steps. I drew my revolver, cocked it, pointed it at his head and told him to drop the knife and hold up his hands. To my utter astonishment he did nothing of the kind. Instead, he backed slowly away.

I did not want to shoot him, nor did I care to get so close to him that he could use his knife on me. I was in a quandary. He backed up to a grocery store and then turned suddenly and ran inside. I ran in after him. There were half a dozen persons in the store, and when they saw me rush in with a revolver in my hand they dodged down behind the counter and boxes and barrels. The man I was after darted out through a rear door.

Before I could follow him, two women ran up to me and threw their arms about my neck. They held me tightly in this embrace while screaming as loud as they could. I attempted to explain the circumstances to them, but my fluency of their language was slight, and not at all usable during exciting occasions like this. When I finally did get into their heads the fact that I was a police officer and only wanted to arrest the man for drunkenness, he had disappeared.

I was mad clear through then. I went at once to the policemen on my force, and ordered them to hunt up the drunken man. They did not seem very anxious to obey, but I spoke imperatively and they started out on the search. I took one of them with me, and we began to hunt in that part of the town where I lost the man. We found him late in the afternoon, asleep in a little adobe house belonging to one of his friends. We went in and arrested him and took him to the "calaboose," but he fought like a tiger all the way. The next morning he had to pay a fine of $10.

This incident, although small in itself, led to more important results. The man whom I arrested was a great favorite with his native townsmen, and I did not make a bid for popularity by taking him to jail. One night a week later, I was shot at in the street. I heard the bullet whistle by my head and hit the door behind me with a thud. I ran toward the place whence the report of the pistol had come, but could find no one there. The streets were very dark.

Half an hour later I was shot at again. Once more I failed to find the man, who had fled, although I hunted diligently. It was getting very uncomfortable. That night I was shot at five times. I told my policemen about it, and they apparently made great efforts to find the man or men.

There was something in the way they went about it, however, that aroused my suspicions, and I, at last, came to the conclusion that they were in sympathy with my unknown assailant. Indeed, I was not sure it was not one of my own men who had been firing at me. Be that as it may, I decided I had had enough of chieftainship, and the next day went to the mayor and resigned.

He accepted my resignation without hesitancy. He did not ask me why I resigned, nor did he ask me to remain on the force. I collected something more than twenty dollars for the time I had been chief of police. It did not take me long to spend that money, and once more I found myself without funds or prospect of getting any.

It was at this time that General Porfirio Diaz was leading the revolution in Mexico against the government under President Sebastian Lerdo. There were several small "battles" in Nuevo Laredo, and

General Porfirio Diaz

President Sebastian Lerdo
Courtesy The Institute of Texan Cultures, San Antonio

the inhabitants of Laredo watched them with interest from the bluffs of the Rio Grande on the Texas side. From the American standpoint the fighting was rather tame. It was not very bloody, but it was interesting to watch, and all the inhabitants of Laredo made it a point to go to the riverfront every time firing began on the other side. The river was less than a half-mile wide at that point.

One morning we were awakened by the sound of firing over in Mexico. It began with two or three savage volleys, and continued with a pattering fire, like raindrops on the dead leaves in a forest. It meant that another battle was in progress, so I dressed as rapidly as I could and hurried down to the banks of the Rio Grande.

Many people were there watching the fight for the possession of the Mexican town. The Lerdists, or Government Party, had been in possession of Nuevo Laredo for about two weeks, and now the revolutionists were attacking them. Should the revolutionists be victorious and drive the Lerdists from the town, it meant a great loss to the merchants there. When the Lerdists had captured the place, in accordance with the regular custom of Mexican warfare—on the frontier at least—they had lost no time in levying a *prestamo*. In other words, they forced the merchants to pay them a large sum of money. The revolutionists did the same thing once or twice earlier in the game.

As a matter of fact, both forces on the frontier

were composed of unscrupulous bandits who only engaged in the war for the money they could force from the merchants. If the revolutionists won the town again, they were sure to make the merchants once more go down into their pockets. There were about two hundred men on each side in this fight. Those in possession of the town had erected barricades across the streets. Some of them fought from behind these barricades, and others went to the housetops and fought from there. On nearly all the flat-roofed houses were raised edges which served admirably for battlements.

The opposing forces had been fighting for about four hours that day, without killing more than two or three men on each side, when it was learned that stray bullets had come over to our side of the river, and wounded two women and killed a boy who was standing in front of his home watching the fight. I reported these incidents to United States Commissioner Peterson, and he sent word to the commanding officer at Fort McIntosh. This officer was Major Henry C. Merriam,[1] later a general in the United States Army.

[1] In May, 1876, Major Henry C. Merriam commanded the 24th U.S. Infantry at Fort McIntosh. He learned that a Mexican bandit named Benavides, together with a force of sixty men, planned to kill U.S. Customs Collector James J. Haynes. Major Merriam crossed over to Nuevo Laredo with one hundred infantrymen, then occupied the town for eight days until the threat was over. See Frank C. Pierce, *A Brief History of the Lower Rio Grande Valley*, (Menasha, Wisconsin: George Banta Publishing Company, 1917), p. 122.

Major Henry C. Merriam
Courtesy National Archives

Major Merriam at once sent a squad of the 24th Infantry into Laredo with an old brass, muzzle-loading twelve-pounder, the only piece of artillery at the fort. This cannon was placed on a highly visible piece of ground near the bluff which over-hangs the river.

There it was—pointed straight at the Mexican town, half a mile or less away. This proceeding interested the Mexican citizens of Laredo so much that a crowd of them gathered around the soldiers and looked at the gun with great curiosity. They had little or nothing to say, but they appeared to be greatly concerned.

Major Merriam would take no further responsibility, however, and said that he would only act under the instructions of the United States marshal or his deputy. Peterson said that I was the only United States deputy marshal in the town and would have to take charge of affairs.

This was interesting for a youth who had only a short time before left the peace and quiet of Philadelphia; but, with supreme confidence in myself, born of inexperience and tickled vanity, I assumed the responsibility without a protest. However, I decided that I would take no action without consulting Peterson. By Peterson's advice, I notified a number of men to act as a posse, among them St. Clair and his partner.

With St. Clair, I went down the river bank to the ferry landing and waited for the boat to be punted over from Mexico. By advice of Peterson, I was going to leave St. Clair at the landing with orders to detain any man who should attempt to cross to the other side of the river with arms.

The ferry landing was under the bluff on which the cannon was planted, but a little further down the river. We had hardly reached the place before we heard the "zip" of a bullet as it sped by our heads. In another moment the sound was repeated. Then we heard three or four bullets come humming by us in quick succession. Although perfectly aware of the futility of such action, I could not refrain from ducking my head a little whenever I heard a bullet pass. It is as natural to do that as it is to close one's eye to avoid something flying into it.

"They certainly must be firing at us from across the river," I said to St. Clair; "those can't be accidental shots."

"Right you are, my boy," he answered; "and the quicker we get away from here, the healthier it will be for us."

We looked across the Rio Grande while two or three more bullets sang by us. One struck in the water in front of us. By this time we had detected a little puff of gray smoke rising from the bushes that fringed the bluff on the opposite bank. I quickly raised the Winchester rifle borrowed from Peterson, and fired at a point a little under the smoke. A moment later a shower of bullets came by us and we did not linger longer in that vicinity. We didn't exactly run, but we certainly did not waste any time getting away.

When we reached the top of the hill where the gun was placed, we found a young lieutenant in charge. His name, I believe, was Glendenning. I told him that we had been fired upon from Mexico, and I added that, in my opinion, a cannon shot would have a salutary effect about that time.

"Oh, I hardly think it was anything more than a few stray bullets," said the lieutenant.

"I am positive they were firing at us," said I.

"Oh, I don't believe they would do that," said he. "It must have been stray bullets."

Before I could answer him, the familiar sound of the bullets as they hummed by our ears made the officer duck his head and jump for safety behind a little adobe house close by. Quickly he straightened up, threw out his chest, and shouted in a commanding voice:

"Put a shell over that town!"

It was beautiful to see the way those soldiers in Uncle Sam's blue uniforms sprang to their positions and made ready to fire the twelve-pounder. They moved like clockwork. Most of the townspeople had moved nearby at this time, and with the greatest interest they watched the loading and aiming of the gun. Then the gunners fell back a few steps, and the next moment the cannon boomed its defiance.

The bullets immediately stopped coming our way. Indeed, the Mexican forces across the Rio Grande were so surprised by the introduction of artillery into their "battle" that they stopped fighting.

There was a sudden clattering of hoofs down the street, and, in a minute, Major Merriam dashed up to the gun on his horse.

"By whose orders did you fire that gun?" he demanded, as the lieutenant saluted.

"Well, sir," said the young officer, "they were firing at us from across the river, and—and this young man, the deputy marshal, asked me to fire, so I gave orders to send a shell or a solid shot over there for every bullet that should come this way."

"I told him to fire, sir," I added.

Major Merriam put his hand to his mouth to conceal a smile. Then he said gravely:

"You have done absolutely right, gentlemen. I have just received orders from San Antonio to do exactly what you have done."

Our attention was attracted at this moment to a rowboat which put out from the Mexican bank of the river. Someone in it was holding a white flag and waving it to attract attention. The boat came halfway across the river and stopped. Major Merriam studied it for a few minutes with the aid of his field glasses. Then he dismounted and walked down to the river bank, followed by an orderly.

They got into a small boat and were rowed out to where the other boat had stopped. There they found the *Comandante* of the Lerdist, or Government Party. The *Comandante* demanded to know why his city was bombarded by the United States authorities. Major Merriam told him the reason, and further informed him that if the bullets continued to come into Laredo, he would resume the shelling.

"If you must fight a battle over there," said Merriam, "you must do it sideways, as they fight on the stage. It won't do to shoot into the audience."

The boats separated and returned to their respective shores. A quarter of an hour later, the "battle" was raging on again, but the combatants seemed to have actually taken the Major's advice and were doing their fighting in such a way as to prevent bullets from flying over into Texas.

Now, although this was highly satisfactory to Major Merriam, it was too tame altogether for the more adventurous spirits among the Americans. A few of us consulted together over the situation, and hit upon a plan to have some fun.

We quietly stole down to a crevice in the bluff on the Texas side of the river, where we could not be seen by the American soldiers. Then we began to fire over into Nuevo Laredo. This soon brought a return fire, some of the Mexicans shooting at the gunners on the bluff. In another minute the cannon was off and roaring again, and this time a solid shot knocked down a little house in the Mexican town.

By carefully putting in our rifle shots where they would do the most good and so drawing a return fire to the cannon, we managed to keep up hostilities all the afternoon, and neither Major Merriam nor the young lieutenant and his soldiers knew that we were the cause of it. Toward nightfall the revolutionists were driven back from the town by the Lerdists. We learned that their entire loss was two men killed and five wounded!

Strange as it may seem, this bombardment of a Mexican town by United States troops did not lead to any international complications. The reason for this probably was that the Mexican government had its hands full taking care of its domestic troubles. Diaz, as everyone knows, finally succeeded in overthrowing the government, and on May 5, 1877, became President of the Republic.

One curious incident in connection with the bombardment of the town by the United States soldiers was that the most damage done was to the United States Consul's house in Nuevo Laredo. Part of one of the shells tore through his roof, and continued right down through the house to the cellar. Luckily, it did not hit anyone on the way. As the Stars and Stripes were flying from the building at the time, the consul thought the attack on his house was inexcusable. The Mexicans looked upon it as a huge joke.

V

I Join the Revolutionists

THE DAY following the bombardment I quarrelled with Peterson. He was intoxicated and in one of his ugly moods, and I was not as indulgent as I might have been, so we parted on very bad terms. Curiously enough, he did not follow his regular practice and challenge me to mortal combat on the field of honor. I should have peremptorily declined if he had done so. It is as well not to indulge a man in all of his foibles, and one should draw the line when it comes to accepting challenges from fancy pistol shots.

I was in another bad predicament. Ross and his brother had given up the market gardening project, and gone back to Atascosa County. I was without money, in a town full of enemies, and knew that as soon as it should be discovered that I had lost the friendship of Peterson, my situation would be desperate. There was absolutely no one to whom I could turn, and I wisely concluded that I should have to get out of town. But that was easier determined upon than accomplished. The only way for me to leave the place was to walk. The distance to the nearest town was several days' journey, and I was without provisions or means to procure any.

While I was puzzling what to do, I met a little Irishman named Ryan. He was almost as badly off as I. He hadn't a cent and he, too, wanted to leave Laredo. But he possessed one decided advantage over me—every man in the place was not his enemy. We talked the matter over without coming to any definite conclusion. We did think of applying to the Commissary Sergeant for rations sufficient to last us until we could reach some other settlement, but before we made up our minds to do so we received an offer which promised at least a living.

A Mexican who was in sympathy with the Diaz revolutionists told us he would see that we received a dollar a day if we would go over to Mexico and join the forces outside Nuevo Laredo. We were in a desperate mood and, consequently, accepted his offer without hesitation.

He led us to a point near the Rio Grande, about two miles above Laredo, and left us in an old dugout, in a bluff near the water's edge. He gave us some bread and coffee, and told us to wait there until we heard from him. We waited two days and, finally, were about to leave the place and go back to Laredo when, on the third afternoon, three men came to our hiding place. They said they had come to guide us to the revolutionists' camp across the Rio Grande. We quietly followed them as they led us to where a little boat was hidden farther up the stream. We stepped into it and were poled rapidly over the river. When we reached Mexico, we had to

walk about three miles before we came to the revolutionists' camp.

The camp was in the middle of a dense mesquite
and cactus chaparral.[1] The revolutionists numbered
about three hundred men; without doubt the most
villainous-looking gang I had the bad fortune to
encounter. They were guerrillas of the worst kind.
They were thieves, cutthroats, and cowards, and did
not possess one redeeming feature, as we very soon
discovered. We were not with them two hours before wishing ourselves to be a hundred miles away.

The man who induced us to join them had told
us we were only wanted for our fighting qualities,
and that we would have an easy time of it. He said
the leaders put great store in the fighting qualities
of Americans. After having watched one or two of
their "battles," I did not doubt that statement in
the least.

When we reached the camp, we quickly discovered that we could be useful to the revolutionists in
other ways than fighting their enemies. We were
compelled to go a quarter of a mile for water, to
collect wood for the fires, and to do all the heavy
work about the camp, while they squatted on their
blankets and quarreled over *monte.* The revolutionists were abnormally lazy and great gamblers.

[1] Chaparral is a dense thicket of shrubs and small trees.
Cattlemen and cowboys were especially aware of its presence in South Texas because its sharp thorns were a constant
hazard to a man on horseback.

They all had horses—sorry-looking, ill-fed mustangs; but when we asked for horses, they laughed at us. They gave us each a revolver, but there it ended, so far as an outfit was concerned.

For three days we worked from dawn until after dark. We did not get the dollar a day which had been promised to us. We barely got enough to eat.

On the fourth day we were told they were going to make another attack on the town. Then they gave us horses, and pretty bad ones they were. Ryan and I did not feel a bit like helping those fellows to capture the town, but we had no recourse. We started out with the troop just before daylight the next morning. When we reached the edge of Nuevo Laredo, the first faint light showed in the east above the horizon. For some reason, which I was at a loss to understand, we did not at once begin the attack. We waited until the sun was up. Then the order to charge was given, and we started into town in a disorganized manner.

As we went up a long, narrow street, the Lerdists, who were on the housetops and in many of the windows of the houses, fired on us. Suddenly my horse gave a jump and bolted ahead like a racer on the homestretch. I tried to rein him in, but could not. He had the bit between his teeth, and was going like the wind. Then I saw that he had been shot through the ear.

By the time I discovered what ailed my horse, I was far in advance of the revolutionists. I had never

led a charge before, and it was not of my own voli-
tion that I led this one; but I did it all the same.
When I found I was in for it, I ceased trying to hold
my horse back. Instead, I urged him to greater exertions. If there was any glory to be won, I thought, I
might as well have the credit of trying to win it. So I
pulled my revolver, and, yelling in true cowboy
fashion, fired at every man I saw.

It was exhilarating and tremendously exciting,
and I lost sight of the danger in the fierce fun of the
dash up that street. When I reached the market
plaza, I burst into it with a wild yell and started
around it fast as I could go, while rifles blazed from
every side. If sharpshooters had been behind those
rifles, I should have fallen before I had gone ten
yards; but, as it was, I was not touched by a bullet.

I soon saw that the streets leading from the plaza
were all barricaded, with the exception of the one
by which I had come into it. I had circled twice
around the plaza when the revolutionists reached it
and came after me with a series of bloodcurdling
yells. Then, on my third round, I darted down the
street by which we had entered, and every mother's
son of those revolutionists followed me. All were
shooting and yelling, and it was exciting to a rare
degree. But I had had all I wanted of it for that
time, and I went out of the town almost as fast as I
entered it.

When we were well clear of the place, I reined in
my exhausted pony and waited for the others to

come up. They stopped when they reached me, and to my extreme amazement were loud in their praises of what they called my "bravery." I did not think it would be wise to tell them that I led the charge solely because I could do nothing about it. If they thought it brave to ride into a town and out again without accomplishing anything, that was strictly their business.

They seemed to think that we had done enough for one day and we rode slowly back to our camp. When we reached it, I thought I would take advantage of my sudden popularity and demand the pay that was due me. I did so, and was told to go and get some water to make coffee. I picked up a bucket and called to Ryan to come with me. As soon as we were out of sight of the camp, I threw down my bucket and told Ryan I was going back to Texas. He followed suit, and we made a beeline for the Rio Grande. We found the man in charge of the boat in which we had crossed a few days before. He declined to take us across the river until he should receive orders to do so from the leader of the revolutionists, so we tried the effect of a little moral suasion in the form of two six-shooters held at his head, and he poled us over to the Texas bank with commendable vigor.

Once more on the soil of the United States, we felt that we were safe from pursuit. It was a warm day and we had been up and active very early, so, following the local custom, we lay down for a *siesta*.

Our couch was the grass-covered prairie and our covering and shelter from the sun's hot rays was a mesquite tree.

We slept long, for it was not until the sun's rays were touching the tops of the mesquite trees with a last golden gleam that we awoke. We did not reach Laredo until after dark. I led the way to St. Clair's house. When we arrived there and went in, St. Clair closed the door quickly and bolted it.

"Where did you fellows come from?" he asked.

"Mexico."

"How did you get away from the revolutionists?"

"Walked."

"Desert?"

"Yes."

"I don't blame you, but you shouldn't have come to this town. You were seen attacking the town over there today, and warrants are out for your arrest for filibustering. You'd better light out of this burg as fast as you can travel."

"Give us something to eat first. We can discuss the other afterwards."

St. Clair made strong coffee for us and toasted some jerked beef over his fire. Jerked beef might not be highly prized as a delicacy in epicurean circles of the large cities of the North, but as it was served to us that night, it seemed a dainty, fit for a king's table. Our appetites were sharp enough to do it ample justice, and St. Clair, good fellow that he was, seemed delighted to see us empty his larder.

We were just finishing the last bit of the supper, when a loud knock came at the door.

"Who's there?" called out St. Clair.

"Open this door instantly," answered a voice which we recognized as belonging to Peterson. "I have come to get two men who were seen to enter your house."

"I'll open my door when I please," cried St. Clair. "There's no one here but myself."

As he said this, he quietly opened a back door and motioned for Ryan and me to go out that way. We did not hesitate long about leaving, but went at once, and found ourselves in a yard surrounded by a high brush fence. As everything that grows in Texas has a more or less wicked thorn, a brush fence in that part of the country is no slight obstacle to surmount, but this was no time to care for a few scratches, so over that thorny fence we scrambled without counting the cost.

We had no sooner reached the further side than we heard a number of men in the yard behind us, and the next moment we saw a bright light back there. It was made by setting fire to a newspaper soaked with kerosene. The light revealed nothing to our pursuers, however, for we were far away.

That night we slept in the brush. The next morning we were both extremely hungry. That may seem curious, after what I have said of the good supper at St. Clair's, but it is a fact that a man is always hungry when he does not know where or how he is to get his next meal. Why this should be I do not know, but anyone who has ever been in such an unenviable predicament will bear me out in my assertion of the fact.

What were we to do? We could not stay out there in the brush and starve to death. We could not go over to Mexico and be shot or hanged for deserting that band of rascally revolutionists. We could not branch out for ourselves and try to walk to another town, for the distance was too great, and we did not know the way. If we went into Laredo, we should surely be arrested for filibustering, and stand a good chance of being convicted and sent to prison. We were in a sad quandary, but it was one from which we must speedily extricate ourselves. We discussed the situation in every light and finally, toward the middle of the day, decided to return to Laredo and face the music. At least, I did; Ryan said he would not return until evening.

I went straight to a restaurant which was kept by an Irishman named McIntyre, and ordered dinner, although I had not a cent to pay for it. I proposed to owe for that meal until I was able to pay for it, with or without the proprietor's permission. I was willing to take the chance of a little unpleasantness with him for the sake of getting a square meal.

Before I had more than half finished my dinner, mine ancient enemy, Gregorio Gonzales, the city marshal, came in. He was after me and had a *capias* for my arrest. When Peterson quarreled with me he made friends with Gonzales, and appointed him a deputy United States marshal.

"Ah," said he, as his eyes fell upon me where I was seated eating my dinner. "I have you at last. I have a warrant for your arrest."

"That's all right," I replied, as I kept eating.

"You must come along with me," said Gonzales.

Now I wanted to finish my dinner before going with him, and so I forthwith began to parley for more time.

"What do you arrest me for?" I asked.

"For going over into Mexico and fighting with the revolutionists."

"That isn't against the law so long as I didn't go across the river with arms."

"You can explain that to Commissioner Peterson, but I have a warrant for you."

"You say you have, but I haven't seen it. Where is the warrant?"

"Here it is."

"Well, I daresay that is right enough, but you ought to do this thing according to the law. You've no right to take me an inch with you until you read that warrant to me. I've been a deputy marshal myself, and I know what I'm talking about."

"You can read it yourself," said the Mexican, offering the paper to me.

"Not at all," I answered, with my mouth full; "the law compels you to read it to me. The United States law is very strict about that."

I knew that Gonzales had an extraordinary respect for the forms of the United States laws, and he probably concluded that I was right, and that he had better be on the safe side, for he began to read the paper. He was not much of an English scholar, and he stumbled through the formal document in a way that I enjoyed hugely. It took him a long time to read it. When he got to the end, I had finished my dinner. I rose and said that I would go with him. The restaurant proprietor, McIntyre, came forward for his pay.

"Mr. Gonzales will pay you," I said.

Gonzales angrily protested that he would do no such thing.

"That is your affair," I said. "So long as I am your prisoner, it is your duty to provide for my wants. Let me go, and I'll pay for the dinner with pleasure; keep me a prisoner, and you'll have to pay for it yourself."

"That's right," put in McIntyre.

With a very bad grace my captor paid the bill, and we left the restaurant.

We went straight to Peterson's office. The Commissioner was very gracious in his manner toward me, but said that he would have to put me under $5,000 bond to answer for crossing the Rio Grande with arms and fighting against the Mexican government, in violation of the neutrality laws. He asked me if I thought I could get a bondsman, and I said it was not at all likely. I asked permission to write several letters at his desk, and he granted it with much courtesy. He seemed to be sorry to see me in such trouble.

While I was writing, Ryan was brought in. He had been arrested as he was entering the town, having decided not to wait until evening before coming in. He was told that he would have to give $2,500 bail. Why my bail was fixed at double the amount of his, I did not inquire. Ryan was no more able than I to get a bondsman, and we had a forlorn prospect before us. Peterson said he would give us until six o'clock to get bail; after that hour we should have to go to the guardhouse at Fort McIntosh. Ryan and I sat in the office talking it all over, and wondering what the result would be. He wasn't as philosophical as I—he hadn't eaten a dinner—but neither of us expected much less than four or five years in a military prison.

As we sat talking, I happened to look out of the open door, and in doing so I saw a man whom I had met in Atascosa County. His name was Crockett Kelly,[2] and he owned a little ranch close to that of John Ross. Kelly was a superb-looking man and a frontier dandy at that time. He was tall and finely proportioned. His face was strong and handsome. His eye was as keen as an eagle's; his hair was black,

[2]Crockett Kelly is not in either the 1860 or 1870 census. Jennings, however, might have been referring to Crockett Cardwell (1812–91), a well-respected, community leader in DeWitt County. See Nellie Murphree, *A History of DeWitt County*, ed. by Robert W. Shook, (n.p.: n.p., n.d.) pp. 73, 133.

and fell in long curls over his shoulders. He looked the border hero of romance, and he became a real hero for me that day. I hadn't known him very intimately in Atascosa County, but we had been fishing together a number of times and were good enough friends. The minute I saw him through Peterson's doorway, I felt that he would in some manner help me. I went to the door and called him. He came at once across the street and greeted me heartily. I told him what trouble I was in. He listened gravely, and when I had finished, said:

"I think I can help you, my boy. How much did you say was your bail?"

"Five thousand dollars, and Ryan's is twenty-five hundred."

"Well, it seems to me that is a little steep, but if the Commissioner will take me, I'll go on a bond for both of you. I know you are not going to run away, and something may turn up in a day or two to get you out of the scrape."

Peterson consented to take Kelly as our bondsman, although I was positive Kelly was not worth anything like the amount of our bail. How he satisfied Peterson that he was good for it, I didn't care to inquire. I did ask, however, who had made the affidavit against us upon which we were arrested. Peterson showed the affidavit. It was signed by the man I had arrested for being drunk and yelling on the street when I was chief of police. In the affidavit he stated that he had seen us crossing the Rio

Grande with arms. This was not true; we had been supplied with arms when we reached the revolutionists' camp, not before.

That evening we went with Kelly to the house of the man who made the affidavit. We found him in and accused him of perjury. He denied it. We had a stormy interview, which was only brought to a close by our making him sign a statement to the effect that his affidavit was a series of lies from beginning to end. I wrote out his retraction, and he signed it with a six-shooter held to his head while he wrote. This may seem to have been a high-handed way of getting what we wanted, but in that country, and in those days, it was not such a peculiar manner of doing business. In those days the revolver was king on the Texas frontier.

Peterson accepted the retraction the next morning as a withdrawal of the charges against us. We had no hesitancy in telling him how we obtained it, but the irregularity of our handling only amused him. He tore up the papers and declared there was no case against us. When I think it all over, I feel confident the Commissioner never seriously intended to push the case, but was merely playing one of his practical jokes on us.

When I visited Laredo in 1892, I learned that Peterson had long been dead.

VI

I Meet McNelly and Join Up

ONCE AGAIN I was confronted with the problem of how to get away from Laredo, and its solution was as difficult as ever. The more I thought it over, the more desperate did the predicament seem. I should have liked to go with Kelly, but, unfortunately, that was not possible, he being on his way on horseback to Camargo, in Mexico. Even if I had a horse, I should not have cared to risk going into Mexico after my experience there. Ryan had obtained employment as a waiter in McIntyre's little restaurant, but I had exhausted all my chances to make a living in the town and my only recourse was to leave it.

But how? The prospect of walking scores of miles over that desolate Rio Grande country alone, depending for maintenance upon what I could get at the widely scattered ranches, was not an enticing one, but I realized that I should have to come to it sooner or later, and the quicker I got away from my enemies the better it would be for me.

While standing on a corner one morning, trying to make up my mind how to start on my perilous and lonely journey, I looked down the street and saw a troop of horsemen coming toward me. At first I thought they were cowboys. But what, I asked myself, were such a large group of cowboys doing together? I counted them as they rode by; there were forty-two of them.

At their head rode a man who was certainly not a cowboy, whatever the others might be. This leader was rather under the average height and slimly built, but he sat so erect in the saddle and had such an air of command that he seemed like a cavalry officer at the head of a company of soldiers.[1]

But it was easy to see these men were not soldiers. They were heavily armed, to be sure, but they wore no uniforms, and were nearly all beardless youths. The leader himself seemed not more than thirty years of age, although he wore a heavy, dark

[1]Leander H. McNelly (1844–77) was born in Virginia. In 1860 he moved to Washington County in southeast central Texas. On September 13, 1861 (at age seventeen), he enlisted at San Antonio in Company F, 5th Regiment, Texas Mounted Volunteers. He served in Thomas Green's regiment of Henry H. Sibley's brigade in the New Mexico campaign in 1862, at the Battle of Galveston in 1863, and then in Louisiana. On December 19, 1863, McNelly was commissioned captain of scouts to raise a company of mounted Texas volunteers. In the spring of 1864 he participated with valor in the Red River Campaign, receiving a slight wound at the Battle of Mansfield (April 8). Several weeks later he skirmished with federal troops led by E. J. Davis, who, after becoming governor of Texas in 1869, appointed McNelly one of four captains in the State Police. Joe B. Frantz, "Leander H. McNelly," *Rangers of Texas* (Waco: Texian Press, 1969), pp. 135–37; also see "Leander H. McNelly," file in Washington County records, Texas Historical Commission, Austin, Texas.

Ranger Captain Leander H. McNelly
Courtesy Western History Collections,
University of Oklahoma, Norman

brown moustache and "goatee," which, at a first glance, made him look slightly older.

I was still wondering what manner of men these were, when I saw the leader suddenly hold up his hand and, at the signal, the troop halted. The leader spoke a few words to one who rode directly behind him; then he turned down a side street and galloped away. The one to whom he had spoken gave the order, "Forward, march!" and in another minute the troop had trotted far down the street and out of the town. Then I asked a Mexican who was standing near me if he knew what horsemen those were. He answered in English:

"Why, those are McNelly's Rangers. They're on their way down the river."

I needed no further explanation. Many times had I heard of the Texas Rangers since I had been in the State, and marvelous were the tales which had come to my ears concerning their reckless courage and wonderful riding. They were the mounted frontier police force of Texas and were noted for their deeds of daring all over the West. I had pictured them as bearded ruffians (going about with bowie knives in their teeth, I half believed), but here they were, a lot of boys of my own age, and led by a captain not much older. I was interested.

"Where are they going from here?" I asked.

"No man can tell that," answered my informant; "but I have heard that they were expected down around Brownsville, and for that reason I said they were going down the river, but they may be just as likely going up the river. No one ever knows where they will turn up. I think they have gone into camp now, just outside the town. I know that Captain McNelly has gone to the hotel with his wife and daughter and son."

I thanked the Mexican for his information and walked slowly away, turning over in my mind a new idea which he had unwittingly put into it.

Why shouldn't I join the Rangers? Here was a chance to get out of Laredo and to gratify my love for adventure at the same time. The men in the troop were of my own age. I was strong, and a fairly good rider. I had seen some little service under fire in the last week or so, and I was willing to see more. I resolved to apply at once to Captain McNelly for a place in his troop. I went straight to the little hotel where he was said to be stopping and inquired for him. He sent word for me to come to his room.

I found him sitting by the window, talking to his sweet-faced wife. A little girl of about twelve years and a boy of about ten were near them.[2] My experi-

---

[2] In 1874 McNelly's wife, Carrie, was twenty-six years old and a native of Texas. Their children were a son, Rivel, and a daughter, Irene. At this time, the girl would have been six and the boy eight. See Ninth U.S. Census, 1870, Schedule I: Population, Washington County, Texas, p. 116; George Durham and Clyde Wantland, *Taming the Nueces Strip: The Story of McNelly's Rangers* (Austin: University of Texas Press, 1962), p. 45; Wilfred O. Dietrich, *The Blazing Story of Washington County* (Quannah, Texas: Nortex Offset Publications, Inc., 1973), pp. 53–54.

ence in Laredo in the last few weeks had not tended
to add to the attractiveness of my appearance. I had
not been shaved for two weeks and my clothing was
almost ragged. I wore a brown handkerchief knotted around my neck in lieu of a cravat, my legs were
encased in high and rather shabby boots, and I carried in my hand a *sombrero* which was somewhat the
worse for hard usage—I had been using it, doubled
up, as a pillow in the brush. I was not prepared to
meet a lady and her presence embarrassed me, but
my business was with the captain and I did not hesitate to state it plainly.

"I have come, sir," I said, "to ask you to take me
into your Rangers. I must apologize for my rough
appearance, but I have had a difficult experience in
this country lately and been without money to buy
food, let alone clothes. I should like very much to
join the Rangers, and if you'll take me, I believe I
can give you satisfaction."

"H'm—what's your name, young fellow?" the captain asked as he looked searchingly at me through
his keen, blue eyes.

I told him.

"You are from the North?"

"I am a Philadelphian, sir."

"That's a long distance from here. What brought
you into this country?"

"I came here to try to make a little money and to
see some wild life and adventure."

"Well, you look as if you'd been doing the latter,

anyhow. If you join my troop you'll see all the adventure you want. Can you ride?"

"I can."

"Very well. Come back to me at three o'clock this afternoon, and I'll tell you my decision."

This was not discouraging, for I thought if he had not had some idea of taking me, he would have said so at once. I determined to be on hand promptly at the hour he named. I wandered aimlessly about town for an hour or so. After awhile, I met St. Clair.

"Hello!" he exclaimed. "I've been looking for you. I saw Cap McNelly of the Rangers a little while ago. He's an old friend of mine. He asked me about you and I cracked you up all I knew how. I told him you went over to Mexico and led the revolutionists in a charge on the town over there, just for the fun of the thing, and it seemed to tickle him. That's the kind of stuff he likes. I think he'll take you in his company."

This was good news for me, and, as it was near the appointed hour, I went to the little hotel. The captain was standing in the doorway.

"I have decided to let you join," were his first words.[3] "You'll have to get a horse, saddle and bri-

[3] Jennings infers that McNelly accepted him into the Rangers in 1874, but Ranger documents list his service from May 26, 1876, to February 1, 1877. Francis T. Ingmire, *Texas Ranger Service Records, 1847–1900* (St. Louis: Ingmire Publications, 1982), III, 72. See also Durham and Wantland, *Taming the Nueces Strip,* pp. 135–36; Webb, *The Texas Rangers,* p. 265n.

dle, a couple of blankets and a six-shooter. The state furnishes your carbine. You'd better ride out to our camp this evening, as we are moving on early in the morning."

Then he turned and went into the hotel. If he had waited to note the effect of his words, he probably would have been astonished, for I must have looked the picture of despair. If he had told me that the entrance fee to his troop was ten thousand dollars in gold, it would not have staggered me more than what he said about the horse, saddle, bridle and blankets, for it seemed to me that such money would have been just as easy for me to obtain. I was completely disheartened, and came away from the hotel in a desperate mood.

I wandered up the street and entered a store kept by an American. I had no reason for going into the store, except, perhaps, to pass away the time with the proprietor, who had always been rather friendly to me. I told him of my hard luck in having a chance to join the Rangers and how my hopes were suddenly extinguished by the insurmountable obstacle of being obliged to provide the horse and accoutrements. He sympathized with me, but could offer no suggestion to help me out of my trouble. I was about to leave when a voice called out from the other side of a canvas wall at the end of the store:

"Come in here and see me, and maybe I can help you out of your fix."

I recognized the voice. It was that of one of the

mounted inspectors of customs who patrolled the banks of the Rio Grande, a young man named Burbank. He lived in a room partitioned off from the store by the canvas wall. I had met him only casually, and knew nothing about him except that he was a remarkably fine billiard player. I went directly into his room when he called to me, and found him lounging on the bed, smoking a cigarette.

"You seem to be in tough luck," he said as I entered. "I've had my eye on you lately, and I know you'll have to get out of Laredo pretty quick or you'll be carried out feet first. I'll get you a horse and whatever else you need, and you may give me an order on Captain McNelly for the amount. He can deduct it from your pay."

I started to express my gratitude, but he interrupted me and said:

"That's all right; don't say a word. I'm willing to help a fellow when I can, and this is only putting out a little money I have no immediate use for. Next time you see a chap in a hard fix, you try and help him out; that's the best way to show gratitude."

Burbank went with me to see Captain McNelly. The captain said he would accept the order on my pay and he'd give Burbank $10 a month until the amount was all paid. Then Burbank and I went and bought a horse. He was a light gray, and as pretty a pony as we could find. He cost $30, a high price for a horse in that country at the time. Within an hour I had everything I needed, and a very fine outfit it was. Burbank treated me to a farewell supper at the restaurant. It was the first meal I had eaten since the preceding day. After supper, I mounted my horse, shook hands with my benefactor, and rode out to the Ranger camp. I was more than happy to leave the town, for I had undergone much misery there and hoped never to see the place again.

It was only about two miles from the town to where the Rangers were camped for the night. It was dark, however, when I started from the restaurant and so the first intimation that I had reached the camp occurred when a voice called to me through the gloom:

"Halt!"

So sudden and unexpected was this order that it made me pull my horse back on his haunches.

"Who goes there?" came the quick demand.

"A friend," I answered.

"Dismount, friend, advance and be recognized."

I threw my leg over the saddle to dismount, but as I did so my horse started violently and dragged me forward with one of my feet in the stirrup and the other hopping along the ground. I was pulled along thus for at least thirty feet before I managed to stop my horse.

"Hi! hold up! What in —— are you doing?" yelled a man, who jumped from the ground where he had been lying. "Do you want to run over me?"

I extricated my foot from the stirrup and explained that my horse had started with me just as I was dismounting and had caused me to lose control momentarily.

"He must have been ridden by a low-life," commented the man whom I had so suddenly aroused. "Someone who has a playful habit of giving a horse a cut with the quirt when they get off him, and he learns to expect this and tries to get out of the way. But who are you, and what are you doing here?"

"That's what I want to know, too," put in another young man, who stood nearby with a carbine in his hands. "I told you to advance and be recognized, but I didn't look for you to come on in such a devil of a hurry. Who are you?"

"I'm a new recruit," I replied. "Captain McNelly sent me out here to join."

"Well, if that's so, I'm glad to see you," said the man with the carbine. "Shake. My name's McKinney—Charley McKinney.[4] This man you tried to kill with your horse is Evans, but he's such a big, ungainly brute we call him 'Lumber.'"

"Thanks a lot, Girlie, for the introduction," said Evans, or "Lumber," as he was always known in the troop. "You mustn't mind what she says," he added as he turned to me. "She's young and foolish. But if you've come to stay, pull off your saddle and make yourself at home. Girlie will stake out your horse for you, seeing it's your first night. Had your sup-

[4]Charley McKinney enlisted in McNelly's Rangers on February 1, 1876, and was discharged on February 1, 1877. Ingmire, *Texas Ranger Service Records*, IV, 51.

per? Good. Well, spread your blankets and turn in; we're going to make an early start in the morning."

While he was talking and I was taking the saddle off my horse, I had an opportunity to observe both young men who turned out to be my closest friends while I was in the Rangers.

Tom Evans[5] was a native Texan, and, by the way, almost the only one in the troop. He was a giant in stature, and as strong as a mustang. Like nearly all very large men, he was exceedingly good-natured and had one of the happiest dispositions. It took a great deal to arouse him to anger, but when once provoked beyond endurance, he was a man to be feared. He was exasperatingly lazy, and it was his habit to sprawl at full length on the ground whenever opportunity offered. This and his great size and clumsiness were what gained for him the nickname of "Lumber." When I first knew him, he was but nineteen years old, and had left school in Austin only about a year before. Like nearly all in the troop, he had joined the Rangers from pure love of adventure and excitement. He always said that he was destined, sooner or later, to be shot in the abdomen—only he didn't express it exactly that way. Lumber certainly offered a superb target in that portion of his anatomy for stray bullets.

[5] Tom Evans also enlisted in the McNelly Rangers on February 1, 1876, and was discharged on January 20, 1877. Ibid., II, 49. See also Durham and Wantland, *Taming the Nueces Strip*, p. 136.

Charley McKinney was the absolute opposite of Evans in every way. He was small and wiry, and as active as a wildcat. He had the prettiest pink-and-white complexion, the mildest and softest blue eyes, golden hair, which curled in little ringlets all over his head; a Cupid's bow of a mouth, and an expression of feminine innocence—except when he was on the warpath. The boys had nicknamed him "Girlie," which annoyed him exceedingly, although he strove not to show that he minded it. He was a general favorite, for he was of a lively, generous disposition, had a quick wit, could tell a good story and sing a jolly song, and, with it all, he was as fearless a daredevil as ever reached the Texas frontier. The man who attempted to impose upon Charley McKinney because of his innocent appearance invariably regretted it.

These two men were the first of the troop I met, and they to this day conjure up fond memories, although for all of my old comrades in the Texas Rangers, I have the most kindly recollections. Further on, I shall take up the troop in detail and show just what manner of men composed it.

Within fifteen minutes after I rode into the camp, I lay down on my blankets and, using my saddle for a pillow, soon dropped asleep. For the first time in many nights, I felt safe and free from care or worry, and slept well.

VII

Ranger Work

THE FIRST faint glimmering of dawn was lighting the sky in the east when I awoke the next morning. The awakening was peculiar. It began with a confused dream, in which I thought myself in a church where all the congregation were singing the hymn, "There's one wide river, and that wide river is Jordan." I remember that I looked about me and recognized many persons whom I had often seen in the church which I attended in Philadelphia, only, instead of being in that church, I was in a little backwoods Sunday school in the mountains of East Tennessee. The singing grew louder and louder, and at last, I awoke with a start. Even then it did not cease, but assailed my waking senses with renewed vigor. I sat up and found myself surrounded by fifteen or twenty Rangers, all of them looking at me and singing about that "one wide river" as loud as they could howl.

It surprised me not a little to see those wild and reckless border riders beginning the day so devoutly, and I looked at them in blank amazement. This seemed to stimulate them to greater exertions, for they not only continued to sing, but presently began to dance with a slow, measured step, as though they were performing some strange religious rite. In time they joined hands as they danced and then formed a circle around me. In time they increased their speed until, in the end, they were all whirling about me in a bewildering, dizzy ring, like a group intent on senseless folly.

Suddenly they stopped and gave a series of wild, bloodcurdling yells, such as are never heard, save in the West. There, the men on the great silent plains feel sometimes that they must let out their voices with all their power, just to break the monotony of that stillness which is one of the most impressive features of a seemingly limitless prairie. Having thus given vent to their feelings in the early morning, the Rangers started off in various directions to attend to their horses and prepare breakfast, leaving me to recover from my astonishment and confusion at my leisure.

"Did the boys wake you up?" asked a voice close to me.

I looked around and saw McKinney regarding me with a grin.

"Oh, no," I answered facetiously, "they soothed me to sleep. Do they always start the day in such a manner?"

"Not unless there's a stranger in camp," he said. "Then they do it to break the ice of reserve which might otherwise congeal about him."

"Thanks for the explanation. The ice is well cracked in my case."

Texas Ranger Camp, c. 1878

Courtesy Western History Collections,
University of Oklahoma, Norman

"Then you'd better go and give your horse some corn. You'll find a sack of corn in the wagon. I wouldn't give him more than two quarts. After you've done that, come back and take breakfast at my dab."

"At your what?"

"Dab."

"What's a dab?"

"Oh, I forgot. Of course, you couldn't be expected to know. We call the messes 'dabs,' in this outfit. There are only four men in our dab at present and we can easily accommodate another. If you want to join it, you're welcome."

I thanked him and told him nothing would give me greater pleasure than to make the fifth man at his dab. Then I went and attended to my horse. When I returned, I pitched in and helped to prepare breakfast. It was like any other camp breakfast in that country: bread, cooked in a skillet or Dutch oven; beefsteak, fried; and coffee. The last was so strong that it was quite black. It was made by putting a pint cupful of ground coffee beans into a two-quart coffeepot, and boiling for half an hour. That coffee would have eaten a hole in a piece of plate glass if it had been given time, but everyone drank a big cupful of it, without milk, and enjoyed it hugely for we were now alert for anything that might happen.

It used to be said in Texas that the only way to find out whether coffee was strong enough to drink was to put an iron wedge into the coffeepot. If the wedge floated, the coffee was sufficiently strong.

We didn't try the test that morning—it wasn't necessary.

As soon as we had eaten breakfast, all the cooking utensils were packed into a box and put into one of the two wagons which were in the camp and which constituted our wagon train. Then the order came to saddle our horses. As soon as this was done, a very young man with a little dark down on his upper lip, in lieu of a moustache, mounted his horse and called out:

"Fall in!"

Instantly every man swung himself into his saddle and began to form part of a long line in "company front." The young man rode up in front of the line and said:

"Right dress!"

The line became straighter.

"Count off from right to left."

It was done.

"Count off by twos."

The men counted as directed.

"Twos right, right forward—march!"

As he sang out the final word, he started off and the troop followed after him in double file. As we turned, I found myself riding on the right side of Charley McKinney.

"Where are we going?" I asked him.

"*Quien sabe?*" he answered. "Sometimes we don't

know when we start the day, but later on along the way we'll be told."

Nearly everyone has heard of the Texas Rangers at some time in his life, but how many know what the Rangers really are, or what are their duties? In a general way, everyone knows they are men who ride around on the Texas border, do a good deal of shooting, and now and then get killed or kill someone. But why they ride around or why they do the shooting is a question which might go begging for an answer for a long time without getting something like a correct one.

At the period of which I write, there were six Ranger troops in Texas. Five of these went to form what was known as the Frontier Battalion, which, at that time, was commanded by Major John Jones, a very efficient and brave officer.[1] Jones's battalion was mainly engaged on the western frontier—near the New Mexico line—against Indian invasion. One or

[1] Major John B. Jones (1834–81) was born in Fairfield District, South Carolina. In 1838 he moved to Texas and grew up on his father's ranch in Navarro County near Corsicana. In 1861 Jones enlisted as a private in Terry's Texas Rangers; in 1863 he rose to the rank of captain and was adjutant of the Fifteenth Texas Infantry. On May 4, 1874, Democratic Governor Richard Coke commissioned Jones as a major in the newly formed Frontier Battalion, consisting of six Ranger companies, and instructed him to rid the northwest Texas frontier of the Indian menace as well as of the state's criminal element. Within four years the Frontier Battalion had accomplished its objectives. See Webb, *The Texas Rangers*, pp. 309–11; and Billy Mac Jones, "John B. Jones," *Rangers of Texas*, pp. 151–59.

two of the troops in the battalion ranged over the southern edge of the Staked Plains, in the "panhandle" of Texas;[2] the others did most of their work along the Rio Grande in the neighborhood of El Paso del Norte.

In addition to the Frontier Battalion, Captain McNelly had organized an independent troop of Rangers. They were known officially as "Company A, Frontiersmen."

This was the troop I joined.

The duties of McNelly's troop were very different from those of the other Rangers. To McNelly's men was assigned the work of protecting the Texas side of the lower Rio Grande from the invasion of Mexican cattle thieves and horse thieves, but these Rangers also had roving commissions which gave them power to make arrests in any part of the state west of the Colorado River. Each man had virtually the authority of a sheriff, and even more, for the Rangers were not hampered by county boundaries.

[2]The Staked Plains is a high plateau extending from the central western part of Texas northward over most of the Texas Panhandle and then into eastern New Mexico. Because of extensive erosion in the region, where escarpments drop from three hundred to a thousand feet (known as Cap Rock), Texans corrupted the Spanish term *Llano Estacado* to mean the "staked plains." Actually *estacado* means palisaded or stockaded. In 1841, Englishman Thomas Falconer, who was a member of President Mirabeau B. Lamar's ill-fated Santa Fe Expedition, referred to the region as the *Llano Estacado*. See Thomas Falconer, *Letters and Notes on the Santa Fe Expedition, 1841–1842* (New York: Dauber & Pine Bookshops, Inc., 1930), pp. 110–11, 133.

Ranger Major John B. Jones
Courtesy Archives Division,
Texas State Library, Austin

At that time, the Texas desperado was in the height of his glory. Large bands of these outlaws were organized all through western Texas, and the honest, hard-working frontiersmen were completely under their rule. The sheriffs were wholly unable to cope with them. Indeed, in a number of counties the desperadoes were in such numbers and held such power that they were able to elect one of their own number to the office of sheriff. In one county they not only elected the sheriff, but also put in their own men as county judge, justices of the peace, and minor county officials.

The United States troops were on the frontier in large numbers, but they were unable to subdue the American and Mexican desperadoes. This was not the fault so much of the soldiers as it was of the military red tape by which they were bound. The cavalrymen had to be careful so as not to ride their horses to death in pursuit, and that alone was a sufficient reason for the ease with which the desperadoes eluded them.

Along the lower Rio Grande, cattle and horse stealing was continually going on. Large bands of Mexicans, very often under the leadership of some American outlaw, made frequent raids from Mexico into Texas and, after gathering all the cattle and horses they could handle, drove them back into Mexico. These men worked together so systematically and were so perfectly organized that they successfully defied or eluded all attempts to bring them to justice. They laughed at the abortive attempts of the United States cavalry to catch them. They could not only outride the cavalry—for the reason I have stated—but they could always escape across the Rio Grande when they were closely pressed, for beyond that natural barrier the soldiers of Uncle Sam could not follow for fear of setting off international complications.

The people living along the border, who had been harassed so long by these marauders, made application to the State Legislature for relief and protection. It was decided to put a troop of Rangers in the field. Captain McNelly, whose fame and daring as an officer in the Confederate service, and later in the Texas State Police during reconstruction days under Governor Davis,[3] was put in command.

There was quite a fight in the Legislature over the bill creating McNelly's troop; the legislators from the eastern portion of the state opposing it as

[3] Edmund J. Davis (1827–83) was elected governor of Texas in 1869. For four years he tried to maintain support for, what most Anglo Texans called, his "carpetbag" Republican administration. To help preserve peace and enforce his orders, the Texas Legislature created the State Police, which Davis organized in July, 1870. The composition of the force was a chief, four captains, eight lieutenants, twenty sergeants, and two hundred twenty-five privates. As previously mentioned, McNelly was one of the four captains. On April 22, 1873, after the Democrats—led by Richard Coke—defeated Davis and drove him from the state, the Legislature repealed the act creating this force. William Curtis Nunn, *Texas Under the Carpetbaggers* (Austin: University of Texas Press, 1962), pp. 43–75.

Governor Edmund J. Davis

Courtesy Archives Division,
Texas State Library, Austin

unnecessary. They said that the sheriffs should be able to cope with any lawless persons in western Texas, as they were in eastern Texas. Finally, the objectors consented to support the bill upon the condition that the Rangers' operations be confined to the country west of the Colorado River. No other authority than that of the sheriffs was needed east of that stream, they said.

There came a time, it may be remarked, when those wise men had occasion to regret the insertion of that clause, for the desperadoes took advantage of it and sought refuge in the eastern part of the State after we had driven them from the west.

As I have said, much individual power was given to the members of McNelly's troop. Any member could summon all the citizens he wished as a *posse comitatus*[4] to assist him in making arrests, but this was a privilege of which the Rangers seldom took advantage. Indeed, I do not remember ever to have known of an instance where outsiders were called upon to assist in making arrests, although occasionally their services were enlisted as guides to some desperado camp or stronghold.

There was one practice of the Rangers which undoubtedly added much to their success in ridding the community of evildoers—they almost invariably arrested men without warrants. The Rangers had no

[4]The term *posse comitatus* refers to any body of armed men which a sheriff or peace officer has enlisted to help maintain the peace of the community.

legal right to do this, however, the condition of the country made it a sensible thing to do. Of course, if warrants were given to the men to execute, they did so, but even in such cases they usually had the papers tucked away in an inside pocket and did not display them in making the arrests.

When a Ranger wanted to arrest a man, his first action was to draw his six-shooter and "get the drop" on his prospective prisoner. It was a simple matter to take him into custody after that, for no matter how desperate a man might be, he would not take the chance of resisting arrest when he was looking into the muzzle of a loaded revolver with a Ranger's finger playing nervously around the trigger thereof.

I heard of but one man who would not give up when a Ranger "had the drop" on him. That particular desperado had sworn that he would die rather than submit to arrest, and he kept his oath. He did die, but not before he had managed to fire his revolver three times at the two Rangers who were after him.

The Ranger privates received $40 a month and rations. The state supplied carbines and ammunition, but the men could choose any style of arms they preferred. Winchesters or Sharp's carbines were the favorite guns, and Colt's, or Smith & Wesson's large-calibre six-shooters were used exclusively for small arms. The Rangers supplied their own six-shooters as a matter of course; for each man

who joined the command owned and carried a revolver just as everyone did in Texas in the '70s.
Two or three of the men had fine breech-loading
shotguns—very effective weapons at close quarters
with nine buckshot to the barrel. Nearly every man
carried a bowie knife, but that was used much more
about camp than for fighting purposes.

The men had to supply their own horses and saddles, but if a horse was killed or used up in the service of the state, the state paid for it—and paid a
rattling good price, too. I never heard of the state
paying less than $100 for a dead horse, and I never
knew a Ranger to pay more than $40 for a live one.
As a rule, $20 to $30 was the price paid. The difference between what the state would pay and what the
Ranger actually paid was, of course, pure profit to
the Ranger. I do not believe such was the understanding in the Adjutant General's office, but I never heard of anyone taking pains to inquire very
closely into the matter.

VIII

My Fellow Rangers

HAVING given some idea of what the Rangers were and what were their duties, I shall, before going into a detailed description of the fights and adventures of the troop, proceed to tell something of the personal history and character of the men and officers composing it.

Our Captain, L. H. McNelly, was well-fitted for the work he had to do. For nearly fifteen years he had lived in the saddle, and had done more than his share of hard riding and fighting in the war and during the troublous reconstruction times. From a number of old comrades of McNelly, notably Mr. W. A. Kerr, of Encinal, Texas, who served in the Confederate Army with him, I have gathered the following incidents of his career.

McNelly was only seventeen years old when the war between the North and South broke out. He was engaged at that time in herding sheep for T. J. Burton, a sheepman, of Washington County, Texas. Captain George Campbell[1] raised a company in the

[1]Captain George W. Campbell commanded Company F of the 5th Texas Mounted Volunteers, C.S.A. McNelly was detached from Campbell's unit to serve as General Sibley's escort. See Martin Hardwick Hall, *Confederate Army of New Mexico* (Austin: Presidio Press, 1978), pp. 180–83.

county to join Colonel Tom Green's regiment, Sibley's brigade, at San Antonio. Young McNelly wanted very much to go to the front, but was such a boy that he found it difficult to persuade Captain Campbell to accept him. At last, he did so, and thereby became an enlisted private in Company F, 5th Regiment, Texas Mounted Volunteers, C.S.A.

The first engagement for McNelly was close to Val Verde, New Mexico, near the Rio Grande.[2] Colonel Green was in command of the entire Confederate forces there and Captain Joe Sayers commanded the Confederate battery of light artillery. Captain Sayers was anxious to find out the exact position of the Federal forces, so that he could turn his battery loose on them, and Green also wished to know their disposition. Young McNelly volunteered to try and get the information, and all day long was on horseback with a few men, pressing the Federal pickets back in order to locate the forces.

Between the lines was open country, and McNelly was in plain view from both sides. He rode all day, thus exposed, amid a storm of bullets. In his shirt was a book he had been reading, and a bullet hit this book and tore it to pieces, but McNelly was

[2]On February 21, 1862, a Confederate force of some two thousand men, composed mostly of Texans and led by General H. H. Sibley, defeated Union troops at the Battle of Val Verde, approximately ninety miles south of Albuquerque, New Mexico. See Alvin M. Josephy, Jr., *The Civil War in the American West* (New York: Alfred A. Knopf, 1991), pp. 52–60, 64–69, 73–76.

Brigadier General Thomas Green

Courtesy Prints and Photographs Division,
Library of Congress

unhurt. He did very valuable service, and when the charge was ordered he was in the front and the first to reach the Federal battery. The Union forces retreated across the Rio Grande and McNelly led in the pursuit.

Colonel Green commended the young soldier very highly for his good work and made him an aide on his staff. When Green returned to Texas, he took his regiment to Galveston and captured the Union forces there. McNelly was on the cotton boat which captured the *Harriet Lane*, and was the first Confederate to board the Union boat.[3] Colonel Green was promoted to General and took his command to Louisiana, and it was there that McNelly did his best work for the Confederacy. He was commissioned to raise a scouting company and he gathered about him a troop of reckless young riders and fighters. His dash and courage became proverbial and his heroic exploits were the subjects of many campfire stories.

[3]The Battle of Galveston began early in the morning of January 1, 1863. Confederate Major General John B. Magruder attacked three hundred Union troops who were behind barricades at the end of Kuhn's Wharf in Galveston and were protected by the naval guns of a Federal squadron including the *Harriet Lane* and the *Owasco*. In the ensuing fight the Confederate navy boarded and captured the *Harriet Lane*. As a consequence, Union land forces decided to surrender to Magruder and, soon thereafter, the remainder of the Federal fleet withdrew from Galveston Bay. See Paul H. Silverstone, *Warships of the Civil War Navies* (Annapolis: Naval Institute Press, 1989), pp. 82–83.

At one time, he was scouting between Brashear City and New Orleans, after the forces under General Green had captured the former place. The young Captain had been sent about four miles from the main command to scout along the railroad. He discovered a large force of Federals in the woods. McNelly had about forty men, and he found that the Federals numbered about eight hundred, together with nearly two thousand Negroes who had flocked to them from the plantations.

There was a long bridge about a quarter of a mile from the Union men. McNelly waited until night and then started his men running back and forth over the bridge, at the same time shouting commands for colonels and generals to move up on the right and left. His men kept galloping and trotting over that bridge for an hour, and by that time the Union men were sure all the Rebs in the country were on them. Then, at daylight, McNelly took the forty men under him, with a flag of truce to the Federal camp and demanded an unconditional surrender. The Union officer was certain he was surrounded by a greatly superior force and was easily convinced to surrender.

It was then that McNelly and his forty men led the eight hundred prisoners to the Confederate lines, four miles off, and delivered them to General Green. After that exploit McNelly, with his picked men of the brigade, harassed the enemy under General Banks continually. Later, McNelly went into Port Hudson[4] as a spy for General Green and obtained valuable information that led to its capture.

He was a thin, palefaced youth, but was very athletic. On one or two of his spying expeditions he was disguised as a woman. During the last eighteen months of the war he had a hundred picked men under him and they did superb scouting work. The Union men called McNelly's scouts "guerrillas." McNelly's command, his old comrades say, took more prisoners and killed more men than any regiment in Louisiana. Most of their work was done inside the Federal lines and they had a fight about every day, generally in the Louisiana swamps.

In 1870, Governor E. J. Davis asked McNelly to take command of the State Police. McNelly went to see Governor Davis and said to him:

"You know I'm a Democrat, Governor, and you are a Republican."

"Yes, I know that," said Governor Davis, "but I'm not looking for a politician, I'm hunting a soldier

[4]Port Hudson, Louisiana, was a Confederate strongpoint guarding the Mississippi River, approximately twenty-five miles north of Baton Rouge. Its first action was on March 14, 1863, when Union Admiral David G. Farragut bombarded it en route to Vicksburg. On May 8–10 Federal gunboats bombarded and silenced the Port Hudson batteries. Then on May 26, Major General Nathaniel P. Banks tried unsuccessfully to capture it, and then laid siege until July 9, 1863, when the Confederates at long last surrendered. *War of the Rebellion: Official Records of the Union and Confederate Armies*, (128 vols.; Washington: Government Printing Office, 1901; reprint ed., Harrisburg, Pennsylvania: National Historic Society, 1971), Ser. I, Vol. 26, Pt. 2, pp. 3–497.

and a brave man. My experience with you on the Mississippi, when I was in command at Morganza and you were on the other side, tells me you're the man I want. You know how I am regarded by all who were in your army. You were there and you might be able to mollify some of my enemies in the State."

McNelly consulted General Shelby and Buck Walton, Davis's most bitter opponents, and they advised McNelly to take the place offered him.

McNelly was wounded only once during the war, but he had countless narrow escapes. When I knew him in the Rangers, he was a very quiet, reserved, sedate sort of a man, but he always had a pleasant word for those under him and was greatly loved by the men. I was his field secretary for a time and was brought much into personal touch with him, and I never saw him lose his temper or heard him raise his voice in anger. Although the life of the Rangers was exciting enough for many of us, it seemed tame, apparently, to our Captain after his experiences. I saw him in several tight places, as will appear later, and a more cool and collected individual under fire would be impossible to imagine.

Such were the traits and actions of our leader, and it is easy to understand that with such experience his choice of men to serve with him was first rate.

For the benefit of my old comrades in the Rangers who are still alive and who may find some little pleasure in the perusal of these pages, I here give the roster of the old troop:

Captain
  L. H. McNelly
First Lieutenant
  L. B. Wright
Second Lieutenant
  T. J. Robinson
First Sergeant
  R. P. Orrell
Sergeants
  J. B. Armstrong
  George Hall
  Linton L. Wright
Corporals
  W. L. Rudd
  M. C. Williams
Privates
  S. J. Adams
  "Black" Allen
  George Boyd
  Thomas Deggs
  T. N. Devine
  L. P. Durham
  Thomas J. Evans
  B. Gorman
  Andy Gourley
  Nelson Gregory
  M. Fleming Griffen
  S. N. Hardy
  N. A. Jennings
  Horace Maben

A. S. Mackey
Edward Mayers
Thomas McGovern
"Cow" McKay
Charles B. McKinney
W. W. McKinney
John McNelly
Thomas Melvin
S. M. Nichols
A. L. Parrott
T. M. Queensberry
Jack Racy
H. J. Rector
W. O. Reichel
Horace Rowe
Jesus Sandobal
G. M. Scott
F. Siebert
D. R. Smith
L. B. Smith
S. W. Stanley
N. R. Stegall
T. J. Sullivan
G. W. Talley
Alfred Walker
David Watson
R. H. Wells
W. T. Welsh
F. J. Williams
James Williams

Jesse Lee Hall,[5] who at the death of Captain McNelly succeeded to the command of the troop, joined it as Second Lieutenant, August 1, 1876, at Oakville. He left the service in 1880 and was succeeded by Captain Ogilsbie. Hall was a famous Ranger captain, and I shall have much to say of his exploits later on.

L. B. Wright left the service in 1876 and became a practicing physician at San Diego, Texas. His brother, L. L. Wright, became the sheriff of Duval County, of which San Diego is the county seat. Both brothers died in the fall of 1892, in the same week. Just prior to their deaths, they furnished me with notes and recollections of their Ranger experiences and I have used them freely in the following pages.

Lieutenant Robinson was killed in a duel in Virginia, his home. He resigned his commission for the sole purpose of fighting that duel. He killed his man and was killed at the same instant. The duel was occasioned by an insult to Robinson's sister in Virginia.

Charley McKinney was murdered in 1890, while attempting to arrest an outlaw. McKinney at the

[5] Jesse Lee Hall was born Jesse Leigh Hall on October 9, 1849, in Lexington, North Carolina. In 1869 he moved to Grayson County, Texas, where at age nineteen he taught school. Unhappy that people continually mispronounced his name as "Lay," he changed the spelling to "Lee." In 1871 he served as city marshal of Sherman, Texas, before joining the Rangers in 1876. See Dora Neill Raymond, *Captain Lee Hall of Texas* (Norman: University of Oklahoma Press, 1982), for the most complete biography of Hall.

*McNelly's Ranger Company around
the Campfire, c. 1871*

Courtesy Barker Texas History Center,
The University of Texas at Austin

time was sheriff of La Salle County. His murderer was afterward hanged at San Antonio.

As soon as the bill constituting the Ranger troop passed the legislature and received the governor's signature, Captain McNelly began to raise his company. He had thousands of applications from men who wanted to serve under him, but he was very particular in his selection of them. He would take only young men who were educated, of good character, and lively disposition. The applicants had to convince the Captain that they possessed courage and were good riders, but the latter qualification was a common one in Texas. Although McNelly was himself a Texan, he was seemingly careful to exclude Texans from his troop and, with the exception of Evans, the McKinney boys, and several others, there were none. He reasoned that Texans might have friends or "kinfolk" among the very men he would have to hunt down, and he knew how important it was that he should be able to place complete reliance upon each individual member of the troop. The consequence was that it was made up of young men from nearly every southern state. I was the only member whose home was north of Mason and Dixon's line.

There was a big group of Virginians; Georgia supplied a good quota; so did Mississippi; so did Alabama. There was one Scotchman (McKay), one Irishman (McGovern), and one Englishman (Rudd). Rudd was a little bit of a red-headed and red-faced

Londoner, who always rode the biggest horse in the troop. He took his corporalship very seriously, but was lively, full of fun, and a great favorite with the boys. When reading Kipling's "Soldiers Three," the Ortheris character has always brought Corporal Rudd vividly to my recollection.

McKay was a splendidly built young athlete and as handsome as a Greek god. His running broad jump was the pride of the troop. He had a sweet tenor voice and sang old Scotch songs in a way to make homesickness epidemic.

Corporal Williams, a royal good fellow, was known always as "Polly" Williams among the men. Horace Rowe was a small, dark, delicately made man. He was a poet of no mean order and had published a book of verse. Adams was also a poet, but rather of the cowboy variety.

Durham was the wit of the company, and as brave a fellow as ever straddled a mustang. Rector was as deaf as a post, but was not lacking in nerve at any time. We used to yell at him in a way which he resented at times, and once I nearly had to fight a duel with him in consequence. Parrott was from the far-off banks of the Suwanee River, given fame in "The Old Folks at Home." I shall give an instance of his courage in another place. Watson was a lame fiddler, but a man of reckless bravery. Boyd had killed his man in Lower California and had escaped by traveling on foot across Mexico to Texas. Later, he went back to California, got out of his trouble there, and fell heir to a large estate. He was a hand-some, jolly fellow and without doubt the best poker player in the troop.

I remember how surprised I was when we rode out from the camp near Laredo that first morning to note the youth of Lieutenant Wright, who, mount-ed on a sturdy, little black stallion, rode at the head of the troop. He certainly was very young to be sec-ond in command. I don't think he could have been more than nineteen years old at that time; but his face was a determined one, and he had a trick of drawing his eyebrows into a straight line and knit-ting his forehead above them which hardened his expression and made him seem older than he actu-ally was. His straight, thin mouth and firm chin de-noted much character, and it did not take a very expert student of physiognomy to see that he was eminently fitted, despite his lack of years, to lead men into danger.

By his side and chatting merrily with him, was a little boy, not more than ten years old. This boy was the Captain's son, and was known as "Rebel" among the boys, with whom he was a great favorite. It was only when we changed our base of operations that the Captain's family joined us on the march. Mrs. McNelly and her little daughter traveled in an ambulance,[6] and the Captain was with them that

[6] An ambulance was a wagon or carriage with spring sus-pensions. Officers would often use such a vehicle for reasons of personal comfort.

morning, so he let Reb ride his horse. Reb was as much at home in the saddle as any cowboy. He was full of mischief, and if he could get any of the men to lend him a six-shooter, he took great delight in blazing away at trees, rabbits, or anything which chanced to cross his line of vision. As he was not a wonderful marksman, his target practice was, at times, a trifle dangerous to others.

Next to Lieutenant Wright was a long, lanky man, with a light sandy, sparse beard and long yellow hair. He was Sergeant Orrell, or, as the boys always called him, "Old Orrell," a Mississippian and as good-natured a fellow as ever breathed. Although continually talking about military discipline, he wisely confined his ideas to words and never attempted to put them into practice. He was brave as a lion and remarkably cool in a tight place, but was also very conceited, and as proud as a turkey cock over his sergeantship. Rudd was almost as precise and martial in his notions as Orrell, but both of them knew the Rangers too well to try to enforce their notions upon the boys.[7]

Armstrong was a Kentuckian and, like many of the sons of the Blue Grass State, was a giant in size. His sweeping blond mustache and pointed goatee would alone have made him conspicuous among so

[7]Sergeant Orrell, according to the Ranger Muster Roll, was R. P. Orrill. He enlisted on July 25, 1874, and was discharged on February 1, 1877. W. L. Rudd served the same length of time. See Ingmire, *Texas Ranger Service Records*, V, 7, 74.

Ranger Sergeant John B. Armstrong
Courtesy Western History Collections,
University of Oklahoma, Norman

many beardless young men, but there was a good deal more to John B. Armstrong than his hirsute charms. He had a singularly mild blue eye, and experience on the frontier has taught me that mild blue eyes usually indicate anything but mildness of disposition. His handsome face was full of character. His carriage was as erect as that of a grenadier and, despite his great size, he was extremely graceful in all his movements. He was a dashing fellow, and always ready to lead a squad of Rangers on any scout that promised to end in a fight.[8]

The rest were, for the most part, beardless boys, full of deviltry and high spirits, and ready at a moment's notice to rush into any adventure, no matter how dangerous to one's life it might be. Their wide brimmed, picturesque cowboy hats; flannel shirts open at the throat; high boots; well-filled cartridge belts with dangling pistol holsters and bowie knife scabbards; their carbines slung at the side of the saddles; their easy manner of riding; their suntanned faces; their air of wild, happy, devil-may-care freedom and supreme confidence, showed that the Captain, indeed, chose wisely when he picked out the men for his dangerous mission.

Here were fellows who would not stop to count the cost beforehand, but would follow their leader

[8]For more about John B. Armstrong, see Thomas Ripley, *They Died with their Boots on* (New York: Doubleday, Doran & Co., 1935), Chapter XIX; Raymond, *Captain Lee Hall of Texas*, pp. 49–53, 86, 88, 90, 107.

with reckless enthusiasm, no matter where he might go. Such was the impression I received in looking at the Rangers that first morning, and it was correct. Only once since then could any body of men be compared to the Rangers—here I refer to Colonel Theodore Roosevelt's regiment of "Rough Riders," which did such magnificent work in Cuba under his command. And among the "Rough Riders" were a number of ex-Texas Rangers, all of whom had given good accounts of themselves in the fighting before Santiago de Cuba.

Colonel Roosevelt has written in his story of "The Rough Riders" the following:

"We drew a great many recruits from Texas; and from nowhere did we get a higher average, for many of them had served in that famous body of frontier fighters, the Texas Rangers. Of course, these Rangers needed no teaching. They were already trained to follow orders and to take responsibility. They were splendid shots, horsemen and trailers. They were accustomed to living in the open, to enduring great fatigue and hardship, and to encountering all kinds of danger."

IX

Our Fight with Espiñoso

A<small>ND</small> <small>NOW</small> for a more detailed story of the work of the command which I had joined after an unusual series of adventures. I shall relate only the more important scouts which were undertaken, with an occasional digression brought about by the remembrance of some noteworthy incident. I shall describe the Texas desperado as I knew him. He may not be all that border fiction has painted him, but the description will be strictly truthful. Even at his tamest, he was sufficiently picturesque.

We went by easy stages across the country to Corpus Christi, the pretty, little old town on the Gulf of Mexico. We were ordered there because Mexican raiders had come across the Rio Grande and spread terror throughout that part of Texas.

We arrived at Corpus Christi on the morning of April 22, 1875,[1] and found the country in the wildest state of excitement. We were told how large bands of raiders were coming from every direction to lay waste the countryside and burn the town.

[1] Jennings was not yet a Ranger during this expedition against the Mexican raiders. Although his account is accurate, it was probably given to him by others in McNelly's command. See Durham and Wantland, *Taming the Nueces Strip*, pp. 34–69.

The most extravagant rumors found ready credence from the terrorized people. The civil authorities seemed helpless. Large parties of mounted and well-armed men, residents of Nueces County, were riding over the country, committing the most brutal outrages, murdering peaceable Mexican farmers and stockmen who had lived all their lives in Texas. These murderers called themselves vigilance committees and pretended that they were acting in the cause of law and order.

We remained encamped near the town for two days, to rest our jaded horses and to try to get a clear idea of the actual condition of affairs.

It seemed that the excitement had been initially caused by a raid made by Mexicans (from Mexico) in the neighborhood of Corpus Christi. These raiders had stolen cattle and horses, burned ranch houses, murdered men and ravished women, and then escaped back to Mexico. The uproar which followed was quickly seized upon by a number of men living in Nueces County as a fitting time to settle up old scores with the Mexican residents of that and some of the adjoining counties. Many believed that some Mexicans had been making a livelihood by stealing and skinning cattle, and the local sheriffs had failed to make any efforts to detect and punish them.[2]

[2] J. Fred Rippy, "Some Precedents of the Pershing Expedition into Mexico," *Southwestern Historical Quarterly*, XXIV (1920–21), 300–01, stated that fifty percent of the Mexican hides exported to the customhouse at Brownsville had been stolen in Texas.

During the evening of April 24th, a report was made to the Captain that a party of raiders from Mexico had been seen at La Parra, about sixty miles from Corpus Christi. McNelly at once called the troop to readiness and in an hour had started to that place and arrived the following day. There we learned that the party reported to be Mexican raiders turned out to be a posse of citizens from Cameron County, who had been brought together by a deputy sheriff so that they "could protect the people of La Parra from further outrages from the citizens of Nueces County," meaning certain lawless bands organized in Nueces County.

McNelly ordered the deputy sheriff to take his posse back and disband it. After some demurring on the part of the posse, this was done. We went into camp and McNelly sent scouting parties out in every direction to disband the various vigilance committees and "regulators" which were roaming through the country.

On April 26th, two companies of civilians, commanded by T. Hynes Clark and M. S. Culver, highly respected cattlemen, came into our camp and said they would like to cooperate with the Rangers by bringing peace to the area.

"We need no one to cooperate with us," said the Captain. "I have heard that some of you men are the very ones accused of a number of outrages committed on Mexican citizens of this State, and you must disband at once and not reassemble, except at the call and under the command of an officer of the state. If you don't do as I say, you will have us to fight."

The Texans didn't like this high-handed way of talking and were disposed at first to dispute McNelly's authority, but the Captain showed them very quickly that he meant business and they disbanded.

We remained in camp, constantly scouting in all directions, until matters had quieted down. When everything was quiet, we went to Edinburg, in Hidalgo County, arriving there on May 16th. Several days later we moved down the Rio Grande.

We found the frontier in a state of great excitement. Reports of a dozen different raiding parties would be brought in daily and the scouting parties had no rest. I was in the saddle almost continually. At night, we would either set camp where we happened to be, or continue riding, in the attempt to head off some party of raiders of whom we had heard. Many of the reports of raiders brought to us were groundless, but the greater number were true. Because of fear of reprisals by the robbers, the law-abiding citizens withheld information which would have insured capture of the marauders.

Many people said that large droves of cattle and horses were stolen and then driven across the Rio Grande into Mexico almost nightly. This, we found, had been going on for years. The United States military authorities had never made a complete effort to put a stop to the wholesale stealing, although the

Martin S. Culver
Courtesy Western History Collections,
University of Oklahoma, Norman

raiders at times would come in close proximity to the frontier army posts.[3]

McNelly continued to keep out scouting parties of Rangers, and this course had the effect of lessening the number of raids, but not of wholly putting an end to them.

While we were encamped at a place called Las Rucias, which we reached on June 5th, a Mexican brought the information to Captain McNelly that a party of raiders was crossing into Texas, below Brownsville, and going in the direction of La Parra. Our camp was located about twenty-five miles from Brownsville. Many Rangers were out on scouts at the time we received this information and only seventeen of us were in camp. This was on June 11th.

---

[3]Chronic lawlessness along the Rio Grande reached an alarming stage in the 1870s. Durham and Wantland, *Taming the Nueces Strip*, p. 41, stated that Mexican raiders killed "in excess of two thousand ranchers and other citizens" and stole "more than nine hundred thousand head of cattle." In June, 1875, President U. S. Grant ordered Navy Secretary George M. Robeson to dispatch the U.S.S. *Rio Bravo* to aid U.S. troops on the Rio Grande. In December, Commander George C. Remey, Captain of the *Rio Bravo*, reported to Secretary Robeson that Mexican authorities were "generally aware of nearly all the thefts" but failed to prevent them. See Robert L. Robinson, "The U.S. Navy vs. Cattle Rustlers: The U.S.S. *Rio Bravo* on the Rio Grande, 1875-1879," *Military History of Texas and the Southwest*, XV, No. II, 44–46; J. B. Wilkinson, *Laredo and the Rio Grande Frontier* (Austin: Jenkins Publishing Co., 1975), p. 332. For further information concerning rustling of cattle and horses along the Rio Grande after the Civil War, also see Chapter 2, footnote 2, p. 17.

The Captain at once ordered us to saddle up, and within fifteen minutes we were following him and a Mexican guide. Lieutenant Wright was in the party as was Lieutenant Robinson.

We camped that night by a little, half-dried-up creek, and early the next morning a Mexican scout came in and said he had discovered the trail of the raiders. We ate a hurried breakfast and started out with the Mexican. In a short time we captured an advance scout of the raiders—one Rafael Salinas—and, by threatening him with instant death if he did not divulge what he knew of the robbers, we obtained much valuable information from him.

A little later we managed to catch another of the raiders and his story agreed with the one the first man had told us. This scout said the raiders had turned the cattle loose, as the men became frightened when the first scout failed to return.

It was three days after that before we managed to head off the raiders. They had fourteen men and we totaled eighteen, including Captain McNelly. We found them with the cattle on a little bit of wooded, rising ground surrounded by a swamp called Laguna Madre. The water in it was eighteen or twenty inches deep.

They were drawn up in line and were evidently expecting us. When they saw us, they drew off behind the rising ground and fired at a range of about one hundred and fifty yards with carbines.

"Boys," said Captain McNelly, "the only way we

Cattle Raid on the Texas-Mexico Border
Courtesy The Institute of Texan Cultures, San Antonio

can get at those thieves is to cross through the mud of the swamp and ride them down. I don't believe they can shoot well enough to hit any of us, but we'll have to risk that. Don't shoot at them until you're sure of killing every time."

Following the Captain, we started across the swamp for the little hill, while the marauders continued to fire at us. When we got near to the hill, the Captain put spurs to his horse and we followed him with a yell as we flew through the mud and up the hill. The raiders answered our yell with one of defiance and a volley. At first, we thought they had not done any execution, but we soon saw they had aimed only too well, for three of our horses went crashing to the ground, one after the other, throwing their riders over their heads. Lieutenant Robinson's horse was one of those shot, but Robinson continued to fight on foot.

Then came a single shot from the invaders, and one of the Rangers—L. B. Smith, popularly known in the troop as "Sonny"—threw his arms above his head, reeled in his saddle for a moment and fell headlong to the ground. We all saw him fall and the sight roused a fury in our hearts that boded ill for the men in front of us.[4]

[4]The Ranger Muster Roll lists a Pvt. L. B. Smith, who served from July 25, 1874, until shot and killed in battle on June 12, 1875. Ingmire, *Texas Ranger Service Records*, V, 117. For more on Smith's death, see Durham and Wantland, *Taming the Nueces Strip*, p. 62; Webb, *The Texas Rangers*, pp. 241, 247–48.

The raiders fired at us again, but this time did no harm. In an instant we were on them, shooting and yelling like demons. They stood their ground for a moment only; then turned and fled. As they left, they leaned forward on their horses' necks and shot at us, but they were demoralized by the fury of our onslaught and could hit nothing.

Crack! bang! bang! sounded our revolvers, and at nearly every shot one of the raiders went tumbling from his saddle. We had ridden hard to get to them and our horses were played out, but we never considered giving up the chase. The remembrance of poor Smith's face, as he threw up his hands and reeled from his horse, was too fresh in our minds for us to think of anything but revenge.

Some of our enemies were well-mounted, but even these we gradually overhauled. We flew over the prairie at a killing pace, intent only on avenging our comrade's death. When we finally did halt, our horses were ready to drop from exhaustion; but the work had been done—every man of the raiders but one was dead. Some of them fought so desperately that even when dismounted and wounded four or five times they continued to shoot at us. Lieutenant Wright killed two men with one shot from his revolver. The men were riding on one horse when he killed them and both were shooting back at him.

The leader of the raiders, Espiñoso, was thrown from his horse early in the fight. McNelly was after him and as soon as he saw Espiñoso fall he, too, sprang to the ground. Espiñoso jumped into a "hog wallow" in the prairie and McNelly took shelter in another nearby. Then they fought a duel. Finally, McNelly played a trick on the Mexican leader. The Captain had a carbine and a six-shooter. He aimed his carbine carefully at the top of Espiñoso's hog wallow and then fired his pistol in the air. Espiñoso raised his head, and the next instant a bullet from McNelly's carbine had passed through it and the bandit was dead.[5]

Espiñoso was the most famous of the raiders on the Rio Grande and one of the head men under the Mexican guerrilla chief, Cortina. Cortina was a Mexican general, and at the head of all the cattle raiding. He had a contract to deliver to Cuba six hundred head of Texas cattle every week. About three thousand robbers were under him, and he was virtually the ruler of the Mexican border.

When we rode back to the hill where we first met the raiders, we soon discovered that we had killed only thirteen of them. The fourteenth was terribly wounded. His name was Mario Olguine, nicknamed Aboja (the Needle) because he had such a quiet way of slipping into ranch houses, on raids, and murdering the inmates while they slept. Aboja was sent to

[5]In their book, *Taming the Nueces Strip*, pp. 56–64, Durham and Wantland graphically tell about McNelly killing an unnamed bandit. But McNelly, in his report to Texas Adjutant General William Steele, lists the death of Guadaloupe Espiñoso, who was one of Juan N. Cortina's "favorite bravos." See Webb, *The Texas Rangers*, pp. 239–41.

jail, but died there, after lingering several weeks. We recovered 265 stolen cattle after the fight. We procured a wagon and took the body of young Smith to Brownsville. The next day the bodies of the thirteen dead raiders were brought to Brownsville and laid out in the plaza.[6] Nearly the entire population of Matamoros, the Mexican town immediately across the Rio Grande from Brownsville, came over to view their dead countrymen. Many were very angry, and we heard threats that Cortina would come across with his men and kill us all. McNelly sent back word to Cortina that he would wait for him and his men even though Cortina's bandits outnumbered the Rangers and the United States forces at Fort Brown about ten to one.

We gave Smith a complete military funeral. The invaders were buried together in one trench. The

[6]The number of dead bandits differs among the various sources. J. Lee Stambaugh and Lillian J. Stambaugh, *The Lower Rio Grande Valley of Texas* (San Antonio: The Naylor Press, 1954), pp. 152–53, state that the Rangers killed sixteen, but only eight bodies were displayed. In Webb, *The Texas Rangers*, p. 240, McNelly reported to Adjutant General Steele that twelve raiders were killed. Pierce, *Lower Rio Grande Valley*, p. 109, stated that fifteen bandits were killed as well as displayed. Durham and Wantland, *Taming the Nueces Strip*, p. 66, listed sixteen dead.

McNelly believed that this type of action would serve as a deterrent against further raids and add to the already notorious reputation of the Rangers among the Hispanic people. See Hinojosa, *Borderlands Town*, p. 116; C. W. Goldfinch, *Juan N. Cortina: Two Interpretations* (New York: Arno Press, 1974), p. 61.

General Juan N. Cortina

Courtesy Archives Division,
Texas State Library, Austin

Mexican inhabitants of the town stood in their doorways and scowled at us whenever we passed, but they were afraid to express their hatred openly. They contented themselves with predicting that Cortina would come over and kill us. Had they but realized, one of our men, Sergeant George Hall, a cousin of McNelly's, was at that very time with Cortina, acting as a spy for us. Hall was on Cortina's boat, waiting with him for the cattle to be shipped to Havana. In the records of the United States government there is doubtless a most interesting report which Hall made to the Federal authorities, since General Grant, who was then President, sent for Hall and personally received his report.[7]

Grant was greatly interested in Cortina's movements, and it was said among those who knew how matters stood on the border and in Washington, that the President would understand the situation if war should break out between Mexico and the United States.[8]

[7]George Hall was definitely assigned to spy on Cortina's activities, but this editor has found no evidence that President Grant summoned Hall to Washington to give a report in person. See Goldfinch, *Juan N. Cortina*, p. 61. Durham and Wantland, *Taming the Nueces Strip*, pp. 42, 47, state that J. S. Rock, a scout and confidant of McNelly, hired George Hall.

[8]Neither Robinson, "The U.S. Navy vs. Cattle Rustlers," pp. 42–52, nor William S. McFeely, *Grant: A Biography* (New York: W. W. Norton & Company, 1981), p. 486, support this view.

X

Jesus Sandobal Becomes a Ranger

AT THE time of which I write, Matamoros was full of Mexican soldiers, and Cortina had put the place under martial rule. No person was allowed on the streets after sunset, except by special permit; that is, no Mexican was allowed on the streets. For some reason best known to Cortina, Americans were not included in the rule, and the Mexican sentries had orders to pass Americans. The Rangers were not slow to take advantage of this state of affairs, and we paid frequent visits to Matamoros after nightfall. We went there for two reasons: to have fun, and to carry out a set policy of terrorizing the residents at every opportunity. Captain McNelly assumed that the more we were feared, the easier would be our work of subduing the raiders. It was understood that we were to gain a reputation as fire-eating, daredevils as quickly as possible, and to let no opportunity pass without asserting ourselves. Perhaps everyone has more or less of the bully inherent in his make-up, for us it was orders we were to follow.

"Each Ranger was a little standing army in himself," was the way Lieutenant Wright put it to me, speaking long afterward of those experiences. Most

Mexicans were afraid of us, and along with their fear was a bitter hatred.

Occasionally several of us would leave camp after dark and cross the river to Matamoros by way of the ferry. If we could find a *fandango*, or Mexican dance going on, we would enter the hall and break-up the festivities by shooting out the lights. This would naturally result in much confusion and, added to the reports of our revolvers, would be the shrill screaming of women and the cursing of angry men. Soldiers would come running from all directions. We would then fire more shots in the air and dash for the ferry, as fast as we could go.

Usually, we'd be followed—at a safe distance— by a company or two of soldiers. Sometimes we would fire back, over their heads, and sometimes they would shoot at us; but we always got back safely to the Texas side. When we reached Brownsville, we would hunt up another *fandango*—some of these dances were going on every night—and proceed, as in Matamoros, to break it up.

The news of our big fight with the raiders soon reached everyone's ears, and no one was so bold as to stand up to us. We accomplished our purpose, for in a few weeks we were feared as men were never before feared on that border. Yet, had we given them an opportunity, we would surely have been exterminated by the bandits, but because there was "method in our madness," we never gave them the chance to get the better of us.

Brownsville, Texas Riverfront
and Ferryboat to Matamoros, Mexico, c. 1880

One of our men came very near paying the penalty of his rashness at a *fandango* in Brownsville. He was passing a house when he heard the music of guitars and a violin, and a voice shouting the figures of a dance. The Ranger knew that a *fandango* was in progress, and he made up his mind to put a stop to it. It was quite a revelation to see how opposed to dancing the Rangers had become. No religious fanatic was ever more active in discouraging round dances than were McNelly's men. The sound of a fiddle playing a waltz was, in its effect, like touching a match to a train of powder. It always roused the Rangers to prompt action, and in ten minutes, at the utmost, the twinkling feet of the dancers were hurrying away in every direction, as fast as wholesome fear could make them travel.

But, previous to the incident of which I write, we had always gone to work to breakup the dances in parties of from four to half a dozen men. No one had ever attempted to carry on the good work all by himself. But this particular Ranger—he was Boyd—did not wish to waste valuable time by going to camp and securing the assistance of some of the other discouragers of terpsichorean revels. Boyd made up his mind to go in and stop that *fandango* at once, and single-handed.

He accordingly turned aside and entered the adobe house where it was in progress. There were about fifty revelers in the place when Boyd entered, but a little thing like that was not sufficient to discourage him when he set his heart on doing a good, moral piece of work. Perhaps he had been glancing once or twice too often upon the *mescal* when it was yellow, but, be that as it may, he did something which no man in his senses would have attempted. He walked into the middle of the room where those fifty-odd dancers were having a good time and, pulling his revolver, deliberately began to shoot at the lamps which were shining brightly from brackets on the walls.

He had fired but three shots when something hit him on the head from behind and he dropped to the floor like a log. A dozen of the Mexicans were on him in an instant, hitting and kicking him, and he certainly would have been killed if something hadn't happened to save him. That something was the entrance of six of the Rangers who, as they were passing the place, were attracted by the noise of the shooting and the melee that followed. They ran in and made their way to the place where Boyd was being beaten. As soon as they recognized it was Boyd, they turned on his assailants.

The blood of the Mexicans was boiling, however, and they stood their ground. A fight ensued, and it was a bloody one. The Mexicans were all armed with knives, and some had pistols. The room was so crowded and there were so many women, that the Rangers would not shoot, instead they used their six-shooters as clubs. They succeeded in rescuing Boyd and running the Mexicans out of the place, but not until some heads had been broken. It was, indeed, fortunate that no one was killed.

This was such a serious affair that it made much talk in the town, and the result was that Captain McNelly ordered a halt to *fandango* raids.

It must not be supposed, however, that the Rangers had nothing to do except terrorize the Mexicans. Most of the men were continually off on scouts of more or less importance. Occasionally, the boys would get into a fight, but more often they would make arrests peaceably enough. Sometimes so many of the men were off on these scouts that not more than two or three would be left in camp at a time. I was almost constantly in the saddle. We did most of our riding at night. This was for two reasons; our movements at night did not attract so much attention, and then, in that hot climate, night-riding is less severe on horses than traveling under the blazing semi-tropical sun. It was on one of these night scouts that we obtained an important addition to the troop. He was a Mexican—the only one who ever belonged to the Ranger troop.

His name was Jesus Sandobal.[1] In appearance he did not differ from hundreds of other Mexicans on

---

[1] Jesus Sandobal, sometimes known as "Old Casoose," enlisted in the Rangers in mid-May, 1875 and was discharged eighteen months later in January, 1877. See Ingmire, *Texas Ranger Service Records*, V, 83. Also Webb, *The Texas Rangers*, pp. 242–266ff; Askins, *Texans, Guns & History*, pp. 49–57; Durham and Wantland, *Taming the Nueces Strip*, pp. 44, 54–55.

the border, except that he was somewhat taller than the majority of them, and was also remarkably thin and angular. His eyes were as black as jet and singularly piercing. He was very sinewy and strong and as active as any man I ever saw. He could mount a pony without putting his hand on him at all. He would simply run alongside of the horse for a little way and spring into the saddle with a bound. I have seen this feat performed at a circus by expert bareback riders, but never with the ease with which Sandobal did it. Once mounted, he was an extremely graceful rider and a daring one.

He came to us as a guide, and after we learned his history, we did not wonder that the Captain had made him a member of the troop. There was no fear that Sandobal would ever betray any of the Rangers to his countrymen. He had no country, in fact. He had renounced all allegiance to Mexico, and he hated the Mexican bandits with such a bitter, consuming hatred that his life was devoted to doing them all the injury possible.

One year before he became our guide, Jesus Sandobal was living at peace on his ranch in Texas, a few miles northwest of Brownsville near the Rio Grande. By hard work and attention to business, he accumulated quite a small fortune in horses and cattle, fenced in a few acres of ground, built himself a commodious adobe house, and was prosperous and happy. He was devoted to his wife and daughter, the latter a pretty girl of fifteen years.

He had had the advantage of a good education at a school in the City of Mexico, but perhaps it was the advantage of his education that caused him to stand aloof from many of his countrymen along the border. As a consequence, he was generally disliked. They resented his haughty bearing, and his air of condescension was galling to them. His actions were too much in the manner of the old-time Spanish *caballero*[2] for them to seek his friendship. He surely knew this, but if so, the knowledge had no effect upon his way of treating his neighbors and others whom he met from day to day. He was always courteous to them, but he did not disguise the fact that he considered himself to be better than them.

One morning, Sandobal left his ranch to go on some business up the Rio Grande, near Ringgold Barracks,[3] almost a hundred miles away. He kissed his wife and daughter affectionately and told them he would ride hard and be back with them in four days at the latest. He left his ranch in the care of a man named Juan Valdez, his chief *vaquero*.[4] Valdez

[2]*Caballero* is the Spanish word for a gentleman worthy of respect.
[3]Ringgold Barracks, located on the left bank of the Rio Grande at David's Landing, just below Rio Grande City, was established on October 26, 1848. Although at first known as the Post at David's Landing, then Camp Ringgold, it finally achieved its name in 1849, honoring Major David Ringgold, Third Artillery, who was killed in the Battle of Palo Alto on May 8, 1846. McNelly used it often as a headquarters. See Roberts, *Encyclopedia of Historic Forts*, pp. 773–74.
[4]*Vaquero* is the Spanish word for cowboy or cattle herder.

had been with Don Jesus for several months and had done his work well, although he seemed of a rather morose disposition. Sandobal trusted him fully.

On the evening of the fourth day from his departure from his ranch, Sandobal returned to it. When he reached a point within a mile of his house, he put spurs to his horse and galloped merrily on in his haste to see his loved ones again. In a few minutes he came within sight of his house, but when he turned his eyes toward it his heart sank within him. Instead of the neat dwelling which he had left a few days before, he saw a heap of ruins. He flew to the place. It was silent and deserted. His home had been totally destroyed by fire and its inhabitants were gone.

At first, he concluded it had been accidentally burned and that his wife and daughter had merely gone to await his return at some neighbor's house or in Brownsville, where they had relatives. But he did not think so long. Upon looking around, he found that his barn was burned, too. His fences were torn down. All his cattle had been driven off.

Then he knew what had happened. He had lived too long on that accursed border not to recognize the work of the dreaded raiders from across the Rio Grande. He knew that his ranch had been destroyed by them and that he was a ruined man. But what had become of his wife and daughter? When he thought of them his heart grew sick, for well he

Ringgold Barracks, c. 1870

Courtesy Archives Division,
Texas State Library, Austin

knew the treatment which women had come to expect from the raiders of the border. He turned his horse's head away from the ruins of his home and set out on a run for the nearest ranch house. Its owner heard him coming and hurried to the gate.

"My wife—my little daughter, Antonita—where are they?" shouted Sandobal, as he pulled his horse up so quickly that it reared back on its haunches.

The *ranchero* looked at Don Jesus and noted the terrible expression of his face—the drawn features and the fierce, glittering eyes—and for a moment he dared not answer him.

"For the love of the good God, speak!" said Sandobal in a hoarse, strained voice. "Do not keep me in suspense. Are they safe? Did they escape? Are they here?"

Still the *ranchero* was silent.

Suddenly Sandobal threw himself from his horse and strode straight up to the man. He looked the *ranchero* in the eyes with a searching stare for a moment; then he grasped him with his strong hands by both shoulders and shook him as a dog would a rat. Between his set teeth he spoke, saying:

"By God, you shall answer me, or I'll strangle you as I would a coyote."

Then the *ranchero* found words to answer him.

"Calm yourself, Señor," he said. "You hurt me. There, that is better. You must bear it like a man, Don Jesus, for there is terrible news for you. Your wife and daughter are alive, but ——"

The *ranchero* hung his head and his eyes sought the ground. He could not tell the husband and father of the foul wrong which had been put upon his loved ones. But he had said enough. Sandobal knew that his worst fears were confirmed. After a pause of many minutes, he said, in a strangely calm voice for the expression which accompanied it:

"Where are they, *amigo mio*?"

"They have gone to the convent in Matamoros. They are with the holy Sisters."

Sandobal pressed his friend's hand with a strong grasp and turned from him without another word. The next minute he was on his horse galloping away toward his ruined ranch. Inquiries were made for him on the following day, but he had disappeared. It was learned that he had gone to the convent in Matamoros and there seen his wife and daughter. After he left the convent, all trace of him had vanished.

In a few weeks, some strange and terrible rumors spread throughout the lower Rio Grande border. It was said that, night after night, a different ranch was burned in Mexico, not far from the big river; that, day after day, some man was found dead on the road in the same neighborhood, with a bullet hole in his head; that the cattle in Mexico were dying of some new and strange disease; that horses were being killed by some unknown hand, and that persons drinking from wells and springs in Mexico had fallen violently ill and died in agony shortly after.

And, in all these cases, the persons who had been shot or poisoned were those who were known to belong to the bands of raiders who lived by their frequent depredations in Texas. It was their ranches which were burned; it was their cattle which died; it was their horses which were killed.

As time went on, these awful happenings did not decrease in frequency. Indeed, they became of more frequent occurrence and the scene of them ever widened. The people became terror stricken. Men banded together to hunt down their common but unknown enemy. They scoured the country for him. They offered large rewards for his detection and capture, dead or alive. But it was all to no purpose. Every few nights a hitherto untouched ranch was set on fire; every day or two, another man was found dead with a bullet hole in his temple. The cattle and the horses continued to die. Springs and wells, and even streams which emptied into the Rio Grande, were found to be poisoned.

For over eight months this kept up. Scores of ranches were burned; forty or fifty men were assassinated, and hundreds of horses and cattle died in that period. And in all that time Sandobal was absent from Texas, save for brief visits which he paid to Brownsville. When anyone would ask him where he was living and where he was working, he would reply that he was "doing things for the Mexican government." He would make purchases of provisions and cartridges and leave the town again, not to return for another month or six weeks. On these occasional visits he always went to the convent in Matamoros to see his wife and daughter.

Why the Mexicans did not sooner suspect Sandobal as the man who had been playing such havoc in the Mexican border region, I cannot imagine, but when, at last, they did couple his name with the outrages, no one doubted that he was their perpetrator. The people had no direct proof that he was the man, but they felt sure of it as soon as it was suggested. A hunt began for him, but he could not be found. It was discovered, however, that he had not been employed by the Mexican government in any capacity, and this tended to confirm the suspicions.

It was while the border country was ringing with Sandobal's name and the hunt for him was being prosecuted that he joined the Rangers as a guide. Of course, he denied that he had been taking such awful revenge for the wrongs done him, but none of us believed his denials. I have good reason to be convinced that Captain McNelly knew, positively, Sandobal was the dreaded border scourge, and I suspect that it was for that very reason he enlisted him in the troop.

Sandobal—we all called him Casoose in the Company—was safe from molestation so long as he was with the Rangers, although direful threats regarding him reached us constantly. Sandobal merely smiled grimly when he heard the threats. His life was too bitter for him to care for them. For hours at a time he would sit in the camp with his back against a tree, brooding over his troubles and lost to all that was passing around him. When, however, anyone of the Rangers spoke to him, he always answered in a most pleasant manner. He absolutely worshipped the Rangers and was ever ready to go to any trouble to please them, collectively or individually.

When any of the boys returned from a scout, he was always the first to greet them and to ask if they had killed any bandits. If the answer was in the negative, he would plainly indicate his disappointment, but if it was in the affirmative, his eyes would brighten, his lips would curve into a smile, and he would pat the men on the back and call them *"muy bravos hombres"* and say that he wished he had been with them. If a bandit prisoner was brought into camp, he was always as carefully guarded to keep Sandobal from doing him an injury as to prevent his escape. This was particularly the case after one of the prisoners complained that Sandobal had threatened to hang him at the first opportunity. I do not doubt that our guide would have done so had he had the chance.

But Sandobal's hunger for revenge on the raiders was destined to be satisfied shortly, for he was to participate in the most exciting and dangerous scout which the Rangers ever undertook, the story of which rang throughout all Texas, and the effect of which was practically to break up the border-thieving on the lower Rio Grande.

XI

Across the Rio Grande

For months we continued to scout from Fort Brown to Rancho Davis and far along the Rio Grande, and the cattle thieves grew more and more cautious, for they knew that the Rangers were in that country for business and would not hesitate to kill them on sight. Late in June we left our camp near Brownsville and went to Santa Maria, thirty-five miles farther up the river, where we heard that a party of raiders had crossed to Texas. The robbers heard of our coming and fled to Mexico.

We were so constantly moving from one place to another, by night as well as day, that the raiders never knew where we would appear and, for the first time in many years, they were checked in their illicit activities. Another good effect of our ceaseless movement and vigilance was that the Mexican settlers on the Texas side of the Rio Grande no longer cooperated with the raiders by withholding information from us and giving it to them. These settlers seemed to realize that a new condition had arisen, and that the State of Texas was determined to set a different course from that which had theretofore been pursued in the border area.

On August 4th we received reliable information

that a band of forty of the robbers were to be at a certain place in Hidalgo County in three days. We prepared to go to meet them and give them a warm reception; but before we started, a scout came in and told us that the leader of the gang had been assassinated by one of his own men on the day they were to start from Mexico, and that the raid had been abandoned. Our later investigation showed this to be true.

Around the middle of August, we moved back from the Rio Grande, so as to entice the raiders over and give them a few more lessons on the danger of invading Texas, and we continued to hunt them with occasional success until November, when we had "the big fight."

We were encamped, November 20th, at Ratama Ranch, about forty miles north of the Rio Grande. Lieutenant Robinson was in command, the Captain having gone near the Rio Grande to reconnoitre. There were about thirty of the boys in camp; lounging about; practicing with their six-shooters at trees and betting with each other on their marksmanship; playing poker with grains of corn for "chips" on a blanket spread upon the ground for a table; or cleaning and polishing their carbines and revolvers, when a Mexican rode hurriedly up and asked to see Lieutenant Robinson.

"I'm Robinson; what do you want?" demanded the Lieutenant.

The Mexican handed him a note which Robinson

hurriedly read. The men knew that something serious was about to take place and gathered around him. Robinson looked up from the note.

"Saddle up, boys," he said. "Don't waste any time about it, for we must be off immediately. We can't wait for dinner. Take what grub you can find that's cooked and bring it along with you. Be sure and girth your horses tight, for you can't stop to do it on the road. We're in for some fun this time, sure. Take all the cartridges you can carry."

The Rangers gave a yell of delight and started on a run for their horses, which were herded close to the campsite. In a marvelously short time we had made them ready, and when, in less than ten minutes, Robinson gave the order to "fall in," every man was in his saddle and alert.

"Now, Jesus," said Lieutenant Robinson to Sandobal, "take us by the nearest road you know to Las Cuevas; the raiders are there and fighting the United States troops."

Sandobal's face lightened up with great joy, and he darted to the front of the column and away toward the south on a gallop. As we swung out after him, the sun was shining directly over our heads. It was exactly noon.

We took an old, unused trail which the recent rains had washed out in many places, and it was very muddy. It would have been a bad road to ride on at a walk, but it was doubly so at the rate we went. From a gallop to a sharp trot, and back again to a gallop, we went, hour after hour, stopping every seven or eight miles for a very few minutes to breathe our horses. We did not go at a walk at all. The mud flew up and plastered the men from head to foot and the horses were coated with it, but we did not pause or slacken the pace.

Sandobal, closely followed by the Lieutenant, rode ahead, and we followed in a long, straggling line. Most of the way it was impossible for the men to ride two abreast and we went in single file. Mile after mile we rode at this killing pace, under the hot Texas sun, and I thought that some of the ponies would drop from exhaustion, but none did. The men were all toughened to hard riding and did not mind it in the least.

Las Cuevas, we learned from Sandobal, was sixty miles away, and it was evidently the intention to reach there that day. Such an undertaking, even on a good road, would have been tremendous, but on that old, rain-washed trail it seemed impossible.

But we did it. Just as the sun was sinking below the mesquite-covered prairie to the west, we arrived at the place. Sixty miles on a bad trail between noon and sundown! Such riding as that had never before been done by a body of men on that border, and I have never heard of it being equaled elsewhere. Horses and men were exhausted, and when we dismounted, we stood by our panting, dripping ponies, glad to get the rest which the change of position gave us.

We had stopped on the bank of the Rio Grande close to the water. All about us the mud was ankle deep, and marked with the hoofprints of hundreds of cattle. On the other side of the river we could just make out in the gathering gloom—for the twilights are very short in that latitude—a flatboat, tied to the bank. As we looked across the quarter of a mile of water which separated us from Mexico, we saw the boat swing out from the shore and go drifting down the river, and as it did so, there came a yell of defiance and derision from the raiders over there. They had crossed all the stolen cattle and horses, and then had turned the flatboat adrift to keep us from following on our horses.

As we stood watching them and wondering just what to do, we heard a sudden pounding of many hoofs, and the sounds of clanking steel and creaking leather, the unmistakable announcement of galloping horsemen. Now, the noises grew louder and closer. They were on our side of the river. The same thought must have flashed through the mind of every Ranger there, for, with a precision like that of men at drill, all turned to their saddles, pulled their carbines from the scabbards, and turned to fight the oncoming horsemen.

"Don't fire, boys; it's the Eighth Cavalry!" yelled Sergeant Armstrong, who was in advance, and the Rangers dropped the carbines to their sides and carefully uncocked them.

Armstrong was right. In another minute thirty

men of Troops H and M, Eighth United States Cavalry, under Captain James F. Randlett, along with Lieutenant Farnsworth second in command, came out of the brush and halted where we stood.[1]

They had left Brownsville at 1 A.M., November 18th, two days before. It took them all that time to come about the same distance we traveled in half a day! No better illustration of the difference between the methods of the Rangers and the regular cavalry could be given. We dared to kill our horses by hard riding, and they did not, which meant the difference between success and failure in the pursuit and capture of border thieves.

Still, we all arrived too late that night to catch the raiders on this side of the Rio Grande, and Rangers and regulars condoled with each other heartily. It was more than provoking to us, who had taken such a terrible ride to head off the thieves, but there was no help for it. We scattered up and down the river-

[1] Captain James F. Randlett, with Lieutenant H. J. Farnsworth, Eighth Cavalry, and eighty troopers, was encamped at Edinburg, Texas. On the night of November 16 they learned that a herd of stolen cattle were being driven south and would cross the Rio Grande near Las Cuevas. The next day Randlett and Farnsworth intercepted the raiders, killing two and wounding a third. Since Mexico was a friendly power, they did not, at first, continue their pursuit of the raiders in the so-called Las Cuevas War. See Webb, *The Texas Rangers*, pp. 258–63; Rippy, "Some Precedents of the Pershing Expedition into Mexico," pp. 305–06; Clarence C. Clendenen, *Blood on the Border: The United States Army and the Mexican Irregulars* (London: The Macmillan Company, 1969), pp. 74–75.

bank to look for a boat, but after an hour's search, gave it up. There was no fodder or grazing for our poor horses, and they had to be content to eat the leaves from the mesquite brush.

About nine o'clock Captain McNelly rode up and joined us. He said he had left Major Alexander with two more troops of the Eighth Cavalry farther on down the river, and that they would arrive, he thought, about dawn, together with Lieutenant Merritt and a detachment of the Twenty-fourth Infantry with a Gatling gun.

Captain McNelly told us that the thieves we were after were under contract to deliver eighteen thousand head of cattle in Monterey, Mexico, within ninety days, and that they had started to gather them in Texas. He said that Cortina had organized all the cattle thieves in Mexico for this purpose, and that he really intended an invasion of Texas. It was clearly our duty to follow the robbers into Mexico, give them battle, and so nip their plans in the bud. He had received assurances that Major Alexander would instruct his men to follow the Rangers wherever they went.

That McNelly had good reason to believe Major Alexander would support him fully, even to the extent of crossing the border and following the marauders into Mexico, there can be no doubt. I know that our Captain had been in direct communication with President Grant regarding the Mexican outrages, and I, in common with many others, was given the impression that Grant would welcome the chance to invade the Republic directly to the south of us.[2] I know also that Major D. R. Clendenin, of the Eighth Cavalry, who was with the troops at Las Cuevas, as well as Major Alexander and Colonel Potter, commanding the District of the Rio Grande, understood that McNelly was to lead all of the Rangers and United States troops into Mexico. I speak of this matter here, so that the reader may understand under what conditions our Captain acted, and that his bitter disappointment at the failure of Secretary of War Belknap to back up his actions may be appreciated.

That night we managed to catch two goats, which

[2]This editor has found no evidence corroborating Jenning's assertion that McNelly was in direct contact with President Grant. The statement "that Grant would welcome the chance to invade" Mexico also cannot be confirmed. For instance, Robinson, "U.S. Navy vs. Cattle Rustlers," pp. 44–45, states that Lieutenant Commander DeWitt C. Kells, who was captain of the *Rio Bravo* in October, 1875, prior to his being relieved of command by Commander Remey, conspired "to foment border trouble and possible war with Mexico." In fact, Clendenen, *Blood on the Border*, pp. 74–75, states that Major David R. Clendenin "positively forbade any crossing by the [U.S.] soldiers" and that Major A. J. Alexander's "first act was to order Randlett [who would cross the Rio Grande two days later to aid McNelly] to return to the American shore at once." Rippy, "Some Precedents of the Pershing Expedition into Mexico," pp. 305–06 also affirms this position of neutrality, as does McFeely, *Grant*, p. 487. McNelly, however, reported to Adjutant General Steele that Clendenin "promised me that in case I was cut off in my attack . . . he would come to my assistance." See Webb, *The Texas Rangers*, pp. 262–63.

President Ulysses S. Grant

Secretary of War
William W. Belknap

Courtesy Prints and Photographs Division,
Library of Congress

we killed and ate for supper. They were very tough, but we were very hungry, and we enjoyed them, although we had no bread or coffee.

At about eleven o'clock, McNelly told Captain Randlett he thought it would be well to try to cross the Rio Grande, so as to be in position to move on the raiders early in the morning. Captain Randlett replied that he would have to await the arrival of Major Alexander before he took the United States troops across the border.

Then it was that Parrott, of our troop, did a most courageous thing. He undressed on the riverbank and swam the Rio Grande to try to find a boat on the other side in which we could cross. We waited quietly for word from him for fully half an hour, and at the end of that time were startled to hear him bawl across the river at the top of his lungs that he had secured a rowboat and would come right over. The wonderful nerve displayed by Parrott in yelling to us while he was on the other side of the river and surrounded by the desperadoes, impressed even the foolhardy Rangers, and he was ever after a hero in the troop.

He came back all right with the boat, and then Captain McNelly got into it with two of the men and started across the stream. Parrott's call had roused the Mexicans and they had probably discovered the loss of the boat, for we could hear them shouting and cursing on the opposite bank. So, when McNelly started across, we and the Eighth

Cavalry troopers formed a line along the bank and prepared to shoot if McNelly was attacked when he reached the other side. We knelt in the mud, with our carbines ready to fire if it should be necessary.

Suddenly, from the opposite bank, just where McNelly and his two men had gone, came the sound of a rifle shot and the flash of a gun. Instantly, we blazed out with a volley from our carbines, firing at the flash. Before we could shoot again, we heard the Captain shouting at us.

"For God's sake, don't fire!" he yelled. "Do-o-o not fire!"

We couldn't understand what he meant by such an order at the time, but afterward we found out that one of the men who was with him in the boat let his carbine go off accidentally as he stepped to the shore. Luckily, we overshot them, but they said our bullets sang very close to their ears.

McNelly and his two men reconnoitred along the bank, but failed to find any of the desperadoes, and then one of the men rowed back and we crossed the river, three at a time. Armstrong swam his own horse over, and he was followed by four of the others, but the water was very cold and quicksands near the banks made this a dangerous proceeding, so the rest of the Rangers left their horses on the Texas side.

We lay on the ground over there, near the river-bank, with no covering whatsoever, although the night was raw and chilly. We were tired, cold, dirty, and wet; but, excepting the men on guard, all slept soundly until a little before daylight. Then McNelly had us quietly awakened. He sent across the river to see if Major Alexander had arrived and to find out if he would cross with his cavalry to Mexico. The messenger returned with the information that Alexander had not yet arrived.

Then the Captain formed us in double ranks and, in a low voice, made us a speech.

"Boys," he said, "I was expecting the United States soldiers to help us in this fight, but I guess we'll have to go it alone now, if we want to do anything before the robbers get away into the interior. I want to tell you, right now, that I'll probably have to lead you into hell for awhile, but I believe I can lead you out again, all right. Still, if there is any man here who doesn't want to come with me, he is at perfect liberty to say so and go back. I won't treasure it up against him, for none of you boys enlisted to fight in Mexico, and you needn't do it if you don't want to."

The Captain paused, but not a man moved or said anything.

"That is just what I expected of you," he went on, in a tone of satisfaction. "Now I'll tell you what we have to do. About a mile from here is the notorious Rancho de Las Cuevas, the headquarters of the Mexican raiders. In that ranch are fine stores of all kinds—silver-mounted bridles and saddles, carved weapons, fine horses. We want to capture the ranch.

It is the headquarters of a gang of ruffians who have lived off the United States for years and years. They have brought up their children to hate us and to prey upon our country. They have murdered our ranchmen and ruined thousands of homes in Texas. Now is our chance to get even. Doubtless, there are many men at the ranch, armed and ready for us. They are expecting our attack, for I sent word to their leader, some time ago, that if he ever made another raid into Texas, we would come over and take his ranch. We will have to fight and they will probably make a desperate resistance, but we can whip them.

"I know the kind of men you are. I know that your courage is unquestioned and I know that there are no better shots in Texas than you. You have plenty of ammunition and, by keeping cool and listening to orders and obeying them strictly, you can take that ranch. We are going to attack it at the crack of day, and when we do, I want you to shoot every man you see and to spare none but the women and children. I want to make an example of these thieves and murderers and ravishers and I depend on you to help me do it."

It was a rather long speech, but it was all to the point, and at its conclusion we knew just what we had to expect. The Captain had a way of taking his men into his confidence at such times, and they appreciated it and served him all the better for it.

When he had finished speaking, we moved slowly off after him, along a narrow path through the willows and brush. The path was only a cattle trail, and it led directly away from the river. We marched in single file. Ahead of the Captain was a Mexican guide who was to show the way to the ranch. We marched in dead silence, treading carefully through the underbrush so as not to make the slightest sound. Armstrong and three others rode their horses and followed directly after those on foot. Jesus Sandobal was also mounted.

Just at the peep of day we came to a fence across the road. The troop halted there, and the Captain walked back along the line and told Armstrong that there was a gate in the fence a little below where we were. He told Armstrong that he wanted him and the other mounted men to go through that gate and ride through the ranch carefully, and then come back and report how matters stood. If they ran across any men, they were to shoot them.

"Shoot at everything you see," was the Captain's direct order.

"Yes, sir," answered Armstrong.

McNelly walked back to the head of the line and Armstrong, followed by the other mounted men, rode by us in the path. As they passed, I heard George Hall, who was on a horse, say to Armstrong:

"Armstrong, the Captain has a difficult job."

"I guess that's right," answered Armstrong, "but we're in for it now and we'll have to stand it."

"Sure," said Hall.

Notwithstanding the seriousness of the situation, the Rangers who were on foot could not resist the temptation to poke fun at the mounted men.

"Goodby, if I never see you again," one loudly whispered.

"Say, Armstrong, bring me a scalp, please," said another.

"I want one of those fancy saddles, covered with gold, Hall; be sure to save one for me before you die," came in soft accents from a third.

"You boys are going to hell in a handbasket this time—better think of your sins," was the encouraging advice from a fourth.

The Captain went with the mounted Rangers and let down the bars at the gate for them. Then he came back to us. Armstrong led the men with him right into the ranch, six-shooter in hand. From him and the others I learned afterward how they fared.

They went about a hundred yards beyond the fence and came to where the road forked. There they found five Mexican soldiers on guard as pickets. The Mexicans called to the Rangers to halt, and were answered with pistol shots. Armstrong rode right on to them and the others followed. There was some quick shooting by those on both sides, and at the end of the exchange, the five Mexican soldiers lay dead.

The five Rangers went straight on and shortly met two other Mexicans, who fired at them. They killed the Mexicans and continued to ride ahead.

Of course, we heard all this firing, and the Captain was quick to act accordingly. He sent half of the troop, with Lieutenant Robinson, to the right flank, and with the rest followed after the mounted men. I was in the Captain's squad. By the time we reached the place where the five dead men lay, the fog was so thick that we couldn't see ten yards ahead. Lieutenant Robinson had circled in and his detachment joined us at that place. They would have fired at us if Sergeant L. L. Wright hadn't recognized us in time and prevented it. We were still at this spot when Armstrong came dashing up on his horse.

"We've taken the place, Captain," he cried, exultantly. "The ranch is ours! We killed all the men we saw—seven of them."

"Seven?" exclaimed Captain McNelly. "Seven? There must be more than seven of them. I think there is some mistake. Let's go on."

We went ahead until we came to a ranch house a short distance from where we had stopped. A woman was standing in the doorway patting a *tortilla*, or Mexican pancake, in her hand.

"What ranch is this?" demanded the Captain.

"Las Cucharas," answered the woman.

"Where is el Rancho de Las Cuevas?"

"*Poco mas abajo, Señor.*" (A bit further on, sir.)

Then our spirits went down to zero. We tried to be cheerful, but the outlook was gloomy for taking the thieves' ranch by surprise, as we had intended.

All the shooting must have put its defenders very much on the alert, and since our task was never an easy one, we felt it was rendered ten times more difficult.

We met a little boy as we were moving slowly along the road the woman had told us led to the Las Cuevas Ranch. The little boy was driving a *burro*, laden with goatskins of water.

We asked him where the Las Cuevas Ranch was and he, too, said:

"*Poco mas abajo*," but he added that there were many men and soldiers there.

We moved along like a funeral procession, for we knew that we had, by our shooting, given fair warning of our approach. About half a mile's march brought us to the Las Cuevas Ranch. There was no mistaking it when we got there. As soon as we came in sight of the houses, we were met by a storm of bullets from the corrals, built of thick mesquite and ebony logs, and bulletproof. We were also greeted with yells and Mexican oaths and abuse of the vilest character.

We halted in the brush, about two hundred yards from the corrals, and for a few minutes returned the enemy's fire; but the fog grew much thicker and soon hid them from sight. Their bullets continued to pass over our heads. The four mounted men sat on their horses to the right of our line and watched the performance with interest, but did not attempt to take part in it. They were waiting for orders.

Corrals at Rancho de Las Cuevas

Restored Home of Juan Flores, Rancho de Las Cuevas
Courtesy Barker Texas History Center,
The University of Texas at Austin

At one time during the firing, I remember to have seen Durham taking very deliberate aim at a shadowy form far ahead, as though he were shooting at a squirrel. There was something so wonderfully cool and collected in his way of shutting one eye and squinting along the barrel of his carbine that it impressed me as comical and I actually shook with laughter at him, although I knew the general run of my thoughts was in a very serious channel.

While we were waiting and wondering what the Captain would next order us to do, a troop of the famed Mexican Rurales[3] dashed out from the corrals and charged directly at our line.

We gave them a volley as they came, and they swung around to the left in a semi-circle.

"Pick off your men, Rangers," shouted Captain McNelly. "I'll kill that fellow riding ahead."

The Captain's Winchester cracked, and the leader of the Rurales pitched from his saddle. A number of his followers' saddles were emptied quickly and the rest of the cavalrymen galloped off out of sight. About twenty-five men were in their troop.

There were evidently so many more of the Mexicans than there were of us that the Captain was puzzled how to act. He called George Hall to him and told him to ride up on a little rising ground, near the corrals, and try to estimate the number of men at the ranch. Hall did as ordered, riding under fire

[3]The Mexican Rurales were the national rural constabulary of Mexico; their model was the Texas Rangers.

all the time. He came back in a few minutes and reported that, as near as he could estimate, about two hundred Mexicans were in sight in the corrals.

"I couldn't see very well, though," he said, "and I may be mistaken as to the number."

The Captain immediately dispatched Armstrong to go closer still and see if he could make an estimate. Armstrong galloped off and went a little closer than Hall had gone. Soon he came dashing back and reported that he estimated there were about three hundred men in the corrals, and that many of them were in the uniforms of the Mexican cavalry.

"Then you think they outnumber us about ten to one?" said McNelly.

"That, or more," answered Armstrong.

Captain McNelly pulled a long, black cigar from his pocket and put it between his teeth. He chewed on the end of it for a minute, in a brown study. Then he turned to the men and said:

"Boys, we are in a dangerous position here and we'd better get back to the river. We only have thirty men and they may get reinforcements at any time. We'll fall back slowly and I shall expect you horsemen to keep the Mexicans off our rear."

We started back, expecting at every step that the entire Mexican force would be down on us and that we should have to make a desperate fight for our lives. But, luckily for us, the Mexicans suspected a trick and thought we were trying to draw them into an ambush. The main body, then, did not follow us

Mexican Rurales

Courtesy Western History Collections,
University of Oklahoma, Norman

immediately, but sent scouts after us, who continually exchanged shots with our little rear guard. By the time we reached the river, however, the Mexicans saw that we were actually in retreat and not playing a trick on them. Then they charged on us.

They came down on us, yelling and shooting rapidly, but we had strung out along the riverbank and behind a little rise in the prairie, which gave us a sort of rude rifle pit, and from there we met them with a murderous fire.

"Pick off the leaders first, men!" cried Captain McNelly. "Don't waste a shot! Kill their leaders!"

We did so. We saw man after man tumble from his saddle, and then we heard the rattle of carbines from the Texas side of the river and the music of Lieutenant Merritt's Gatling gun. United States troops were firing over our heads at the enemy.

It was too much for the Mexicans, and they wheeled and dashed back into the brush in full retreat, leaving the Alcalde of Camargo, Juan Flores, and a number of others dead on the field. These bodies lay in full sight from our lines, on a little open space which was free from the chaparral. The Mexicans formed in line on the other side of this open ground, and all the morning we kept up the firing, back and forth, across it. Twice they dashed out and tried to recover the body of the Alcalde of Camargo, but both times our steady fire drove them back quickly.

XII

McNelly's Ultimatum

DURING the morning a number of the officers of the Eighth Cavalry came over to us and joined in the firing, but they took the precaution to remove their coats, on which were their shoulder straps, so as not to appear with us in an official capacity. They wanted the excitement of the fighting and they wanted to help us against the superior number we were facing, but they were with us without orders, Major Alexander having refused to cross the Rio Grande with his soldiers without direct instructions from Washington.

Among the officers of the Eighth who came "unofficially" to our assistance was Captain S. B. M. Young, the same man who, as Brigadier General of Volunteers, led the Second Brigade, U. S. A. in the Santiago de Cuba campaign. Roosevelt's "Rough Riders" were part of Young's Brigade, and it was by Young's orders that the fight at Las Guasimas, the first in the Santiago campaign, was made.

Henry Guy Carleton, the playwright and littérateur, who comes of a long line of fighters, was a lieutenant in the Eighth Cavalry, and was also with the command under Major Alexander. It was he who, by order of Major Alexander, tapped the telegraph

wire which ran along the Texas bank of the Rio
Grande and established direct communication on
that afternoon with the Office of the Secretary of
War in Washington.

About three o'clock in the afternoon, a messenger came across the river bearing a telegraphic dispatch for Captain McNelly. I am able to provide it
and the answer it received, verbatim. The dispatch
handed directly to Captain McNelly was in Lieutenant Carleton's writing and was as follows:

> Fort Brown, November 20, 1875
>
> To MAJOR ALEXANDER, Commanding at the Front
>
> Advise Captain McNelly to return at once to this side of
> the river. Inform him that you are directed not to support
> him in any way while he remains in Mexican territory. If
> McNelly is attacked by Mexican forces on Mexican
> ground, do not render him any assistance. Keep your
> forces in the position you hold now and await further
> orders. Let me know if McNelly acts upon your advice
> and returns.
>
> (Signed) POTTER,
> Commanding
> District of the Rio Grande

McNelly was white with anger when he read this
dispatch. He had received secret instructions from
the Commanding General of the Department of
Texas to follow the thieves into Mexico and, at the
same time, had assurances that he would be supported in such action by United States troops. He
knew that Colonel Potter and Major Alexander
had seen his instructions. He had relied on their

Captain S. B. M. Young

Colonel Joseph H. Potter
Courtesy National Archives

197

support when he crossed the Rio Grande so bravely with thirty Texas Rangers. Now that he was on Mexican soil and under attack, he was deserted "by order of the Secretary of War" (Belknap). He was mad right through, and in his rage he took a bit of torn brown wrapping paper and a stub of a pencil, and wrote this in reply:

At the Front near Las Cuevas, Mexico,
November 20, 1875

To COLONEL POTTER, Commanding District
of the Rio Grande, Fort Brown, Tex.

I shall remain in Mexico with my Rangers until tomorrow morning—perhaps longer, and shall recross the Rio Grande at my own discretion. Give my compliments to the Secretary of War and tell him the United States troops may go to hell.

(Signed)   L. H. McNELLY,
Commanding Texas State Troops, Mexico

In the official reports of this affair, on file in the office of the Adjutant General of Texas in Austin, is the following from Major D. R. Clendenin, Eighth Cavalry, to Adjutant General Steele:

I did not deem it best to interfere with McNelly, who had secret instructions from the Commanding General, Department of Texas, which Colonel Potter, commanding the District, had seen, as had also Major Alexander of my regiment.

(Signed)   D. R. CLENDENIN,
Major Eighth Cavalry

When Captain McNelly saw Major Alexander before our raid, the latter said to him:

"If you are determined to cross, we will cover your return, if we do not cross to help you," but, in spite of this promise, Captain McNelly and the Rangers were told officially in the telegram from Colonel Potter that they would have to get out of their predicament as best they could.

Captain McNelly showed us the message he received and explained the situation to us. The men felt as bitter in their anger as did the Captain. Like the Captain, they expressed themselves vigorously by saying, "Let the United States soldiers go to hell; we'll stay and fight it out by ourselves."

We were not all alone, however, for the United States army officers who were with us "unofficially," remained with us, and a few of the troopers of their regiment also contrived to come over to our assistance. They said they "gloried in our spunk."

The firing slacked up about 3:30 P.M. and we could find nothing to shoot at. The Mexicans were out of sight in the brush and had ceased firing almost entirely. McNelly put up with this inactivity for about half an hour, and that was as long as he could stand it.

"Let's get out into the open and draw their fire," he said coolly to Armstrong. "Then we can see what to shoot at."

The next minute he and Armstrong were walking deliberately out into the open space between the lines, just as though there were no Mexican bandits or soldiers within a hundred miles of them. They

Fort Brown, c. 1870

Courtesy Archives Division,
Texas State Library, Austin

strolled leisurely to and fro, far out from our lines, but not a shot was fired at them. After awhile they came back to us, and then McNelly went over to Texas to send dispatches, leaving Lieutenant Robinson in charge of the troop.

I know that McNelly attempted to establish direct communication with President Grant when he crossed the Rio Grande, for our Captain knew better than any other man at the front how Grant felt about the Mexican border outrages. He was certain the President would back him up in his action in crossing, for that his "secret instructions" had been inspired by the Silent Man in the White House was an open secret to all those concerned in the Las Cuevas affair.[1]

Before McNelly could contact the President by wire, however, we were surprised to see a flag of truce carried out from the Mexican lines, and a man was at once sent by Lieutenant Robinson to the Captain to request his return. With the flag of truce were five men. They rode halfway to our lines and halted, and Lieutenant Robinson detailed Armstrong and four men to go out and see them and find out what they wanted.

The leader of the Mexicans with the flag of truce was an American. He was a tall, handsome man,

[1] Although McNelly expected U.S. Army support, no evidence can be found that President Grant and the Ranger captain corresponded. See Webb, *The Texas Rangers*, pp. 255–80, for the most thorough account of the "Las Cuevas War."

about forty years old, but his hair and long beard were as white as snow, giving him a most patriarchal appearance when seen at a distance. A closer view showed he had a youthful, ruddy complexion and deep, soft blue eyes. He wore a fine, white linen suit and a broad, white *sombrero*. He introduced himself as Dr. Headly.

With a bow of much courtliness, he handed Armstrong a carbine with a letter fastened to it under its hammer. Then he said in English:

"We have come to treat with you, gentlemen, and that is our message to your commanding officer."

"The commanding officer is on the other side of the river," said Armstrong. "We have sent for him and he will be here soon."

"Where shall we await him?"

"Right here, where we are."

"Very well," said Dr. Headly, "but, in the meantime, suppose we take a smile."

He put his hand in the nosebag tied to his saddle and drew forth a bottle of *mescal*, which he politely offered to Armstrong.

"Thank you," said Armstrong, "but I cannot drink while I am on duty."

The white-bearded doctor raised his eyebrows in mild surprise and offered the bottle to each of the other Rangers, but all declined to drink.

"Ah," said Dr. Headly; then with a bland smile, "you gentlemen must be afraid of poison. I am an American myself, and I would not play such a trick as that upon you, and to convince you that the liquor is all right, I here drink to your good health."

He suited his action to his words and drank from the bottle. Then his Mexican companions, two of whom were in officers' uniforms, drank from the bottle, each in Spanish politely wishing the good health of the Rangers. When they had all drunk, the doctor again handed the bottle to Armstrong, but again it was politely declined. The handsome doctor then became very talkative and asked Armstrong a number of questions, but Armstrong told him he was under orders not to converse with him and begged to be excused.

Presently Captain McNelly came, and the letter fastened to the carbine was handed to him. While he was reading it, the Mexicans and their American leader drew off a little distance. The Captain was still reading the communication when one of our men came hurrying from our lines with a message to Armstrong from Lieutenant Robinson. The messenger whispered something to Armstrong and then stepped aside and waited.

"What's up?" called out Captain McNelly, who had observed the action.

"Lieutenant Robinson sends word that the enemy is advancing," cried Armstrong in a voice loud enough for all to hear. "He says the Mexicans are advancing on our right. He can hear them close by, in large numbers, and he expects the firing to begin at any minute."

"Very well," said the Captain; "instruct your men to kill every one of this flag of truce party if there is a shot fired."

Dr. Headly, who heard all that passed, seemed greatly perturbed.

"My God!" he cried; "Captain, you don't intend to have us murdered, do you?"

"My men will obey my orders; you may call it what you please," answered McNelly.

"But," said Dr. Headly, "our troops have orders not to shoot and not to advance while this flag of truce is here. Some of them have been drinking hard, and it may be that some reckless, drunken fellow will shoot; but, I can assure you, there will be no attack. I must insist upon you countermanding that order to your men. It isn't fair, while we are standing under a flag of truce, to shoot us down as if we were dogs."

McNelly looked Dr. Headly full in the eyes and answered:

"The life of one of my men is worth more than one thousand such as yours and your fellows. We are not here for fun."

"Well, will you permit me to send one of our officers back to prevent any accident of this kind?" asked Dr. Headly.

"Yes," said McNelly; "and I should advise him to go in a hurry."

Dr. Headly spoke quickly to one of the officers who hastened away. He seemed very glad to have the chance to get off, for he and his companions fully understood the Captain's orders, Dr. Headly having translated them for their benefit. After the officer had disappeared in the brush, Dr. Headly turned to McNelly, and said:

"Do you know how many of our men you have killed?"

"No," said the Captain.

"You have killed twenty-seven already," asserted Dr. Headly, gravely; "and this matter is getting serious. It is time some settlement was made. You have invaded our country and attacked the citizens and soldiers of your sister Republic, and ——"

"Stop!" commanded McNelly, abruptly. "I am not here to listen to any long-winded harangue. We have come here to recover horses and cattle which your men have stolen from Texas. If you return them, we shall go back to Texas; otherwise, we shall stay here in Mexico."

"How many men have you?" asked Dr. Headly. "I may as well tell you that three regiments of Mexican troops are on their way here from Monterey and from Matamoros to drive you out of Mexico."

"Yes? Well, you'll need them all," said McNelly, with a smile.

"Why, how many men have you?"

"Enough," said the Captain, "to march from here to the City of Mexico, if necessary."

It was a beautiful bluff, and it worked. The treating party lost no more time in coming to terms. It was quickly decided that all the stolen livestock should be turned over at ten o'clock the following morning to the Rangers at Rio Grande City—fifteen miles farther up the river. When Dr. Headly and the others had signed a paper to that effect, the Mexicans were permitted to carry away their dead.

Just at sunset we all recrossed the Rio Grande, and we were very glad to be once more on friendly Texas soil.

We were tired and hungry, but we were happy, for we had won a big victory. With thirty men we had gone five miles on foot into Mexico, fought over ten times our number, killed twenty-seven of the enemy, brought them to terms and reached Texas again without the loss of a man. The Mexicans said afterward that they would certainly have annihilated us in Mexico had they known how few we were; but they never thought for an instant that we would be such fools as to invade their country with but thirty men to fight three or four hundred.

That night we had some of a freshly killed cow for supper. Epicures will tell you that beef is not fit to eat until it has been kept a number of days after being killed, but I never remember to have tasted any better than we had that night. We cooked it by thrusting a sharpened stick through a piece of it and broiling it in front of a campfire. We had no salt, but our appetites furnished the seasoning, and the supper was delicious to us.

After supper, Captain McNelly told Armstrong

to pick out fifteen of the horses best able to travel and take their riders up the river, so as to be at Rio Grande City in the morning in time to receive the cattle. The poor horses were nearly famished, but we managed to get fifteen that would go the fifteen miles required, and started off that night, arriving at Rio Grande City before daylight. McNelly went with us. We camped outside the town and gave our horses some much needed grazing.

In the morning we got breakfast at Rio Grande City, and, at ten o'clock, started down to the ford to receive the cattle. All the townspeople and the soldiers stationed at the nearby post knew what we had come for, and the bluffs on the riverbank were lined with people.

At the ford, we met a small boy who told us he had a note for us from the commanding officer of the Mexican soldiers at Camargo. McNelly read the note. It was long and, with much circumlocution, stated that as it was Sunday, it was not customary or proper to transact business, and so the cattle would not be turned over to us until the following day.

McNelly wrote an answer to the note, in which he said he had arranged to receive the cattle that Sunday morning; that he had negotiated with officers—soldiers, and had supposed that they were gentlemen. Their conduct, he added, in now refusing to give up the cattle showed that they were anything but gentlemen, and he would not treat with them any further, but would take matters into his own hands. He read his answer to the Rangers, and said:

"The cattle are in that pen, over on the other side of the river, near the bank. What shall we do?"

"Go over and take them," answered the boys.

"That's just what I wanted you to say," said the Captain; "but, as it is a rather risky undertaking with our small force, I preferred that the decision should come from some of you."

We dismounted and went across the river in the ferryboat. There were five or six of the Rurales, as many customs officers and about forty regular Mexican soldiers guarding the cattle when we reached the other side of the Rio Grande. These men drew up in line to receive the Rangers, and their commander stepped forward to talk to Captain McNelly. The Captain quickly stated the reason for his visit. The Mexican officer said he had no orders to deliver the cattle that day, and the chief customs officer said export duties would have to be paid by us before he could let the cattle go.

This kind of talk did not in the least improve McNelly's temper, and he began chewing on the end of a cigar, a sure sign that he was excited and dangerous.

"Those cattle are going to be turned over to us now," he said. "As for the claim for duty, there was no duty paid when they were stolen and brought over here and, by the Eternal! there shall be no duty paid now."

It looked very like a fight then, and Armstrong, at a signal from the Captain, gave the command:

"Attention! Load carbines! Ready!"

The effect was ludicrous. As the Rangers brought their guns to their hips, preparatory to taking aim, the desperadoes threw up their hands and told us to take the cattle as soon as we pleased.

"No," said the Captain, "we do not propose to take them; you'll deliver them properly to the other side. Now, if you don't drive those cattle across the river as quickly as possible, we'll shoot every one of you."

The Captain marched us farther from the river, so that we had the men and the herd between us and the water. Then we made the Mexicans swim the cattle across to Texas. In this way they crossed two hundred and fifty head. We gave a cow to the ferryman for taking us back, then thanked the Mexicans for their assistance, and went away from the ferry, driving the cattle before us.

The soldiers from Fort Ringgold, who were interested spectators of our movements, cheered us heartily, and the people of Rio Grande City joined in with yells of approval.

Later, we turned over the cattle to their owner, Richard King, the wealthiest ranchman in the West at that time. He sent Captain McNelly a check for $1,500 as a reward, and this was divided up among the men, giving us $50 each.

McNelly's chagrin at the manner in which the

United States military authorities failed to back him up in his attempt to destroy one of the most notorious of the raiders' ranches in Mexico took form about two weeks later in the following letter, which he wrote when he returned to Brownsville:

Brownsville, December 2, 1875

GENERAL WILLIAM STEELE, Adjutant General,
Austin, Tex.

Sir: The condition of this frontier is pitiable in the extreme. The lives and property of our citizens are entirely at the mercy of the Mexican hordes of robbers that infest the banks of the Rio Grande. The State forces, be they ever so active, can only protect the country in the immediate neighborhood of their camp. The hour the camp is moved, it is known on the opposite bank of the river, and the thieves positively steal stock from the site of the camp before the next night. Then, with scarcely an exception, all the male population of the ranches on the opposite bank, from Matamoros to Piedras Negras, are directly engaged in this cattle stealing business; and three-fourths of the population of this border, for one hundred miles back, are the beneficiaries of this illicit traffic. So we cannot reasonably expect any very active or efficient assistance from the better disposed class of people living on the border.

The thieves are getting bolder than ever. For a time, immediately after my arrival, I evidently alarmed them by throwing out hints of the approach of several companies of State troops, and that, on their arrival, these long-time robbers would be dealt with severely; but the troops never came, and now crossing cattle seems to be going on by wholesale.

On November 15th, one hundred and twenty-five head were crossed, one mile below Ringgold Barracks. From the 19th to the 21st, two herds, numbering some four or five hundred in all, were crossed below Brownsville. About the 9th, one herd crossed nine miles below Edinburg. And so they cross, every full moon. They have done the same thing for the last ten years, and they will continue to do so until the robbers are followed to their fastnesses in Mexico and taught that there is no refuge, even in the land of "God and Liberty," for the perpetrators of such outrages.

The policy pursued so long by our Government, of policing our border so ineffectually that the raiders may cross cattle as they please, must now be admitted by the most obtuse of its stupid originators to be a miserable failure. Criminal I call it, for it has permitted our people to be robbed and impoverished, our men murdered and our women outraged.

Shall this condition of affairs continue? It rests with the authorities of the State to answer, yes or no. Let the Governor make one more demand on the President; and then, in case the Cuban question, or some other *Fish* affair, prevents the President from giving us the protection to which we are entitled under the Constitution of the United States, let the Governor order out the militia of the State to repel these invaders.[2]

Although our State is poor—not yet recovered from the effects of the war—I will warrant that enough men and

[2]The "Fish affair" refers to Secretary of State Hamilton Fish and his continuous concern for American neutrality in regard to Cuba. Despite provocation, such as the *Virginius* affair in 1873, wherein the Spanish government executed thirty-six men, including Americans and British subjects, for carrying arms to Cuban rebels, Secretary of State Fish would not recognize Cuban belligerency. See Allan Nevins, *Hamilton Fish: The Inner History of the Grant Administration* (2 vols.; New York: Frederick Ungar Publishing Co., 1936), I, 102-29ff; II, 667-94.

money can be raised to put a stop to these diabolical outrages, from Texas and by Texans. I, for one, will guarantee to raise one company for ninety days that shall not cost the State one dollar.

This may look like an extraordinary course, but, General, this is an extraordinary condition of affairs. These people are American citizens, Texans. They are being murdered, robbed, driven from their homes. Now, shall we wait for the political clock to strike the hour to put a stop to it? When will the hour come? We have waited ten years, and ten long years they have been to the people of this desolated border; and still no signal, no sign of relief. God help our frontiersmen if they have to wait ten years more!

With my present force, I can do but little. These raids are made from seventy-five to one hundred miles from my camp, and by the time I receive information and get to the crossing, the raiders are over the Rio Grande and safe from our men, as at almost any point on the whole line of the river, from Matamoros to Piedras Negras, they can gather from one hundred to two hundred men to resist us if we attempt a crossing. And, now that the regular Mexican cavalry have come from Monterey, it will be much worse, as they are anxious to have revenge for our crossing at Las Cuevas and forcing them to submit to such humiliating terms.

The regular troops tell the thieves that if we ever dare cross again, they will never let one of us return to Texas; but, with two hundred men, I could recapture any herd of cattle they might cross, in spite of raiders or regular troops, and unless this can be done, I would respectfully recommend that this troop be ordered elsewhere, or disbanded. It is too humiliating to follow the thieves to the bank of the river and see our stock on the opposite bank, and have the raiders defy us to cross, but crossing with my present force is almost certain destruction.

I was very much annoyed at all those false reports put out by the Mexican officials of Matamoros about our being surrounded and asking for quarter at Las Cuevas. The idea of Texans asking quarter from robbers, assassins and ravishers! On the contrary, it was *they* who asked for terms, and granted *our* demands, and were happy when we left their side of the river. They admit having twenty-seven killed and nineteen wounded, and our loss was one horse wounded. As one of the boys remarked, "We went over and came back with our heads and backs up."

Very respectfully,

(Signed)   L. H. McNelly

XIII

A Quiet Border

DESPITE Captain McNelly's gloomy views, as expressed in the characteristic letter I have given from his pen, the result of the Las Cuevas fight was highly satisfactory to the cattlemen, for the raids practically ceased while we remained on the lower Rio Grande. We had done our work so effectually that we were forced to have a very prosaic time for months. We went upon many scouts and did plenty of hard riding, but we seldom got a chance to do any fighting. The border thieves simply would not resist us. If we wanted any of them for past offenses, all we had to do was find them, and they submitted to arrest with painful humility.

The border was quieter than it had been since the independence of Texas was won. Less than fifty young men had done more to enforce order on the Rio Grande than thousands of the United States troops had been able to do in years. Tireless riding, deadly shooting, and utter disregard for danger caused the Rangers to be dreaded by evildoers, far and wide. The good people of the frontier, the hardy settlers and cattlemen, were loud in their praises of us, and the wealthy ranchmen vied with each other in rewarding us for recovering stock.

But the Rangers were not pleased. The quieter life was entirely too tame for us. We had had so much exciting adventure that the habit had grown on us. The routine of camplife was not to our taste. We wanted a chance again to do active work at the mechanical end of a carbine. Shooting blue quail and wild turkeys around camp was good enough exercise in its way, but the blue quail and the turkeys couldn't shoot back, and the exciting element of danger was missing. Solitaire is a dull game, after poker.

Speaking of poker reminds me that the Rangers were, one and all, inveterate poker players, and the money we received for recovered cattle, and which was equally divided among the men, was ever changing hands. So it was with our pay of $40 a month. In a day or two after payday, it was not unusual for four or five of the more lucky ones to have about all the money in camp, the rest of the boys going without funds, or borrowing until payday came around again. I was never one of the lucky ones and was "flat broke" for months at a time, while some of the successful fellows were squandering my pay.

Captain McNelly did not approve of the gambling, and one day he sent word from Brownsville that he would discharge any man who played poker thereafter. A week later, we sent him a round robin, in which we stated that all the signers were confirmed poker players. It was signed by every member of the company, excepting the commissioned officers. As we expected, we never heard anything further from Captain McNelly about the gambling, for he had taken too many pains to select his men to discharge all of them for such an offense.

We practiced shooting a great deal and bet on our marksmanship contests. The men were nearly all remarkably fine shots, both with their carbines and six-shooters. One of our favorite methods of practicing was to ride at a full run past a tree and try to put all six shots from a revolver into it as we sped by. We also spent much time in practicing the gentle Texas art of "drawing a gun" quickly from its holster. It isn't the best shot who comes out ahead always in an impromptu frontier duel; it is the man who gets his six-shooter out and in action first.

One of our most popular forms of amusement was playing practical jokes on each other, and some of them were of a pretty rough character. I remember one joke we played on Rector, a jolly and useful member of the troop, albeit so deaf one had to yell at him to make him hear. The boys called him "Reck."[1] He was fond of natural history, and was never so delighted as when he captured a curious insect, or shot a rare bird, or killed a fine specimen

[1]Private H. G. Rector enlisted twice in the Rangers, the first time from July 26, 1874, to October 31, 1876, and the second from January 25, 1877, to his final discharge on February 28, 1878. See Ingmire, *Texas Ranger Service Records, 1847–1900*, V, 46. See also Durham and Wantland, *Taming the Nueces Strip*, p. 40.

of a snake. One day, one of the boys asked Reck if he'd ever gone "sniping."

"Shooting snipe?" said Reck. "Lots of times."

"No, no," said the Ranger, "not shooting them; catching them in a bag. I thought nearly everyone knew about 'sniping.'"

"Never heard of it," said Reck. "How can anyone catch snipe in a bag?"

"Oh, it's simple enough when you know how," explained the other. "A party of half a dozen or more men start out about sundown and go to some marshy place, near a river, where the snipe are apt to be night. They take a bag—an old gunnysack is best—and some candles with them. They select a likely spot and, when it is quite dark, one of the party holds the mouth of the bag open and places a lighted candle in front of it, on the ground. The others go off and make a large circle, which they gradually narrow as they approach the one who is holding the bag. They beat the chaparral and make all the noise they can as they get near to him, and they frighten all the snipe and start them running toward him, too. The snipe are attracted by the light from the candle and, as they get close to it, are blinded by its rays. They run straight into the mouth of the open sack. It's great sport, and I know a place, about three miles from here, where the snipe are as thick as hops. Let's get up a party to go after them tonight."

Reck was delighted with the idea and a party of

nine snipe hunters was quickly made up. Strangely enough, all of the men except Reck had often been on sniping expeditions and knew all about them. I was in on the secret and became one of the party.

We started soon after sundown and went up the river, led by the Ranger who proposed the sport. He took us, by winding, roundabout paths, to a swampy piece of ground where we sank to our ankles at every step. The place was swarming with mosquitoes. When we reached what we agreed was a favorable spot, we stopped and had an animated discussion as to who should hold the sack. We all wanted to hold it, apparently, because it was so much more fun to bag the snipe than to go tramping around in the brush, beating up the birds. Finally, someone said that it took more skill to flush the snipe than it did to hold the sack and, as Reck was green at the work, perhaps it would be better to let him have the coveted part. The rest agreed to this as a fair solution of the question and two candles were lighted and stuck in the marshy ground, while Reck squatted down and held the mouth of the sack open behind them. It took both his hands to hold the sack properly, and when we left him, the mosquitoes were already singing in high glee about his head.

And so we went away from him. To beat up the snipe? Oh, no; to get by the nearest way out of that mosquito-infested marsh and back to camp. We reached there shortly, and the boys howled with wicked delight as we drew graphic pictures of poor Reck holding on with both hands to that sack, while every mosquito in the swamp within sight of the candles made a beeline for the spot.

Reck came into camp about midnight. He got lost in hunting it and came near having to pass the night in the brush. He brought the sack with him and went straight to where the man who had invited him to go "sniping" lay asleep. He woke him up and all near him with a wild war whoop.

"Hello, Reck!" exclaimed the practical joker, as he sat up; "did you get any snipe?"

"You bet your boots I did!" cried Reck, as he suddenly shook the contents of his sack all over the joker. "Look at all these fine fellows."

The man gave a yell and scrambled to his feet. Reck had shaken about two quarts of big, black ants all over him, and he knew from experience that ants in Texas bite like fiends. Reck had stumbled over an ant hill in wandering back to camp and gathered a lot of them into his sack, so as to get even with the sniping party. He did it very effectually, for the ants spread in all directions and made things decidedly uncomfortable for us the rest of the night. That was the last "sniping" party we ever had in the Rangers, but it was far from being the last practical joke played. I invented one myself and worked it with wonderful success for a long time before I was found out.

I discovered, one day, quite by accident, that I

could perfectly imitate the peculiar trilling hiss of the rattlesnake. This I came to believe was a unique accomplishment; at least, I have never met anyone who could do it. The sound is made by a trilling tongue movement and a hiss. The first time I tried it was one day while riding quietly along the road from Brownsville to our camp. It must have been a very fine imitation of the rattlesnake, even at that first attempt, for my horse gave a great leap and nearly unseated me, as he shied off about ten feet to one side. That set me to thinking, for I felt that if I could deceive a horse with the imitation, it would be a simple matter to fool a man. Having so reasoned, I practiced for awhile and then waited until later that evening.

When we had all "turned in," except the one Ranger who stood the first two hours of guard duty, I thought it time to try the effect of my new accomplishment on the boys. Some of them were asleep, but most were awake. I began to hiss very softly, as I lay on my blanket, and gradually increased the volume of the sound, until it seemed as if a very angry rattler must be close by. Four or five of the men sat bolt upright and listened. I waited for a few minutes, and then "rattled" again. This time more of the men bolted up and, so as to avoid suspicion, I did likewise.

I kept on hissing and the excitement in the camp grew. Two or three jumped up and pulled on their boots, and I did the same. We began a cautious hunt for the rattlesnake, and whenever I was far enough away from the others I started the rattling again. In a short time the entire camp was in commotion. We hunted the elusive snake for nearly an hour, and most of the boys sat up for an hour or two longer after it ceased to rattle, for I stopped after awhile and went to sleep.

I played this interesting game four nights in succession before I was caught at it. Then the boys entered into a conspiracy to keep me awake. For two nights, whenever I tried to sleep, they got around me and woke me up. They relieved each other at the work. The third night I took a blanket, slipped off into the chaparral and slept about half a mile from the camp.

If any of the boys attempted to take a *siesta* in the afternoon, as was quite natural in the lazy life about camp, he had a miserable time of it. One favorite way of awakening a sleeper was to run close by his head, dragging a saddle over the ground and shouting "Whoa!" at the tops of our voices. The sleeping man would think a horse was running away close to him and would invariably start up in alarm. I have seen a man awakened in this way twice within an hour, and he was every bit as frightened the second time as the first. It was impossible to get used to waking up that way.

Another little pleasantry practiced was for one of the boys to wait until a number of the others had found a comfortable place around the campfire after supper, and then approach and toss a few pistol or carbine cartridges into the fire. The resulting scramble to get away from the fire was always a source of pure delight to the cartridge thrower. We became used to this after awhile, however, and would rake the cartridges out of the fire and keep them. We learned that a cartridge will not explode under such circumstances for a minute or two, and so we rescued them for better use.

The above are but a few of the thousand and one practical jokes which the Rangers in McNelly's command were ever perpetrating.[2] We were boys, not only in appearance, but in our amusements as well. I do not remember any instance where practical joking led to bad feeling between the joker and his victim. Reckless and daring though they were, ever ready to jump into the middle of a fight against a common enemy, the Rangers seldom or never quarreled among themselves. We were like a great band of brothers, and our affection for each other was genuine. There was not an unpopular man in the troop. All were received into the common brotherhood. There was no backbiting, there were

[2] Jennings certainly understood Ranger practical jokes. George Durham, who was with McNelly during these years on the border, stated that Jennings was from the "East" and "had come down with some money." To relieve Jennings of his money, "Boyd taught him the finer points of draw poker, and among us we taught him all about snipe hunting and badger fighting and all the things a Yankee must learn when he comes to Texas." See Durham and Wantland, *Taming the Nueces Strip*, p. 136.

no petty jealousies. Unlike most practical jokers, each man was willing to be occasionally a victim himself to the sport of the others, or, if not exactly willing, he never openly objected.

There was one other good reason for treating a practical joke in a good-natured way. Every man understood that a rebuff by any one of his comrades would mean a duel to the death. I don't believe any knew the A B C of "the noble art of self-defense" with nature's weapons. Our only weapons of offense or defense were those which worked with a trigger.

XIV

The Capture of King Fisher

THE MEMORY of the camp life on the lower Rio Grande is a pleasant one to me, but it is hardly of such a character as to furnish material for a story of adventure, so, without lingering, I shall pass over the time which intervened between our big raid into Mexico and the day when orders came for us to remove our camp permanently to another portion of Texas. We had done all that was possible with our small force to subdue the border thieves, and Captain McNelly was of too active a temperament to be content to rest quietly while there was work to do in other places.

The American desperadoes were swarming all over western Texas, and the sheriffs in many counties were powerless to do anything toward their suppression. The Captain decided that the time had come for us to take an active part in the problem of restoring order in those counties which were over-ridden and terrorized by fugitives from justice of nearly every State in the Union. So, one day, the welcome order came for us to move camp and we started on a long ride up the Rio Grande.

We traveled slowly—not more than twenty-five miles a day—and we went as straight as possible to

Laredo. My feelings upon riding into that town were very different from those with which I had last ridden out of it. Almost the first man I met was Gregorio Gonzales, the City Marshal. He treated me with marked deference, which, I regret to say, I returned with scant courtesy. I was not so ready to pass politely over old scores as he seemed to be.

It was May 25, 1876 when we arrived at Laredo, and we camped near the town for three days. Then we continued our journey on toward the Nueces River, where we camped not far from the place where I had helped Peterson lay out homestead sections, over a year before. Here we remained for a few days to rest our horses, and then began our work of running desperadoes to earth—the work which has since made western Texas a law-abiding, safe country in which to live.

At the camp near the Nueces River, we learned first about the desperado, King Fisher,[1] and his notorious gang of horse thieves, cattle thieves, and

[1] John King Fisher, better known as King Fisher, had an obscure and blurred early life. He was born in the early 1850s, most probably in Kentucky, although one account claims his birthplace as Collin County, Texas, "in 1853, or thereabout." By the 1870s Fisher was recognized as the "chief" or "king" of the outlaws from Castroville—near San Antonio—to Eagle Pass on the Rio Grande. See O. C. Fisher, *The Texas Heritage of the Fishers and the Clarks* (Salado, Texas: The Anson Jones Press, 1963), pp. 53–58; Askins, *Texans, Guns & History*, pp. 64–67; Webb, *The Texas Rangers*, pp. 286–87. Raymond, *Captain Lee Hall of Texas*, p. 55, states that Fisher, when age twenty-six, "boasted that he had killed a man for each year of his life."

John King Fisher
Courtesy Western History Collections,
University of Oklahoma, Norman

murderers. Fisher lived on Pendencia Creek, near the Nueces, in Dimmit County. He had a little ranch there, and about forty or fifty of his followers were nearly always with him. These men, too lazy or too vicious to work for themselves, preyed upon the substance of the toiling settlers. They stole the ranchmen's horses and cattle and robbed their corn cribs, and they did not stop at murder to further their ends. Captain McNelly (I was then his field secretary) wrote, in a letter to the Adjutant General, from this part of Texas:

"You can scarcely realize the true condition of this section, from Oakville to this point. The country is under a perfect reign of terror from the number and desperate character of the thieves who infest this region. The country is rich in stock, but very sparsely settled, and the opportunities and inducements for anyone to steal are very great.

"This county (Dimmit) is unorganized and is attached to Maverick County for judicial purposes. About one-half the white citizens of Eagle Pass are friends of King Fisher's gang. The remainder of the citizens there are too much afraid of the desperadoes to give any assistance in even keeping them secure after they have been placed in jail, and they would never think of helping to arrest any of them. On my arrival here, I found the people greatly terrified, and on the eve of deserting their homes and property to save their lives—the homes which for years they had defended against Indians and invading Mexicans alternately, and never once thought of leaving. Some of the oldest and best citizens told me that, in all of their frontier experience, they had never suffered so much as from these American robbers. For weeks past they have not dared to leave their homes for fear of being waylaid and murdered.

"Every house in this part of the county has been repeatedly fired into by armed men, from fifteen to twenty in number at a time. The ranchmen's horses and cattle have been driven from their range, and even from pens at the houses, until the people are left almost destitute of means of support. If anyone had the temerity to protest against being robbed, he was told that he had just so many days to live if he did not leave the county. Some of those who had the courage to remain have been foully murdered.

"As the country is so sparsely settled, there are not enough good citizens to defend themselves, even if they united to do so. They seem perfectly willing to assist me, provided the desperadoes are properly secured and tried where they will get justice. They will not get justice here, even if they are brought to trial, which is doubtful. Should they be let loose and return here, this county would be in even a worse condition than it is now. No persons can be found who will dare to testify against the desperadoes, and I am told by the Circuit Judge that he is convinced no jury in the three counties—Dimmit, Maverick, and Live Oak—can be found to convict them, notwithstanding all their lawless, brutal conduct and the many complaints made against them.

"There is a regularly organized band of the desperadoes, from Goliad to the headwaters of the Nueces, numbering four or five hundred men. The band is made up of men who have committed crimes in different portions of this State and farther east and who have run out here for safety. When they get here, they go to robbing for a livelihood. They divide up into parties of twenty-five to forty men and form settlements in the different counties, communicating with each other constantly. They pass stolen horses along the line continually, and are in communication with other gangs to the north of this place and far to the west."

Some idea of the extent to which the desperadoes swarmed over the western portion of Texas may be obtained when I state that the Rangers had a printed book, containing the names of over three thousand fugitives from justice who were known to be or to have been in that country. And of the three thousand names in the book, the large majority were those of men who were "wanted" by the authorities for crimes of most serious character, like murder, arson, highway robbery, burglary, and horse and cattle stealing. More than a thousand were murderers, with rewards on their heads ranging from a few hundred to ten thousand dollars.

As undoubtedly there were very many desperadoes in the country whose names were not in the book, it will be seen how formidable were their numbers.

To break up the organized bands of these lawless, desperate men; to hunt them down, to arrest them and put them in jail, or to drive them out of the country, was the work we had cut out for us. We had less than fifty men; they had thousands. But we were backed by the law and the good will of all the honest frontiersmen—a big factor in our favor. And then we made up in self-confidence and reckless disregard of danger what we lacked in numbers. Our successes on the lower Rio Grande gave us the feeling that we were invincible. We not only did

not fear the result of a conflict with the desperadoes; we were eager to try conclusions with them.

The fourth morning after arriving in camp, we
started for the Pendencia, to arrest King Fisher and
those of his gang who should happen to be with
him. The Captain had received information from
some of the less timid ranchmen that Fisher was at
his ranch, making ready, they thought, to go on another raid and gather cattle to drive north. These
men said that Fisher had about thirty men with him
at that time at his place. His house was at Carrizo
Springs.

McNelly divided the troop into two squads when
we started, and we proceeded in the direction of
Fisher's stronghold, the two squads being about two
miles apart and traveling in parallel lines. Scouts
were sent out about a mile in advance and told to
ride half a mile apart and arrest all the men they
saw. In this way, a number of men were picked up
and turned over to the main troop for safekeeping.
We wanted to take Fisher and his gang by surprise,
and we did not propose to be thwarted by his
friends apprising him of our coming. We went very
rapidly over unused roads and trails, and succeeded
in arriving at a point in the chaparral about a quarter of a mile from Fisher's house without being seen
by any of his men.

Both squads came together at this place, but Captain McNelly divided us again and sent part of the
troop through the chaparral, around to the other

side of the house. Then, at a prearranged moment, all of us dashed for the house at full speed, six-shooters in hand. A fence was in our way, but the horses went over it like hunters after the hounds, and before Fisher and his men perceived us we were within a hundred yards of the place.

Most of the desperadoes were playing poker under the shed-like extension in front of the ranch house. They jumped up and started for the house proper to procure their arms, but before half of them succeeded in getting inside the door, we were around them and our six-shooters were cocked and pointed at their heads.

"You'll have to surrender or be killed!" cried McNelly to Fisher, who stood halfway out of the door, with the lieutenant of his band, one Burd Obenchain, but known to his companions as Frank Porter.

Fisher did not move, but Porter half raised his Winchester, and coolly looked along the line of Rangers.

"Drop that gun!" yelled McNelly. "Drop it, I say, or I'll kill you."

Porter looked McNelly squarely in the eyes, half raised his rifle again, and then slowly dropped it to his side, and with a sigh leaned it against the side of the house.

"I reckon there's too many of yer to tackle," he said, calmly. "I only wisht I'd a-seen yer sooner."

The other men gave up without a struggle. They

were badly frightened at first, for they thought we were members of a vigilance committee, come to deal out swift justice to them and hang them by lynch law. They were agreeably disappointed when they discovered we were the Rangers, officers of the law of Texas.

There were only nine of the desperadoes at the house at the time, but a precious gang of outlaws and cutthroats they were. Here are their names: J. K. Fisher, known as "King" Fisher; Burd Obenchain, alias Frank Porter, wanted for murder and cattle-stealing, as desperate a ruffian as ever the Texas border knew; Warren Allen, who shot a Negro in a barroom at Fort Clark for drinking at the same bar with him, and then deliberately turned and finished his own drink and ordered another; Bill Templeton, horse thief; Will Wainwright, Jim Honeycutt, Wes Bruton, Al Roberts, and Bill Bruton. All of them were "wanted" for numberless crimes. They were the head honchos of the gang of murderers and all-round criminals.

Porter, as an example, had followed a man all the way from Kansas to southwest Texas to kill him. He rode up to where his enemy had made camp one evening and dismounted.

"Howdy," said Porter.

"Howdy," said the man.

"I haven't seen yer fur some time; how're yer gettin' along?" said Porter.

"Oh, so-so," replied the man. "How're you doin'?"

"Only tol'ble," said Porter; "I'm plumb wore out, ridin' an' campin' on yer trail. I reckon yer know what I've come fur?"

"Yes," said the man, "I reckon I do. Ain't yer goin' to gi' me no chanst?"

"Nary chanst," said Porter; "I'm a-goin' ter kill yer right where yer be, but I ain't in no hurry ef yer don't move fur yer gun. Le's have supper first; I wanter talk to yer."

Then this villain calmly ate his supper at the man's campfire, and, after he finished it, deliberately shot and killed his host.

A few weeks before we arrested them, King Fisher and Frank Porter, by themselves, stole a herd of cattle from six Mexican *vaqueros* who were driving the herd for its owner, near Eagle Pass. Fisher and Porter rode around the herd and killed every one of the six Mexicans. The *vaqueros* were all buried together, and I saw the place where they were buried. It was known as "Frank Porter's Graveyard."

Fisher was about twenty-five years old at that time, and the most perfect specimen of a frontier dandy and desperado that I ever saw. He was tall, beautifully proportioned, and exceedingly handsome. He wore the finest clothing procurable, but all of it was the picturesque, border, dime novel kind. His broad-brimmed white Mexican *sombrero* was profusely ornamented with gold and silver lace and had a golden snake for a band. His fine buckskin Mexican short jacket was heavily embroidered with gold. His shirt was of the finest and thinnest linen and was worn open at the throat, with a silk handkerchief knotted loosely about the collar. A brilliant crimson silk sash was wound about his waist, and his legs were hidden by a wonderful pair of *chaparejos*, or "chaps," as the cowboys called them—leather breeches to protect the legs while riding through the brush. These *chaparejos* were made of the skin of a royal Bengal tiger and ornamented down the seams with gold and buckskin fringe. The tiger's skin had been procured by Fisher at a circus in northern Texas. He and some of his fellows had literally captured the circus, killed the tiger and skinned it, just because the desperado chief fancied he'd like to have a pair of tiger skin "chaps." His boots were of the finest high heeled variety, the kind all cowboys loved to wear. Hanging from his cartridge-filled belt were two ivory-handled, silver-plated six-shooters. His spurs were of silver and ornamented with little silver bells.

He was an expert revolver shot, and could handle his six-shooters as well with his left hand as with his right. He was a fine rider, and rode the best horses he could steal in Texas or Mexico. Among the desperadoes, the stolen horses were known as "wet stock"—that is, horses which had been stolen in Mexico and swum across the Rio Grande to Texas, or *vice versa*.

We took the men with us at once to Eagle Pass and put them in jail there. We tied the feet of the prisoners to their stirrups and then tied the stirrups together under the horses' bellies. We also tied the desperadoes' hands to the pommels of their saddles and led their horses. Before we started, Captain McNelly told us, in the hearing of the prisoners and of Fisher's wife—a pretty girl, with wonderfully fine, bold black eyes—that if any of our prisoners attempted to escape or if an attempt was made to rescue them, we were to kill them without warning or mercy. That is, or was, known on the frontier as *la ley de fuga*, the shooting of escaping or resisting prisoners.[2] It was well understood among the outlaws, and was a great protection to the officers who were compelled to escort prisoners over long distances through the sparsely settled country. The knowledge of this condition of the border prevented members of a desperado gang from attempting to rescue prisoners, for such an attempt meant instant death to the captives.

It was about forty miles, in a westerly direction, from Carrizo Springs to Eagle Pass, the county seat of Maverick County, situated on the Rio Grande, directly opposite the Mexican town of Piedras Negras, now called Ciudad Porfirio Diaz. Only a small part of the Ranger troop went with the prisoners; the others, including Captain McNelly, went into

[2] *La ley de fuga* is a Spanish phrase which means "the law of flight." In other words, Texas Rangers—without penalty—could kill a suspect or prisoner resisting arrest or attempting an escape. See Webb, *The Texas Rangers*, p. 227; Durham and Wantland, *Taming the Nueces Strip*, p. 38.

camp, and scouting parties were sent in various directions to try and capture other members of the Fisher gang. As soon as the prisoners were turned over to the Sheriff of Maverick County and put in the jail in Eagle Pass, the Rangers who had guarded them returned to Carrizo Springs.

Two days later, while we were on our way to Eagle Pass with more prisoners, we met King Fisher and his men going home to Carrizo Springs. They were out on bail, although charged with murder and many other serious crimes. Fisher calmly told Captain McNelly that he was out under $20,000 bail, and that any member of his gang could get all the bail he wanted at any time.

"Very well," said McNelly, "if the people of this section want such men as you running over their country and stealing and murdering, they are welcome. There is no use in working my men night and day for such a farce as this. Turn the prisoners loose, boys."

We untied the bonds of our new prisoners and let them go. Afterward, we learned that Fisher had sent some of his friends around to the merchants and wealthier citizens of Eagle Pass with the message that he wanted them to go bail for him and the other prisoners in the jail. The merchants well knew that if they refused Fisher's "request" they would probably be robbed and murdered, and so they hastened to do as he wished. A scared justice of the peace and a timorous sheriff made the arrangements for providing the bonds, and the men were quickly freed to continue their work of terrorizing the country where they had held sway for so long.

McNelly was not through with the desperadoes of Fisher's band, but he knew that he would have to deal with them in another way and at another time, and he wisely concluded to draw off his forces and so give them a feeling of security which later would bring trouble upon them.

"If we ever come up here again, we'll come to kill," was all the Captain said to Fisher, "and if you keep up your system of robbery and murder, you'll be hearing from us."

Fisher laughed, and said he would be delighted to see the Rangers at any time and entertain them to the best of his ability. Then we rode away.

XV

Lieutenant Hall Arrives

W E STRUCK out across the country toward the
southeast and made many arrests, here and
there, in La Salle, McMullen, and Live Oak Counties, and also in Frio and Atascosa Counties. Most of
the men we arrested were fugitives from justice
from other parts of the State, and we were constantly employed taking them to the county seats, where
they were turned over to the sheriffs for safekeeping
until peace officers from counties where they were
wanted came for them. All this section of Texas was
in a lawless state, and I remember that, in Atascosa
County alone, there was a murder nearly everyday.
Men were waylaid on the roads and shot down or
murdered in their homes by assassins shooting at
them through the windows.

Every man went armed. A woman buying calico
or groceries in one of the country stores was waited
upon by a clerk who had a six-shooter dangling
from his belt. Schoolteachers carried their guns with
them to the schoolhouses. Ministers—parsons they
were called, as a rule—went armed to church and
preached to armed congregations. Men placed their
revolvers, rifles, or shotguns within easy reach before retiring for the night.

Even women carried derringers in many parts of the country, particularly the wives of ranchmen. When the husbands were away from the ranches, the women knew that their best protectors were those provided with easy-working triggers. The country was "on the shoot," to use a colloquial bit of slang, and the six-shooter was the supreme arbiter of most disputes. Little boys were taught to handle and discharge pistols and rifles with accuracy long before they were taught the alphabet.

I wish to emphasize the fact here that, with the passing of the desperado from Texas, the necessity for going armed disappeared, and at this time, no person, except an officer of the law or a wild and quarrel-seeking cowboy, still believes it requisite to "tote a gun." More pistols are carried now by men in New York City than in Texas. Life is as safe in the Lone Star State as in any metropolis in America, and all old Texans will bear me out when I say that it was the Texas Rangers that made it so.

We went on to Oakville and made our camp there, scouting in squads throughout Live Oak and the adjoining counties, and making many arrests of men who were "wanted." There was no difficulty in finding them or in arresting them when found, for already they were beginning in that part of the country to have a wholesome respect for the Rangers with their ever-ready six-shooters. The outlaws had long laughed the sheriffs and their deputies to scorn, but they found in the Rangers a wholly new force with which it was not so easy to deal.

We put in several months at this work, and it was while we were in camp at Oakville that Jesse Lee Hall joined the troop as Second Lieutenant, having been appointed to that office by the governor. Hall succeeded McNelly to the command of the troop in the following year, upon the death of McNelly,[1] and it is generally agreed that our new lieutenant became one of the most feared punishers of evildoers ever known in the Southwest.

Jesse Lee Hall was born in Lexington, N.C., in October, 1849.[2] He came of old Revolutionary stock by both his parents. His ancestors had settled in North Carolina in the early part of the eighteenth century, coming from the northern English colonies where their forefathers had lived since early in the seventeenth century. Among Hall's ancestors were the famous General Giles Mebane, and Governor Stanford of North Carolina.

Hall went to Texas when he was nineteen years old, and shortly after became a deputy sheriff in Grayson County on the line of the Indian Territory, where he did such good work that his fame as an officer attracted wide attention. During the winter of 1876, Hall was appointed sergeant-at-arms of the lower house of the Texas Legislature, and as such

[1]Captain McNelly died at Oakland, Texas, on September 4, 1877. See Dietrich, *Washington County*, pp. 53–54.
[2]See Chapter 8, footnote 5, p. 122.

became well acquainted with Governor Hubbard.[3] His appointment to the lieutenancy of the Rangers soon followed.

I shall never forget the afternoon he first rode into our camp, just below Oakville. We had heard that he was coming and that he was a hard man to deal with, but we soon discovered that he was a splendid fellow, full of fun, of charming manners, and only "nasty" when dealing with outlaws. His hair was bright red, and he soon received the nickname of "Red" Hall, which clung to him ever after. As he rode into our camp that afternoon, early in August, 1876, he first called out:

"Say, have any of you boys got a chew of tobacco? I'm Hall."

All of us liked that, and we invited him to join us and have something to eat. He did so. Then we

[3]Richard Bennett Hubbard (1832–1901) was born in Walton County, Georgia. He graduated from Mercer College in 1851 and Harvard Law School in 1853, then established a law practice in Tyler, Texas. In five years Hubbard became the U.S. district attorney for the Western District of Texas; in 1859 he was elected to the Texas House of Representatives; and, during the Civil War, he fought for the Confederacy as a colonel, commanding the Twenty-Second Texas Infantry Regiment. In 1873 and again in 1876 he was elected lieutenant governor. In December, 1876, he became governor—after Governor Richard Coke resigned to become a United States senator—and would serve in this position until January, 1879. See Jean Sutherlin Duncan, *Richard Bennett Hubbard: Texas Politician and Diplomat* (Ann Arbor: University Microfilms, 1990); and Martha Anne Turner, *Richard Bennett Hubbard: An American Life* (Austin: Shoal Creek Publishers, Inc., 1979).

Ranger Lieutenant Jesse Lee Hall

Courtesy Archives Division,
Texas State Library, Austin

beguiled him into telling us some stories of his life as sergeant-at-arms at the State Capital. We didn't want to hear the stories so much, but we did want to have a little fun with our new lieutenant, and we had it. When he began telling stories, he had an audience of about thirty Rangers. Pretty soon, one of the boys got up and went away. Then another arose and quietly moved off. Then a third stole from the circle. In two minutes, Lieutenant Hall was telling his yarns to the campfire, all by himself.

He stopped, and the boys howled in sheer delight at his discomfiture.

"You're a tough lot," said Hall with a grin.

I think it was while we were camped at Oakville that I had a little turkey shooting adventure which caused much hilarity in the camp. I had been off hunting some horses which had strayed away from our range and was returning to camp, not having found them. Suddenly, I heard the gobble of a turkey, off to one side, in the mesquite chaparral. The country was full of wild turkeys and quail, and they made a welcome addition to our usual camp fare.

As soon as I heard the turkey, I slipped from the saddle, pulled my carbine from its scabbard under the stirrup leather and crept off into the chaparral. I had not gone far before I spied the big turkey gobbler with half a dozen turkey hens. I took very deliberate aim at him and fired. The gobbler fell over and fluttered about on the ground for a minute, but I rushed up and grabbed him and wrung his neck.

He was a gigantic bird, and I felt good as I carried him back to where my horse was standing and tied him to the saddle. I was just tying the last knot when I heard a shout. I turned my head and saw, not twenty yards away, a ranch fence which I had not noticed before. A man was coming toward me, shouting and gesticulating wildly. In only a second, I realized the situation. I had shot his tame turkey gobbler. Wild turkeys and tame turkeys look very much alike, particularly when they are running in the brush, and the mistake was a natural one. But I didn't believe I could explain it to the owner's satisfaction at that time. He didn't look as if he was amenable to reason. He was swearing like a trooper and saying unkind things. I did not have a cent to pay him for his turkey and I didn't want to fight him for it.

So I waved my hand in a careless, happy farewell to him and started off on a gallop, the turkey flopping up and down behind me in great style.

When I reached camp, I flung the turkey off and the boys began plucking it in a hurry. They wanted to cook it for supper. No one seemed to notice that it wasn't a wild turkey and I didn't enlighten them as to its domesticity.

We fried the turkey and were eating it in full enjoyment of its lusciousness when my friend, its former owner, rode into camp.

"Which one o' you fellers shot my turkey?" he called out from the saddle.

"Get down and have some supper," answered Durham, who grasped the situation instantly.

"I don't want no supper; I want the man who shot my turkey."

"Well, you must have come to the wrong place, friend," said Durham. "No one here has shot your turkey. I haven't seen a turkey in a month. Any of you boys seen a turkey around here?"

Durham held a leg of the turkey in his hand as he asked the question. The boys all answered in the negative with their mouths full of turkey.

"Why, doggone ye," said the farmer, "all of you are eatin' my turkey right now!"

"You are mistaken, sir," said Horace Rowe, carefully picking a wing of the bird; "this is a *Meleagris Americana* which we are devouring, and we beg that you will accept our poor hospitality and join us in getting away with it."

This display of learning seemed to stagger the farmer. He dismounted and sat down on the ground with us. Soon he was eating a piece of the turkey. He picked some of the feathers up and carefully examined them.

"That was my turkey all right," he said, gravely.

"Very well," I put in, "if one of the boys really did shoot your turkey, you point him out and we'll arrest him and take him to the justice of the peace in Oakville."

"Yes; pick him out, show him to us!" cried all the others.

The man looked all around at the faces and finally picked out Rector.

Rector proved an alibi by half the men in camp. Then the farmer pointed out another man; but we said he couldn't go on guessing that way, and he, himself, agreed it wouldn't be quite fair. At last, he gave it up in despair. Then I gave him a dollar, which I borrowed, and he went away satisfied.

But I kept on hearing about that turkey for a long, long time afterward. The Rangers had a pleasing little way of keeping any awkward episode fresh for an unbearable length of time.

In the latter part of August, Hall took eleven men and went in command of them on his first scout as a Ranger officer. He went to Goliad and did the sheriff's work during the suspension of that officer for malfeasance in office. Hall and his men made about twenty arrests of desperate men on the trip.

Hall also gave assistance to the sheriffs of other counties in quieting a few disturbances which arose among the cattlemen. Among those he arrested were George McCarty, Wesley Bruton, and Charles Bruton, all desperadoes of the worst type. He turned them over to the sheriff of Dimmit County and they were turned loose on straw bail at the demand of King Fisher.

As I was not with Hall, I cannot give anything but a bare record, in a general way, of his work at this time; but that it was good and showed him to be a fearless and efficient officer there can be no doubt, for, at a later date, I had an opportunity to see him under circumstances to try the nerves of the bravest man, and he was chillingly cool.

Those of us who were left in camp at Oakville grew very tired of our life there, for it was anything but active. Most of my time was put in herding horses. I remember that I stampeded them one afternoon by shooting at an antelope, and it was a weary hunt I had before I got them together again.

Early in September, we received word that a Mexican had been murdered near a sheep corral about twelve miles from camp. Sergeant Orrell took six or seven of us with him to investigate the matter. We arrived at the corral after dark and camped for the night. The weather was insufferably hot, and I could not sleep for a long time. It was not only the heat which kept me awake, but a horrible odor which came from I didn't know where. At last, I fell asleep and dreamed about some hair-raising adventure. When I awoke, utterly unrefreshed, I looked about me, and there, not six feet from where I lay, was the body of the murdered Mexican.

I had slept with that corpse almost within arm's reach all night. He had been shot in twenty places and presented a terrible appearance, for the body had lain in the hot sun all the afternoon. My breakfast was limited strictly to black coffee that morning. We never succeeded in catching the murderers of the man. They escaped to Mexico.

XVI

The Fight at Lake Espantoso

Late in September, Sergeant Armstrong[1] told us, one afternoon, that we were to go on a long and important scout with him—McNelly had become sick and had gone to San Antonio. Then he added, "I believe we'll be lucky enough to have a fight before we get through."

He was right. We not only had the fight, but we succeeded in breaking, at last, the reign of terror which King Fisher and his gang had established.

It was raining the morning we left camp, twenty-five strong. Our route started on an old, unused trail along the Nueces River. All day long the rain poured down in torrents, wetting us to the skin. I remember how, after emptying the water out of my

---

[1] John Barclay Armstrong (1850–1913) grew to manhood in McMinnville, Tennessee. He came to Texas in 1871 and joined McNelly's Rangers on May 20, 1875. Because of his performance in the field he was promoted to sergeant and, when Lee Hall took command of McNelly's special force of Rangers in January, 1877, Armstrong was appointed second lieutenant. Together, the two became a formidable force against Texas desperadoes. In fact, Webb, *The Texas Rangers*, p. 294, stated that Armstrong "was a man after McNelly's own heart." See also Raymond, *Captain Lee Hall of Texas*, pp. 49, 53, 86–88; Askins, *Texans, Guns & History*, pp. 87–98.

pistol holster two or three times, I cut the end of the holster off, so that it would not hold water.

When we camped that night, it was hard work to start the campfires, for everything in the way of fuel was soaked. Our plan under such circumstances was to get a piece of deadwood and split it so as to get the dry core. This we cut up fine and so started a little blaze which had to be carefully nursed until, by adding larger and larger pieces, enough of a fire was under way to receive wet sticks.

I lay in two or three inches of water that night, and protected my face with my hat to keep the cold raindrops from hitting it. My clothes and blankets were wringing wet, but so were those of every man in the party. The next day the rain continued as hard as ever, and so it was for the ten days we were on the march along the Nueces. There was not a minute that it cleared off. The river, which ordinarily was a small enough stream, was so swollen that it was three or four miles wide in places. Every night we lay in the rain and every morning we started out again to ride in it.

In any other place, the sick list would doubtless have been a large one under such conditions, but the Rangers suffered no ill effects from the continuous drenching. Horace Rowe,[2] who was inclined to

[2] Horace Rowe enlisted as a Ranger private on September 10, 1876, and was discharged on January 15, 1877. Ingmire, *Texas Ranger Service Records, 1847–1900*, V, 73; Durham and Wantland, *Taming the Nueces Strip*, p. 136.

be consumptive, improved wonderfully in health on the trip and gained weight. The spirits of the men never lagged for a moment. We were all as happy as so many ducks in a mud puddle, and more practical jokes were played than there is room to tell about. I remember, one evening, two of the men and I hunted for an hour for a fictitious shepherd's hut to sleep in, carrying our blankets with us through the chaparral until we gave it up in despair and lay down on the ground to sleep until morning. The next day the boys who played the trick had a good laugh at our expense.

All the way along the Nueces we took every man prisoner we met and made him fall in with us. By the time we reached Carrizo Springs we had over a score of these prisoners, but we effectually prevented the news of our advance upon Fisher's stronghold from becoming known, for it was his gang of desperadoes we were after.

On the night of October 1st, we reached a point near Fisher's house, and succeeded in capturing one Noley Key, a member of his gang. I know not what threats Armstrong used on Key, but he, at last, willingly acted as our guide. He told Armstrong that Fisher and his men had left home and were not expected back for some time. We surrounded the settlement and closed in on it, however, we found that Key told the truth and that no one was there but the women and children.

But Armstrong would not give up. He took Key

aside and drew from him the information that a band of horse thieves were in camp on the banks of Lake Espantoso,[3] six or seven miles distant. Key told Armstrong that seven men were in the band, and that they had forty or fifty stolen horses which they were planning to drive farther north to sell in a few days.

Armstrong immediately divided his men, sending eighteen of the Rangers down to another desperado settlement and taking six with him to go to the lake. The six were Devine, Durham, Evans, Boyd, Parrott, and myself. Key acted as our guide and we started off. The rain had finally ceased during the afternoon and a full moon was in the heavens.

We rode quite slowly for about an hour and then turned off into some woods, where we dismounted. Key pointed out the location of the thieves' camp and then was told to remain where he was with Devine and Evans, who were left in the woods to protect the horses.

"Boys," said Armstrong to the four of us who were left with him, "we are going to capture those thieves or kill them. The reason I did not bring more men along was because I was afraid that these

[3]Lake Espantoso (in Spanish means "frightening") is not listed in Walter Prescott Webb and H. Bailey Carroll, eds., *The Handbook of Texas* (2 vols.; Austin: The Texas State Historical Association, 1952). But Durham mentioned a "Lake Espantoso," which was "some ten miles to the northwest" of present-day Carrizo Springs in Dimmit County. See Durham and Wantland, *Taming the Nueces Strip*, p. 138.

fellows wouldn't resist us if we were so many. Key tells me that they stood off the sheriff and his posse a few nights ago, and so they'll be looking for officers and be prepared to fight. That's just what we want. If they will only fire at us, we can rush in on them and kill them all. Nothing but that will break up this gang of cold-blooded desperadoes. I only hope they'll show fight. Now, come along and don't make any noise."

We advanced slowly and cautiously through the brush, and soon came to a wide, open space near the lake. We looked across the open space and saw the campfire of the horse thieves' camp, but could see no one stirring. Very cautiously, bending down and moving as swiftly as we could in that position, we approached the fire. We were within twenty-five yards of it, when suddenly a figure rose and a yell split the silence.

"Here they come, boys! Here they come!" shouted the man who had arisen. In an instant the seven men at the camp were up and the one who had shouted fired at us.

I heard Armstrong cry, "Damn you, you'll shoot at an officer, will you?" and then the firing grew furious on both sides. We rushed in on them and there was a continual blaze from the firearms.

Just in front of me was a man emptying his six-shooter at me, and I raised my carbine and fired at him. The moment before I fired he had his mouth wide open, yelling curses at me; but with my shot he dropped like a log. I thought I had killed him and turned my attention to the others, but, except for one man with whom Boyd was having a fierce hand-to-hand fight with knives, all were either dead or had jumped into the lake.

Over and over rolled Boyd and the desperado, but in the end Boyd jerked himself loose, his knife dripping with blood from the thief's heart.

The fight lasted not more than three or four minutes, but in that time fully two hundred shots were fired. We turned over the bodies of the dead men. They were all well-known desperadoes—John Martin, alias "One-eyed John;" "Jim" Roberts, and George Mullen. The man whom I shot was named McAlister. I was bending over and looking at his face, when I saw his eyes move.

"Hello!" I cried; "this man isn't dead."

McAlister looked straight at me and began to beg for his life.

"For God's sake, gentlemen, don't kill me," he begged piteously. "For God's sake don't kill me!"

"No one wants to kill you," I said. "We are not murderers. Would you like some water?"

He murmured that he would, and I took a tin cup from beside the campfire and went down to the lake and dipped it full of water. When I returned to him, I put it to his lips and he drank. He told me he was wounded in the leg and a part of his jaw was also shot away. I thought he would surely die, but we promised to send a wagon for him and made him as comfortable as we could before we left him. Then we returned to where we had left our horses with Devine and Evans.

As I was walking silently along in the woods with the rest of the boys, I heard suddenly, close in front of me, the sharp click of a gun being cocked, and the quick command:

"Halt!"

I stopped so quickly that I nearly fell over backward. It was Devine who gave the command, and in a moment we told who we were. Evans stood close to Devine.

"Where's Noley Key?" asked Armstrong.

"Dead," said Devine.

"Dead?"

"Yes. When he heard the firing, he jumped up and started to run, and we fired at him. One of us killed him, for there's a bullet hole in his back."

We went over and looked at Key where he lay, face downward. I felt badly about him, for on the way to the camp he had been talking in a pleasant voice to me and I had passed him some tobacco. He was not an important loss to the community, however, for he was a well-known horse thief.

Before I go on with the record of this night's adventures, I may say that McAlister recovered and, so far as I know, is alive to this day. When I went to Texas, in 1892, he turned up one day in San Antonio and told some men in a barroom that he was there for the express purpose of killing me.

"I've been camping on his trail for sixteen years," he said; "and now I'm going to kill him for shooting my jaw off that night."

I was told of this, and I lost no time in getting a six-shooter. Then I went on a hunt for McAlister. I thought I would know him, with his disfigured face, a good deal quicker than he would know me, and I relied on the virtue of "the drop," the Texas way of expressing the advantage of being prepared to shoot before the other man is ready.

It got to McAlister's ears that I was after him, and several of my old friends told me that he left town in a hurry. Captain Hall told me afterward that he knocked this same man down one day, a few years before, for using threatening language to reputable people. I am afraid that Brother McAlister is just a trifle revengeful and ungrateful.

As soon as we mounted our horses again, that night of the fight, we rode over to a ranch, about three miles away on the banks of the Nueces. We found four men sleeping in the yard of the ranch house, and we awakened them by uncovering them with the muzzles of our carbines. It must be a little alarming to wake up suddenly in the dead of night and find a number of heavily armed strangers yanking the covering from one by the aid of gleaming gun barrels. If I remember correctly, those men did not look pleased at the proceeding; but they did not protest very loudly. They just lay still and shivered with fright until we told them to get up. We had only been looking under their blankets for arms, so that they would not attempt any resistance, for we had had enough bloodshed for one night. Armstrong decided that he wanted two of the men, and we made them saddle their horses and go with us. Then we returned to where we had parted from the other squad of Rangers.

Going back along the road, I was on the right hand of one of our prisoners. I believe Boyd was on his other side. We were supposed to guard them, but both Boyd and I went to sleep as we rode. We were completely tired out. Suddenly I was awakened by a confused sound of shouting voices and the rattling of a wagon. For a moment I hadn't the least idea where I was or what the noise could be, and I was panic stricken. My nerves, after all the shooting and fast action, were, I suppose, in a shaky condition, and the sudden awakening was horrible in the extreme.

That I was not alone in experiencing these sensations I discovered later, for nearly every man on that ride was asleep. Our prisoners could have escaped with ease if they had dared. Boyd described his awakening to me that night in a manner more forceful than elegant. He said that for a few seconds he imagined himself in the regions infernal—only he didn't put it in that way exactly.

When we got back to camp we found the other eighteen Rangers there. They had had a little rumpus, too, and killed a man who resisted arrest. He was Pancho Ruiz, wanted for murder at Corpus Christi. I believe Corporal Rudd[4] was the one who killed Ruiz. We were all so tired out and sleepy after our long march in the rain and the excitement which followed it, that we slept until late in the afternoon, each man standing guard for twenty minutes at a time. It was difficult for anyone to keep awake even as long as that.

That evening Armstrong and I wrote a report of the fight, then we started with three others and our two prisoners to Eagle Pass, some forty miles distant. We had captured about fifty head of stolen horses and a lot of cattle late in the afternoon, near the thieves' camp. As my horse was tired, I decided to give him a rest and ride one of the stolen horses to Eagle Pass. I picked out a fine, big brown horse and saddled him. Armstrong and the other three men also took stolen horses for the ride, but none as fine in appearance as the one I had.

Alas! it is not always well to judge by appearances. I quickly discovered that my horse was a hard trotter, and under no circumstances would he go in a gallop. All the other horses were galloping, with a motion as easy as the rocking of a cradle, but my old fellow did nothing but trot, and that in a way to

[4]W. L. Rudd's two Ranger enlistments overlapped slightly. His first was from October 1, 1874, to February 1, 1877, and his second from January 25, 1877, to February 28, 1878. See Ingmire, *The Texas Ranger Service Records, 1847–1900*, V, 74. See also Durham and Wantland, *Taming the Nueces Strip*, pp. 26, 59, 136.

almost jolt the teeth from my gums. I stood it as long as I could, and then adopted a plan to save myself from being shaken apart. I would make my horse walk very slowly until the others were far ahead—a mile or so; then I would go on a full run until I caught up with them. By adopting this plan and repeating it over and over again, I made that forty miles with some degree of comfort.

We reached Eagle Pass about daylight and made camp in the wagon yard of the little hotel. While we were eating our breakfast, two guests of the hotel came out and began talking to us. One of them seemed especially curious to learn our business and all about us. After awhile, he turned and said he would go in and get his breakfast.

"Why not take breakfast with us?" said Armstrong, cordially.

"No, thank you; I'll go inside," said the man.

"Better stay and eat with us."

"No; I'm much obliged, but I think I'll go in the hotel."

"I think not, my friend."

"Why not? You're not going to arrest me, I hope. I haven't done anything."

"No," said Armstrong, who was looking through our book of fugitives from justice; "no, we won't arrest you because, you see, you have been under arrest for the last fifteen minutes."

The man's jaw fell and he began to tremble, but he tried to bluster and brave it out.

"This is an outrage," he said. "I'm a traveling man and a guest of this hotel."

"Yes, I know you're a traveling man," said Armstrong with a smile. "You've traveled all the way from Missouri on funds you stole from a bank there. I don't think you'll travel much farther south, my friend. You'll do your traveling in the other direction now."

The man grew ashy-white, but he saw it would be useless to resist. He was an escaping bank cashier and had been wanted for some months. He was kept in jail in Eagle Pass until officers arrived from Missouri and took him back with them.

XVII

A Threatened Ambush

THAT MORNING Armstrong sent the report by wire to Captain McNelly at San Antonio. I later saw it in the San Antonio *Express* under a big "scare" headline. We soon discovered that the news of the Lake Espantoso fight had reached Eagle Pass long before we told about it, and a number of desperadoes in Fisher's gang had gone across the Rio Grande to Piedras Negras as a matter of safety. Armstrong went over the river in the afternoon by himself and did not return until well after sunset. He was agog with excitement as well as elated when he reached us.

"I've found out where those outlaws are," he told us, in a tone of much joy. "They're all big men, too—rewards on every one of them. They go to a little *jacal*[1] every night and play cards. We can steal across the river tonight, about nine o'clock, and corral the whole lot while they are playing. If they resist us, we can kill them."

"How many of them are there?" I asked.

"Nine," said Armstrong; "and every one is wanted for murder or horse stealing."

"How do you propose to get them?"

[1] *Jacal* is the Spanish word for "shack."

"Go to their shanty and break in the door. Then we can get them."

"What will they be doing during the time we are breaking in?"

"Oh, I suppose they'll show fight, of course."

We four Rangers who had come to Eagle Pass with Armstrong exchanged glances. Then we all looked at him. Finally Boyd said in a quiet tone:

"John Armstrong, you're a —— fool."

He didn't mean to show any disrespect to a superior officer. He simply wanted to give voice to his opinion of the sergeant's plan. Armstrong seemed to be hurt.

"I thought," said he, in an injured tone, "you boys would follow me anywhere."

"We will," said Boyd; "you know that. But we think you're a —— fool, all the same, and you're going to get us all killed."

"Nonsense," replied Armstrong, much relieved. "Five Rangers can lick nine of those fellows any day of the week, and you know it. We'll go over tonight about nine o'clock and get them."

"And bring them back here with us, I suppose?"

"Certainly—if we don't have to kill them."

"All right," said the boys, "we're with you."

We had supper and spent some little time in carefully inspecting our arms to see they were in complete order, and at about nine o'clock that night proceeded quietly to the ferryboat landing and were soon poled across to Mexico. Armstrong

A Mexican Jacal

Courtesy Barker Texas History Center,
The University of Texas at Austin

led us along the dark streets of the little Mexican town and across a plaza. We halted on the plaza, and our leader told us in a low tone that the desperadoes were in a little house, about halfway down one of the streets which led off from it.

"We'd better go down on the other side of the street from the house," he said, "one or two at a time, and then make a break for it when I give the word. I'll smash in the door with the butt of my carbine, and you fellows pile right in after me. I needn't tell you to shoot to kill if they start to make any trouble."

Armstrong went ahead to show us the way, and we followed at short intervals. When we arrived opposite the house, he silently pointed it out, and then we swiftly moved across the narrow street, carbines in hand, ready to fire at an instant's notice. Without a word, Armstrong lifted his carbine and dealt the door a smashing blow with its butt.

Crash! it flew in and, without a second's pause, we dashed into the room. A smoky lamp on a table, which was covered with a jumble of playing cards and poker chips, some rush-bottomed chairs, one overturned on the hard dirt floor and, more significant than all else, the unmistakable fumes of recently smoked corn shuck Mexican cigarettes, showed that the room had been occupied but a short time prior to our coming; but when we entered it with such a flourish of arms, it was empty, so far as desperadoes were concerned. The birds had flown, doubtless having been warned, in some mysterious way, of our advent.

I don't believe any of us regretted their absence except Armstrong. He was deeply chagrined, for he had counted upon bagging those nine desperadoes, or killing them. I think he would have preferred the latter method of dealing with them. We returned to Texas as soon as we realized our errand was fruitless and an hour later were sound asleep in the wagon-yard of the hotel, one man, of course, standing guard, for we were hardly safe without one.

The next evening, the telegraph operator told Armstrong that a band of desperadoes had gone out on the road to Carrizo Springs, for the purpose of waylaying the Rangers on their way to Eagle Pass. We had made no secret of the fact that the rest of the men were coming to the town, and the telegraph operator said the desperadoes had determined to shoot them from ambush on the road.

"We'll have to warn the boys, and quickly," said Armstrong, when we received this news. "Here, Boyd, Jennings, Mayers, saddle up as fast as you can and ride to Carrizo. You'll probably meet the boys on the way, as they were to leave this afternoon. You know the general direction, but don't take the road. Cut across the prairie, and ride like hell!"

In a very few minutes we were on our horses and away. I took a white horse which Armstrong had ridden, for I did not relish going that forty miles again on my stolen trotter. It was after sunset when we started, but the moonlight made the country almost as bright as day and we flew over the prairie to warn our comrades of the danger which awaited them. We dashed through the mesquite chaparral and cacti, tore over flower-spangled open spaces, skimmed just under the low-hanging boughs of live oaks and cottonwood trees, always keeping the road a good quarter of a mile or so to our left and going, as Armstrong suggested, by "general direction."

So, for over two hours we rode, slowing down now and then to let our horses get their wind, and then darting ahead once more. At last, we came to the thickly wooded banks of a stream and found that we could not cross it. The banks were very steep and covered with brush and driftwood in a great tangle.

"There's just one place we can cross this creek," said Boyd, "and that's at the road."

"And that's just where those men will be waiting to do their waylaying," said Mayers.

"We'll have to risk it," I said. "We can't wait here, and we must get across."

We rode back from the creek for a few hundred yards and then went slowly toward the road. When we reached it we tossed a coin to see who should go first, who second, and who last. It fell to my lot to go first, but I would willingly have relinquished the honor. I drew my six-shooter and cocked it; Boyd, who came next, and Mayers, who was last, followed my example.

"Now," said I, "we'll go for all we're worth through that place. Shoot at anything you see that moves. One of us may get through anyhow, for it's so dark in there under the trees we won't be much of a mark."

I remember regretting very keenly then that I had taken Armstrong's white horse instead of my brown trotter, but it was too late to remedy matters and I consoled myself by thinking that even if my horse was shot I might escape.

"Are you ready?" I whispered.

"All right," said Mayers.

"Let her go," said Boyd.

I dug the spurs into my horse, leaned well forward in the saddle and started on a full run, straight for the ford. Down the bank and into the blackness I dashed, my pistol held at half-arm and ready; into the foot or so of inky water I splashed, across it and up the hill on the other side, Boyd close at my horse's heels and Mayers following.

Up, up, up! The top of the hill was gained! Hurrah! I was already tugging at the bridle to slow down my horse, when ——

God! Right in front of me, drawn across the road, were many men on horses—waiting. I could see the barrels of their six-shooters and Winchesters gleaming in the moonlight as they made ready for the fight. I jerked my horse back on his haunches and flung myself from the saddle to the ground. In a second, Boyd and Mayers followed suit. We darted quickly into the brush at the side of the road, knowing that in that way only could we escape. It was folly to try to fight all those men.

Bang! crash! and many bullets whistled over our heads and close to us, clipping the bushes all around where we lay. Then came the pounding of scores of hoofs and the men were on us. I had just raised my six-shooter to fire at the leader of the desperadoes, when I recognized him. It was Corporal Rudd.

"Rudd! Rudd! Don't shoot!" I shrieked. "Look! I'm Jennings! We're Rangers!"

My voice carried far and clear and was answered by a whoop and a series of joyful yells. We were safe and with our comrades.

We rode back along the road to Eagle Pass with the men, throwing out scouts on either side of the road ahead, but saw no sign of the waylaying party. We concluded that the telegraph operator must have been misinformed, but he said not, later. It may be that the desperadoes did not care to risk the attempt to waylay twenty of McNelly's Rangers, for the fame that came from our prowess had become a mighty advantage for us.

The Rangers remained for two or three days in camp just outside of Eagle Pass, and then started down the Rio Grande. We only rode about ten miles, however, and then turned back and went close to the town. As soon as night fell, some of us stole quietly into the town to see if we could pick up some of the men we wanted. Bill McKinney and I were sent to Bruton's saloon to see if we could run across any of the desperadoes there. We succeeded. We were not in the place two minutes before King Fisher himself walked in.

"Whoopee!" he yelled. "All the Rangers have gone down the river. Everybody come up to the bar and take a drink."

McKinney went to the bar and got on Fisher's right hand and I placed myself at the left of the desperado chieftain. He was pouring out a drink of whiskey for himself when he saw McKinney standing by him and recognized him. He turned to me and looked me up and down. Then he smiled easily and said:

"Well, gosh durn my chaps; I thought you boys were all down the river, and here you are back again. D'you want me for anything?"

"Yes," I said, "we do."

"All right," said Fisher, grinning again. "Here are my guns. What'll you have to drink?"

He unbuckled his belt and gave up his two white-handled six-shooters without a murmur. Then we had the drinks and took him to our camp, and that night went with him and several of the Rangers to a *fandango*. Fisher, as usual, gave bail the next day and was released. He didn't mind being arrested very much; it was so very easy for him to get out of trouble again.

There was yet another fugitive from justice in

the same barroom where we arrested King Fisher, but McKinney didn't know it and I had good reasons for not enlightening him. That man was Bill Thompson, the one who came to my assistance when I was fleeing from the Mexicans of the *fiesta* the first night I was in Nuevo Laredo. I recognized him instantly and made myself known to him.

"I suppose I ought to tell who you are," I said, "but I won't. I want to warn you, however, that your description is on our list, and if you don't get back over into Mexico pretty quick you are liable to be taken in."

Thompson thanked me and left the room. I was glad to see him take the hint so quickly, for although I truly felt I owed him a debt of gratitude, it went against my official conscience to connive at his escape.

In a few days we all started back to Oakville again. Armstrong had heard of some Mexican raiders who were killing cattle for their hides on the Nueces River near Fort Ewell, and he determined to raid their camp, which was on our way back. We drove the fifty stolen horses we had captured, the main body of men riding ahead and the horse herders following a mile or so behind. We were scattered along the road for a couple of miles as we were riding as we pleased.

One morning Armstrong said we were not very far from the raiders' camp, and he ordered us not to make any more noise than possible, as we might

scare them off. We had a liking, common to cowboys, Rangers, and plainsmen of all kinds, of yelling like wild Indians at times, for nothing at all
except to give vent to our exuberant spirits, born of
the free, big life of the prairies.

Early that afternoon, I was riding with Adams, a
good half a mile behind Armstrong and the few
Rangers who were ahead with him. A rattlesnake
crossed the road in front of us and coiled with an
angry rattle. Without any thought of the conse-
quences or of what Armstrong had said about keeping quiet, I pulled my six-shooter and took a shot at
the rattler. I missed him, and Adams fired. Then
Durham, Parrott, Devine, and Griffin came galloping up to see what was the matter. They all began
shooting at the snake from their horses, and at last
somebody succeeded in killing it with a bullet.
Then we realized we had disobeyed orders and
would get into trouble.

We rode slowly ahead—all but Devine—and presently came to where Armstrong had halted and was
waiting for us.

"What was all that shooting about back there?" he
demanded.

"We were shooting at a snake," said Durham.

"I certainly hope you killed it," said Armstrong,
sarcastically.

"We did."

"I'm glad to hear it. You've probably scared off
those raiders, who must be camped near here."

He looked sternly at us for a few moments and then added:

"Durham, Adams, Jennings, Griffin, and Parrott, you will report to Corporal Rudd for extra guard duty for a week."

He had not finished speaking before Devine came galloping up at racing speed, his six-shooter in his hand, excitement written all over his face.

"What's all the shooting about?" he panted, as he reined in his horse. "I thought there must be a fight."

Armstrong looked at Devine narrowly for a second. Then his lips curved in a dry smile and he added:

"Devine, you will also report to Corporal Rudd for extra guard duty for a week."

Armstrong was not an easy man to fool.

We had lots of fun with that extra guard duty. We stood the first and last reliefs by turns, but most of the night we all slept the sleep of the just and took chances. The first of the six culprits to wake up in the morning—we were all early risers—would scramble to his feet and begin pacing about with his carbine, and no one outside of the six knew that a strict guard had not been kept all through the night. We might have been more careful in a country where we were looking for trouble, but we felt safe enough to run the risk there.

We found the raiders' camp, after all, and arrested six men in it. There was one who wanted to fight, but a crack on the head with the butt of a six-shooter changed his notion.

Devine nearly lost his life on the way back, by swimming across the Nueces River when a freshet was making the stream boom. He swam across to get a boat and was caught in some thorny bushes, locally known as "catclaws," and nearly drowned.

XVIII

The Sutton-Taylor Feud

THE FULL Ranger company left for San Antonio shortly after we arrived at the Oakville camp, however, I was detailed to go on a scout commanded by Sergeant Orrell to Gillespie County for the purpose to arrest J. B. Johnson, charged with cattle stealing. We surrounded Johnson's house one night, broke in the door and arrested him. He had sworn he would not be taken alive. We searched the house to see if any others of his gang were there in hiding. I remember going into a bedroom and approaching the bed cautiously to see who was sleeping there. When about six feet from the bed, I heard a noise almost at my feet and, looking down, saw an enormous dog glaring at me in the uncertain light, and evidently prepared to give battle if I advanced another step. I did not advance, but kept my carbine pointed at the big dog's head and cried out to Johnson to call the animal off, which he did. All the time during this upheaval two children were fast asleep in the bed.

We started for San Antonio with our prisoner, but that morning learned that an old man had been murdered in the night near Fredericksburg, and we rode to his ranch to see if we could be of any help in hunting down whoever was responsible. When we reached the ranch, we found about two hundred excited Germans there—the county was largely settled by Germans—and they were holding an inquest. The murdered man had been a sort of patriarch of the colony, and all the men gathered there were determined upon avenging his death.

The inquest did not disclose the name of the murderer, but a number of the Germans came to the conclusion that our prisoner, Johnson, was the guilty party. A committee waited upon Sergeant Orrell and informed him they were going to hang Johnson, then and there.

"Oh, you are, are you?" said Orrell. "What do you suppose we'll be doing all that time?"

"What do you mean?" asked the spokesman of the proposed lynching party.

"I mean," said Orrell, "that this man is my prisoner and under my protection. I don't believe he killed the old man, but even if I knew him to be the murderer I wouldn't give him up."

"You'll have to do it," said the German. "You only have four men with you and we have about two hundred. We'll take him from you."

Without a word in answer, Orrell handed a six-shooter to Johnson, who was shaking with fear.

"Here," he said, "you take this and defend yourself, if you have to."

Then, turning back to the Germans, the sergeant coolly said:

"Now, gentlemen, if you care to take that man from us, start right in. But I want to tell you one thing first: before you take him you'll have to kill five of McNelly's Rangers, and if you do kill five of McNelly's Rangers, I can only ask God to help you and your settlement!"

The Germans knew that Orrell meant every word he said, for there could be no doubting the determination of his tone and manner. They also knew that if they killed us—or even one of us—there would come a fearful day of reckoning when our comrades heard the story. They drew away to the side and consulted together, and soon came to the conclusion that they would not have a lynching-bee that afternoon.

Shortly after, we rode away; Johnson, with a Ranger on either side of him, two Rangers ahead, and Orrell coming behind as a rear guard. We landed Johnson in jail in San Antonio, and he was soon tried for cattle stealing and sent to the penitentiary.

For the next month or so the Rangers went on short scouting trips and made many important arrests of outlaws. Squads of men were riding here and there over the country, turning up when least expected and terrorizing the desperadoes, just as the desperadoes had for years terrorized the settlers. Lieutenant Hall was doing great work in Karnes County. There he arrested eleven of a gang of bank robbers, and many men charged with cattle stealing, horse stealing, and murder.

On December 7th, Sergeant Armstrong and J. W. Deggs went in a buggy from the San Antonio camp to arrest John Mayfield, at a ranch about twelve miles distant, for a murder committed in Parker County. Mayfield had sworn he would never give up, but would die before submitting to arrest. So many desperadoes had made this same boast and then had given up quietly that neither Armstrong nor Deggs expected any trouble in taking Mayfield.

They found the man in a corral near his house. He was breaking in a colt, but before Mayfield saw them, both Armstrong and Deggs had him covered with their six-shooters. Then Armstrong called out:

"You are under arrest; we are Rangers."

Mayfield turned quickly and looked squarely at the two men.

"Put up your hands!" commanded Armstrong.

"I'll see you both in —— first!" shouted Mayfield, pulling his six-shooter and firing at Armstrong.

Just before he shot, Deggs fired and struck Mayfield on his pistol-arm, thus saving Armstrong's life. Mayfield fell, dropping his pistol. He immediately picked it up with his left hand and fired at Deggs, but this time Armstrong shot him and he fell dead, cocking his six-shooter with the last bit of strength he had.

The shooting aroused the settlement around Mayfield's place, and the two Rangers noticed men coming in every direction with their guns. They knew that Mayfield had many friends, and thinking discretion to be the better part of valor, jumped into their buggy and drove quickly away, arriving at our camp two hours later. Lieutenant Wright and ten men immediately started back with Armstrong and Deggs to the scene of the shooting, but when we arrived there, we found that Mayfield's body had already been taken away and buried. No one could be found who would tell us where the murderer was buried, although it was very important for us to know. There was a sizable reward of four thousand dollars on John Mayfield, dead or alive, but we were unable to collect it, for we could not produce the body.

A few days after this occurrence, I was sent with a number of the men to join Lieutenant Hall's detachment at Clinton, DeWitt County, where a state of great lawlessness had existed for many years.

DeWitt County was notorious for a feud which, for over a quarter of a century, had existed between the Taylor and Sutton factions. The Taylor-Sutton feud began back in the 1840s, in Georgia, moved to Texas with the opposing families, and was flourishing at the time of which I write, 1876. No vendetta of Corsica was ever carried on with more bitterness than was this feud in Texas. Scores of men had been murdered, nay, hundreds, on both sides, and still the war kept up. Every man in the county had to choose sides in the feud. A new settler was anxiously watched to see which faction he would choose to align himself with. Every man went armed to the

teeth. Midnight murders were of frequent occurrence. Waylaying along the road was considered
permissible and shooting from ambush was taken
as a matter of course.

Matters had quieted down a bit in the few years
preceding 1876, but in the months just prior to
the Rangers' advent, the feud raged more desperately than ever. There were over one hundred and
fifty indictments for murder in the DeWitt County
sheriff's office, but not a single one had ever been
acted upon.

Hall had been carefully getting at the facts for
some time, and when he sent for reinforcements, he
was ready to act. He made up his mind to break up
the feud and restore order in DeWitt County.

It was a tremendous undertaking, but Lee Hall
had perfect faith in his ability to carry it through
successfully. I know of no better illustration of the
confidence which the Rangers put into their own
powers than the fact that Hall set about his task
with only eighteen men. There were at least five
hundred men directly and indirectly engaged in the
Taylor-Sutton feud at the time.

Shortly before our arrival in the county, a despic-
able murder was committed by members of the Sutton party. They went at midnight to the residence
of Dr. Brazzell, an educated, refined old gentleman,
dragged him from a sick bed in the presence of his
wife and daughter, and then murdered him in cold
blood. At the same time, they killed his son.

Pitkin Taylor and Wife Susan

Courtesy Western History Collections,
University of Oklahoma, Norman

Hall, in a report to Adjutant General Steele, dated December 16, 1876, wrote:

"I am confident of arresting the murderers of Dr. Brazzell and his son. I hold now thirty-one murder indictments and know where I can find the men. All of these criminals have friends throughout the county, because more than half of the county is mixed up in this matter. They are so involved in deeds of blood that they cannot afford to have any member of the brotherhood sent to prison. The people are completely terrorized and cowed by the assassins and cutthroats who got their hands in, shedding blood during the Taylor-Sutton troubles, then joined so-called vigilant associations, and are now killing off witnesses and intimidating juries by threats of violence, so that we believe it is impossible to secure a conviction."[1]

[1] The Taylor-Sutton feud was the "longest and bloodiest" feud in Texas history. Legend has persisted that troubles between the two families first began in the Carolinas, and then moved to Georgia before starting anew after the Civil War in Texas. In November, 1867, Creed Taylor's two sons, Hays and Doboy, made the Union army's "most wanted" list for killing two soldiers near Mason, Texas. In turn, during March of 1868, Deputy Sheriff William Sutton killed a Charles Taylor while searching for horse thieves. Later, at least two more Taylors died at the hands of Suttons. Retaliation on both sides occurred with increasing frequency until 1875, when family leader, Jim Taylor, died in a street fight. Then in September, 1876, after the senseless murders of Dr. Philip Brazzell and his son George, the Rangers arrived and brought to trial eight Sutton men. See Raymond, *Captain Lee Hall of Texas*, pp. 59–78; Chris Emmett, *Shanghai Pierce: A Fair Likeness* (Norman: University of Oklahoma Press, 1953), pp. 50–51, 67. For a detailed account of the feud, see C. L. Sonnichsen, *I'll Die Before I'll Run: The Story of the Great Feuds of Texas* (Lincoln: University of Nebraska Press, 1961).

It was about this time that Hall first met Judge Henry Clay Pleasants,[2] the district judge whose district took in DeWitt County.

"I want you to do your part," said the old judge to Hall, "and I will see that the courts deal justice. Together, we can bring order out of chaos."

Judge Pleasants was of an old Virginia family— one of the F. F. V.s—and was a courtly, dignified, delightful gentleman. He was not only a strict and impartial judge, but he was as brave as a lion, too; and the latter quality was, perhaps, needed as much as the others at that time in DeWitt County.

On the evening of December 22, 1876, Lieutenant Hall rode out from Clinton to our camp, near the town, and told us to saddle up.

"We won't go far," he said, "so you needn't take any blankets. We'll be back tonight."

It was drizzling at the time and very cold for that part of Texas. Two of the men were sick and were in a house in the town for shelter, so that meant only sixteen men went with the lieutenant. As we rode along through the dark night, Hall told us that we were going to arrest seven men who had just been

[2] Judge Henry Clay Pleasants (1828–99) was born in Richmond, Virginia. He came to Texas in 1854, settling in the small community of Cuero. In 1877, at the time of the Brazzell murder trial, Pleasants was district judge of the Twenty-third District. In 1892 he was elected to the Texas Court of Civil Appeals of the First District, where he served until his death in Galveston on November 17, 1899. See Raymond, *Captain Lee Hall of Texas*, pp. 72–75, 77; Emmett, *Shanghai Pierce*, p. 90; Webb, *The Texas Rangers*, p. 290.

Judge Henry Clay Pleasants

Courtesy Archives Division,
Texas State Library, Austin

indicted for the murder of the Brazzells. He said that one of the indicted men was Joseph Sitterlee, the Deputy Marshal and Deputy Sheriff of DeWitt County, and that Sitterlee was being married that night. We were going to the wedding at the house of the bride's father and should expect to find all of the Sutton gang there.

When we reached a point about two hundred yards from the house, we dismounted and Hall told us we were probably going to have a pretty hot fight in a few minutes. He produced a bottle of whiskey and we each drank to the success of the undertaking. Then we silently stole toward the house. As we got nearer, we could see that it was brightly lighted up and that a dance was in progress. A fiddle was squeaking, and through the windows we could see the dancers. A great many men were in the house, which was a large double one, with a gallery on each side of it.

Hall placed his men in a wide circle all around the building. I was put right in front of it in a shaft of light which streamed from one of the windows. As soon as I discovered this fact, I stepped a yard or two to one side, out of the light. At the ends of the long porches, Hall placed four men with double-barreled shotguns. Then he made a rapid round of the lines to see that every man was in his place. He came to me and asked, pleasantly:

"Well, how's the fighting Quaker getting on?"

"Bully," I said.

"Good. Now don't let a man escape past you. I'm going into the house in a few minutes and then there is going to be fun. Some of them will try to get away, but if they come your way, stop them. Don't shoot unless you have to."

He disappeared in the darkness and I waited. In a few minutes, I saw the tall form of the lieutenant pass in at the open door of the room where the dance was going on. He held a carbine in his hand. Instantly the music stopped, and I could see many six-shooters being flourished in the air. The women screamed and there was a sudden rushing to and fro of men and the sound of angry voices.

"Do you want anyone here, Ranger?" called out Sitterlee, as he faced the officer at the doorway.

"Yes," cried Hall in a loud voice; "I want seven men for murder. I want you and William Meadows, the Marshal of Cuero, and Dave Augustine, Jake Ryan, William Cox, Frank Heister and Charles Heidrichs, all charged with the murder of Dr. Brazzell and his son and indicted this day."

At these words, the uproar redoubled and Hall was forced back on the gallery which divided the two parts of the house.

Meadows raised his voice above the others and, going up to Hall, demanded, excitedly:

"How many men have you got?"

"Seventeen, counting myself," said Hall, calmly.

"Well, we've got over seventy and we'll fight it out," roared Meadows.

"Yes, yes; let's fight it out, let's go after them!" came a chorus.

"That's the talk," shouted Hall in a delighted tone. "Move out your women and children and be quick about it. I'll give you three minutes to get them out of the way. We don't want to kill them, but it is as much as I can do to restrain my men. We came down here for a fight and we want it."

A silence followed these bold words.

"Get ready, men," Hall yelled to the Rangers. "You with the shotguns sweep the porches when I give the word. The rest of you can shoot to kill. They're going to move out their women and children and then we'll have at it."

Meadows was crying with anger and mortification by this time.

"We don't want to kill you all," he blurted out.

"Then give me your gun—quick, and right now!" said Hall, sharply, reaching out his hand and disarming Meadows before that worthy knew what had happened.

Hall was quick to follow up his advantage. He grabbed six-shooters out of men's hands, right and left, and called to two of the Rangers to come up and help him take them. In two minutes a dozen men were disarmed and the Rangers were forcing their way through the crowd, taking guns and pistols as they went.

Not a shot was fired, and in five minutes we had disarmed the entire Sutton gang.

"You're not going to take us tonight?" asked Sitterlee. "You might let us finish our dance. I've just been married."

"All right," said Hall. "Finish the dance if you want to, but if any man tries to get away, we'll kill him as certain as you stand there. We'll take you to town at daylight."

The dance was resumed and we stood guard around the house all night, going in two at a time to eat some of the wedding supper. I observed that everyone seemed to be having a good time and the prettiest girls there were the ones who seemed to take pride in dancing with the accused murderers.

I neglected to say that, at the beginning of the rumpus, one fat, old fellow came plunging out of the house wildly in the dark and ran as hard as he could straight for me. I punched him in the stomach with the end of my carbine, and he doubled up and turned like a hare back to the house. This man, it turned out later, was the parson who had performed the marriage ceremony.

Soon after dawn, we took our seven prisoners, all mounted, to Clinton and put them in a room in the jail there, two of the Rangers remaining in the room with them to guard them and four other Rangers standing guard outside the building. We had three reliefs of six men each, four hours during the day and four hours at night. Hall had informed all at the dance, as we took the prisoners away, that we would kill the prisoners first if there was any attempt at a rescue and that afterward we would attend to the rescuing party.

It was hard work, guarding those men in the Clinton jail, which was a little old, rickety building, so on the second day Hall removed them to the upper floor of the fine, big courthouse, where it was much easier to look after them.

Habeas corpus proceedings were begun in their behalf in a few days and the court sat for a week hearing them. Every day the courtroom was crowded with members of both the Taylor and Sutton parties, but as we were careful to disarm every man who entered the building, there was no clash.

As the proceedings drew to a close, we received information that the members of the Sutton gang were determined that their comrades should not be sent to jail. Judge Pleasants received a few anonymous letters in which the threat was made that he would be shot and killed if he decided against the accused murderers. Hall decided to run no chances, and accordingly sent for more Rangers. They arrived the night before the day Judge Pleasants was to render his decision. With the reinforcements, we had thirty Rangers, enough to take care of every "bad man" in the county, if need be.

When court was called to order, the room was crowded with men, and everywhere it was whispered that Judge Pleasants would be shot if he decided against the prisoners and sent them to prison to await trial, instead of admitting them to bail.

The old judge took his seat on the bench amid a profound silence. One could feel the suppressed excitement in the courtroom and see it reflected in the faces of the spectators. Just before the judge arose to give his decision, six of the Rangers stepped up to the bench and stood on either side of the judge. I was one of the three on his right and was next to his side. Like the other five men, I had my carbine in my hand and, like the others, I threw a cartridge into the breech and cocked the gun in plain sight of all in the courtroom. Then we stood at "ready" while Judge Pleasants addressed the crowd of men in the room. With supreme dignity he stood and looked at them for a full minute before he spoke. Then he said, in a calm, distinct voice whose every tone carried conviction:

"The time has arrived for me to announce my decision in this case. I shall do so without fear or favor, solely upon the evidence as it has been presented. This county is and has been for years a reproach to the fair name of the State of Texas. Over it have roamed bands of lawless men, committing terrible outrages, murdering whomever met their disdain, shooting down men from ambush in the most cowardly manner possible. Here in this very room, listening to me now, are murderers who long ago should have been hanged. At this time, I do not speak of the prisoners at the bar, but of you who yet are free. You are murderers, bushwhackers, midnight assassins.

"Some of you have dared to threaten me with cowardly, unsigned letters, and I have needed to bring state soldiers into this court of justice. I learn that you have blamed the sheriff of this county for calling upon the Rangers to assist in restoring order. No, it was not the sheriff who had the Rangers sent here; it was I. I called for them and I am going to see that they remain here in this county until it is as peaceful and law-abiding as any in the State—as quiet and orderly as any in the Union. I tell you now, beware! The day of reckoning is surely coming. It is close at hand. When you deal with the Texas Rangers, you deal with men who are fearless in the discharge of their duty and who will surely conquer you.

"I shall send these men at the bar to jail to await trial for as wicked and cowardly a murder as ever disgraced this State. It is but the beginning. Others will soon follow them. The reign of the lawless in DeWitt County is at an end!"

Never shall I forget how the gray-haired old judge's eyes flashed and how his fine voice rang as he pronounced these words. Angry looks came onto the faces of scores of men in the courtroom, but they knew better than to make any demonstration.

"Lieutenant Hall, clear the room, sir," ordered Judge Pleasants, when he concluded. The order was quickly obeyed, and those who were determined to create trouble were fast leaving the town.

It was the beginning of the end of their power.

XIX

Catching Famous Desperadoes

FROM THAT time, the Rangers were exceedingly active in DeWitt County and hundreds of arrests
were made. The desperadoes could no longer find
shelter there. A guard of four men went with Judge
Pleasants whenever he rode through the county,
and wherever he held court, the Rangers were always present. Gradually, the worst characters in the
county were either jailed or run out, and in a few
weeks' time peace and order were restored and the
long-standing feud was a thing of the past.

On January 26, 1877, Captain McNelly, who had
become an invalid, resigned his command, and the
Ranger company was reorganized at Victoria under
command of Lee Hall.

On the day we were reorganized, I had a few
words with Rector that became quite serious. We
both had pulled our six-shooters and were about to
fire, when Armstrong and one or two others got between us and we were disarmed and placed under arrest. We decided to fight a duel at daybreak the
following morning with six-shooters, beginning at
twenty paces and advancing. It was to be a duel to
the death.

That afternoon, I was standing on the street in

Victoria with Griffin,[1] when a doctor drove up in his buggy and got down. He looked at us for a moment closely and then asked:

"Say, aren't you boys feeling a little under the weather?"

We both said we were feeling ill. I had been ill for two days, but had thought little of it.

"Well," said the doctor, "I believe you both have the measles. The best thing for you to do is to go and get a big drink of whiskey and hot water and go to bed at the hotel. I'll come around later and see how you are getting on."

We followed his directions, and that night I was delirious. I was out of my head for two days, and on the third Rector came around and we made up our quarrel and shook hands.

The reader may be curious to know why we were going to fight and what caused our quarrel. Strange as it may seem, I cannot remember at this time why we quarreled. I only know that we had a few words about something at camp, but what that something was I do not remember. It is only another illustration of the reckless kind of fellows we were in those good old days of Ranger life, ready to fight at the twitching of a finger, for little or nothing.

After the reorganization of our Ranger outfit, we

[1] According to Ranger records, W. H. Griffin's two enlistments overlapped by a week, the first time from August 1, 1876 to February 1, 1877, and the second time from January 25, 1877, to February 28, 1878. See Ingmire, *Texas Ranger Service Records, 1847–1900*, II, 105–06.

returned to DeWitt County and continued to arrest men for whom indictments were prepared. We also went into other nearby counties, everywhere arresting desperadoes. I have copies of the reports made to the Adjutant General, and find in them that in a little more than two months we arrested over eleven hundred men.[2]

We had no fights and so did not kill anyone. We couldn't get into a fight in those days because we couldn't find any men who would fight us. We had been so uniformly successful and had come out victorious so often against heavy odds that whenever we ran across desperate characters, so called, they would submit at once. It became too tame to be interesting—certainly too void of excitement to be worth recording. I shall, therefore, depart from the continued narrative of the Ranger life and only give those incidents which were of extraordinary interest and importance.

The arrest of Ham White, stage robber, was one of these. Captain Hall personally made that arrest.

---

[2] Jennings did not exaggerate that the Rangers "arrested over eleven hundred men." At the beginning of Governor Richard Coke's term in January, 1874, Ranger headquarters in Austin compiled a "Fugitive List" which contained three thousand names and descriptions of "wanted men." By January, 1876, even though law enforcement officers had imprisoned seventeen hundred of these desperadoes, the "List" had expanded to about five thousand names. See Raymond, *Captain Lee Hall of Texas*, pp. 29–39; Askins, *Texans, Guns & History*, pp. 87–88; Webb, *The Texas Rangers*, pp. 233–391ff.

Ham White was a genuine knight of the road. He was as fine in his methods as even Claude Duval, that prince of highwaymen, dared to be. It is related by Macaulay how, at the head of his troop, Duval "stopped a lady's coach, in which there was a booty of four hundred pounds; how he took only one hundred, and suffered the fair owner to ransom the rest by dancing a coranto[3] with him on the heath."

Now, although Ham White probably never did "dance a coranto" in his life, and would not have known a "coranto" if he had seen one, he was much more gallant than Duval, for he refused to rob ladies at all. He hadn't any "troop," but worked absolutely alone.

He did not stop ladies' coaches, but held up the regular stagecoaches that carried Wells Fargo Express boxes and Uncle Sam's mail pouches. Twice in one day in the latter part of March, 1877, White robbed the stagecoaches between Austin and San Antonio. He did not get much booty from the first coach, so he waited for the other. It was filled with passengers and a guard was riding on it, but Ham White with his six-shooters was a match for them all, and they surrendered without a struggle.

He made the passengers get out and cut open the United States mailbags and hand him the registered

[3] Jennings obviously was referring to the word "courante" (koo rant), which was an old-fashioned French dance dating back to the seventeenth century and characterized by running or gliding steps to an accompaniment in triple time.

packages. While they were thus engaged, White discoursed to them upon the enormity of their action.

"Don't you know how wicked it is to rob the mailbags?" he asked, facetiously. "I certainly would make a complaint against you, but I haven't the time to fool around the courts as a witness."

A man who handed every bit of his money over to White—some three hundred dollars—said to him:

"I should like to get my watch back, as it was a present to me from my brother, who is dead."

"I would not think of taking it from you, if that is the case," said White. "Here, take this ten dollars, so that you will have enough to live on, a day or so, when you reach San Antonio."

To a lady who was one of the passengers, he said:

"Madam, there is no reason for your alarm. I can assure you, I have no intention of taking a cent from you."

To the stage driver he said:

"I'd like to swap my horse for that off-leader of yours. My horse is really a better animal, but yours is fresher, and I may have to do some fast riding when I leave you."

Of course, the trade was made, and it was due to the exchange of horses that White was captured. The stage horse he took had a broken shoe and, consequently, was easy to track. Captain Hall was informed that evening of the robbery, and early the next morning took up White's trail at the place where he had held up the stagecoach. With three of the Rangers, Hall tracked White for a day and a half. That brought the pursuing party to Luling.

In the livery stable there, Hall found his man. The three Rangers were at dinner at the hotel when Hall met White in the stable. White reached for his pistols, but Hall threw himself on the man and bore him onto the floor. They had a rough-and-tumble fight, at the end of which, Hall was sitting on the helpless White and relieving him of about $4,000 in gold coins.

White was quickly tried and received a sentence of ninety-nine years in a military prison, for robbing the United States mails. White turned out to be a relative of Secretary of the Navy Goff, under President Hayes, and Hayes pardoned the stage robber. It was the last act of Hayes's official life.

White returned to southwest Texas and made threats that he would have Captain Hall's life, but Hall started out to find him and White disappeared. He next turned up in Colorado under the name of H. W. Burton, and began robbing stages between Lake City and Alamosa. Then, with ten or twelve men, he robbed trains in Colorado. He was caught and again was sentenced to life imprisonment, but on an appeal, escaped on a legal technicality. He disappeared for awhile, but finally was arrested in Ohio for killing the man who had killed his father. He escaped from the Columbus, Ohio jail and the last heard of him, he was robbing stages in California in 1892, and always alone. White has been confused at times with the notorious Black Bart, but was far more daring than that other "knight of the road."

In April, 1877, I was one of nine Rangers who guarded Frank Singleton in the little two-roomed jail in Beeville, prior to his execution for murder. He was the first of the murderers to be sentenced by Judge Pleasants, and it was important that the sentence of the court should be carried out without a hitch. Singleton had a large following, and many threats were made that he would never be hanged. The date of his execution was set for April 27th.

He was as cool a man, under such a situation, as I ever knew, and my experience as a Ranger and, many years later, as a New York newspaper reporter, brought me into personal contact with many condemned murderers. Singleton made an absurd will a few days before his execution. In it he bequeathed his skin to the prosecuting attorney of the county with the suggestion that it be stretched into a drumhead and beaten at the door of the courthouse on the anniversary of his execution, "as a warning to evildoers." The rest of his body he bequeathed to the doctors to be used in the cause of medical science.

On the evening before the day of execution, nine more Rangers came to Beeville and joined us. That night I passed in Singleton's cell with him. Three other Rangers were also in the cell. The jail was a wooden affair and the sheriff had chained Singleton to the floor. The chain was fastened to heavy iron shackles which were forged around the prisoner's ankles.

During the long night I played "seven-up" with Singleton. We played for $10 a game—on trust. Singleton owed me $40 at the end of the games.

"I don't know where I'm going," said he, "but wherever it may be, I'll try and have that $40 for you by the time you come along."

When the sheriff came to remove the shackles from Singleton's feet, the murderer said:

"Sheriff, I wouldn't use those leg irons again, if I were you."

"Why?" asked the sheriff.

With a shrug, Singleton picked up the shackles and with his thumbnail removed some soap from a crack in them, thus revealing how he had managed to nearly saw them in two.

"I'd have been away from here long ago," he said, "if it hadn't been for these Rangers. They watched me too closely. I had a file and a little saw and a bottle of nitric acid. I softened the iron with the acid and sawed away at night."

"Where are these tools?"

Singleton put his finger in a crack between the boards which made the inner wall of his cell and pulled up a string to which the saw, file, and a bottle of acid were attached. He would not say how he obtained them, but he presented the file to me.

"You may keep that to remember me by," he

said. "And you may need it someday if you ever get into a fix like mine."

I thanked him, despite the rather dubious suggestiveness of his estimate of my character.

He was executed in front of the jail, and people came from all over the county to see him hanged. Many women and children were in the crowd. The Rangers formed a circle around the high scaffold to keep back the crowd. We put on such a display of force that a plan by his friends to rescue Singleton at the last moment was not attempted. He was smoking a cigar as he walked up the steep steps of the scaffold. As the blackcap was put on his head, he threw the cigar away, saying:

"You and I'll go out at about the same time."

A few minutes later he was dangling at the end of the rope, dead.

John Wesley Hardin, of DeWitt County,[4] was the

[4] John Wesley Hardin (1853–95) was born in Bonham, Fannin County, Texas, the son of a Methodist circuit-rider preacher. During his short but violent career, Hardin made the mistake of killing Deputy Sheriff Charles Webb of Comanche County on May 26, 1874, thus putting the Rangers on his trail. After being apprehended for trial and convicted, he escaped and vanished until 1877 when he was captured by private detective John Duncan. After serving sixteen years in jail, where he underwent a complete character change, Hardin was pardoned in 1894. On August 19, 1895, during a visit to El Paso, he was shot to death by Constable John Selman. See *The Life of John Wesley Hardin As Written by Himself* (Norman: University of Oklahoma Press, 1961); Webb, *The Texas Rangers*, pp. 297–304; Askins, *Texans, Guns & History*, pp. 94–104.

worst of the "bad men" Texas produced in such numbers during the stormy reconstruction days. He was probably the worst desperado ever in Texas, at anytime. When the Rangers captured him, late in August, 1877, he was known to have killed over a score of men. He himself placed the number at twenty-seven.

The name of John Wesley Hardin was dreaded from one end of Texas to the other. Let it be rumored that Hardin was in a county, and that county became panic-stricken. When he rode into a town, the town and all its inhabitants were at his mercy and hastened to do his bidding. If any person dared to thwart his will, another "killing" was added to Hardin's list. And all the other "bad men" were as much afraid of John Wesley Hardin as peaceable citizens were afraid of them. He was a marvelous shot with a six-shooter. He could shoot with his left hand as well as with his right. He could take a six-shooter in each hand and put all twelve bullets in a playing card at twenty yards with lightning rapidity. He could handle his favorite weapon as a juggler handles painted balls. He could twirl a six-shooter around his finger by the trigger-guard so rapidly that it looked like a wheel and then, at the word, fire and hit the mark. He could fire a Winchester repeating rifle so rapidly that a continuous stream of fire came from the muzzle and four or five empty shells from the ejector were in the air at the same time, falling at different heights, to the ground.

John Wesley Hardin

Courtesy Western History Collections,
University of Oklahoma, Norman

He killed men on the slightest provocation, and on no provocation at all. He never forgave an injury, and to incur his displeasure was simply suicide.

Out of the many tales of John Wesley Hardin which were current in Texas, I have selected two or three which I know to be true.

On one occasion, he met a sewing machine agent in the country. The agent was driving a wagon in which were two or three sewing machines. Hardin made the agent take one of the machines from the wagon, place it in the dusty road and sew on it. The desperado took off his jacket, ripped it up the back, and made the agent sew it up again. He amused himself in this way for two hours and then sent the agent about his business with the remark:

"I'm feeling pretty good-natured today, so I won't kill you if you get away quick."

One day Hardin found himself short of money. He came to a country store where a number of men were congregated. He told them he wanted to get money by raffling off his horse and saddle. For two dollars a chance the men could participate. Some were afraid not to take a chance, and some tried to curry favor with the noted desperado by taking two or three chances apiece. Hardin took the money and told them to begin throwing the dice. While they were doing so, Hardin walked out, mounted his horse and rode away. Not one of his victims dared follow him.

At Cuero one day, he was in a saloon drinking.

He stepped to the door and saw a stranger sitting on a dry goods box, two blocks away.

"I'll bet you the drinks I can kill that fellow with the first shot from my revolver," said Hardin to a companion standing nearby.

The bet was accepted and Hardin pulled his six-shooter and fired. The man fell dead. Hardin went into the saloon and took his drink, as calmly as though nothing unusual had happened.

A sheriff got the drop on Hardin once and arrested him. He kept the outlaw covered with his six-shooter and ordered him to slowly hand over his revolvers. Hardin took his pistol and, holding it by the barrel, handed it, butt first, to the sheriff. The sheriff extended his hand for the weapon, but just as his fingers were closing on it, Hardin gave it a sudden flirt and a twist and fired, sending a ball through the sheriff's heart.

At another time, he was arrested and five soldiers were taking him to jail. During the night, Hardin managed to get his hands untied. He crept behind the man on guard and stunned him with a blow from a heavy stick. Then he deliberately murdered all five soldiers.

He began murdering men when he was only fifteen years old. He grew into a short, stocky man of great activity and strength. He was a perfect rider. His face was broad. He had little, pig-like eyes, which had the glitter and very much the expression of a rattlesnake. They were ever moving here and there and were not quiet for a moment. This habit of glancing continually right and left and behind him was caused by the constant outlook he had to maintain against surprise, for he had many bitter enemies who would not have hesitated to kill him from behind, although they dared not face him.

Hardin's parents were good, simple folk, his father being a preacher of the frontier sort, who mingled the occupation of ranchman with that of his sacred calling because his pay as a preacher was never sufficient to support his family. His intention was to make a preacher of his son, and the name John Wesley was given him in memory of the great founder of Methodism. The son, however, turned out to be the heaviest cross any preacher was called upon to bear, but despite the boy's wickedness, he was always beloved by his parents.

Another illustration of his cold-blooded character came to me in Texas, well authenticated. One night Hardin was awakened in a lodging house by the snoring of a man on the other side of a thin wooden partition. Having fixed the precise point where the sleeper lay, Hardin fired through the partition, killed him, and then turned over and slumbered peacefully for the rest of the night.

A few months before Hardin's capture and conviction, a young man was walking on the streets in Cuero with a young woman to whom he was engaged to be married. The couple met a noted town bully, who was on a periodical tear. He met and passed them, and then deliberately turned and shot the young man dead. A more wanton murder was never committed, for the two had not exchanged a word, and never saw each other before. Nothing was done with the assassin in the feud-ridden county. He was not even arrested. The brother of the victim was so enraged when he learned of the murder that he started out with a shotgun, swearing he would kill the assassin or be killed himself.

While he was searching through the various saloons for the bully, he met Hardin, who inquired about his business. The young man, almost beside himself, explained.

"You can't work it," said Hardin, with a warning shake of the head; "that fellow'll get the drop on you quicker'n lightning."

"I don't care. He murdered my brother, and I'll never rest till I shoot him."

"Well," said Hardin, "I'll go along and see that you get a square deal."

At this moment, the young man caught sight of the miscreant on the other side of the narrow street. He took deliberate aim and fired, but was so excited he missed his man. The desperado whirled around like a flash and had the drop on the young man before he knew his danger.

"So you're looking for me are you?" he asked with a grin; "wal, I'll give you just two minutes to say your prayers in."

And he held his pistol on a dead level, while the

trembling youth could do nothing but stand in his tracks, helplessly awaiting his fate. But the bully failed to note another figure, standing a few paces behind the youth, calmly watching the proceedings. Before the two minutes had expired, Hardin fired and the other desperado rolled over with a bullet in his brain.

Among the many deaths which had been inflicted by Hardin's pistol or Winchester, this is the only one for which an impartial jury would have acquitted him.

XX

Proud to Have Been a Ranger

WHEN the Rangers began to make things so hot for the many desperadoes in and near DeWitt County, Hardin disappeared. Try as we might, we could learn nothing of his whereabouts. He was a prize worth capturing, too, not only because he was such a notorious desperado, but also because the State offered a reward of $4,000 for him, dead or alive. Connected with the Rangers, and on the payroll, were two or three men who were only known to the Captain. They were the detectives of our force. One of these men was John Duncan.

By the order of Captain McNelly, Duncan had, months before, taken the job to find John Wesley Hardin. To this end, Duncan hired the ranch adjoining that owned by Hardin's father, the preacher. The Ranger detective cultivated the friendship of the old man, but did it with such deliberation and naturalness that his identity or purpose was never suspected.

For days, weeks, and months the two met in the evening, smoked their pipes, and talked over matters such as naturally occurred to them; but never once was reference made to John Wesley Hardin, the son. The detective, however, was biding his time, and it was not until five months had passed that the chance for which he was waiting came. One afternoon, just as it was growing dark, Mr. Hardin remarked that he had a letter to mail, and would walk to the post office, which was in a grocery store at the junction of the highway, half a mile away.

"I may as well take a stroll with you," said the other, rising to his feet. Hardin was glad to have him, and they entered the store together. Hardin asked for a pen with which to direct the letter, which was written in pencil and enclosed in an envelope. The postmaster handed him a pen, and Hardin began writing the name slowly and with great care. Just before he finished, the pipe of the detective went out, and he leaned over the shoulder of the unsuspecting Hardin to get a match. As he did so, he gave one quick glance at the envelope. It was enough, for he read the name and address and was sure to remember them.

Duncan and Hardin walked home together, conversing on the way on various matters. A few days later, Duncan said he would have to go to St. Louis to see some cattlemen there. Instead of going to St. Louis, however, Duncan went straight to San Antonio, where he met with John Armstrong, Charley McKinney, and two other Rangers. The party at once started for Florida, for the address on the letter the old man had sent was "William Jones," at a little place near Pensacola, Florida.

They arrived at Pensacola, August 18th. Duncan

took the train for the little station to which the letter was addressed. He saw Hardin at work in a field
on a farm, but passed him by without apparent notice. Duncan came back to Pensacola. He had taken
the telegraph operator at the little station into his
confidence, however, and had arranged with him to
send a dispatch notifying him when Hardin would
take the train for a station nearer Pensacola. The
operator told Duncan that Hardin would usually
take this train about once a week, as he was paying attention to a farmer's daughter who lived near
the second station.

On Saturday, August 23rd, Duncan received the
telegram he expected, and he and the four Rangers
went at once to a point up the railroad where Hardin's train was scheduled to stop. When the train
arrived, Armstrong entered the car where Hardin
sat, walking in at the forward end. Hardin and a
companion were the only occupants of the car. Another of the Rangers entered the car at the rear door
and took the seat immediately behind Hardin and
his friend. The other officers remained outside, near
the car doors.

Hardin paid no attention to Armstrong and the
other Ranger until Armstrong reached the place
where the desperado was sitting. Then Armstrong
looked Hardin straight in the eye and said:

"How are you, John Wesley Hardin?"

With a motion as quick as a flash, Hardin threw
back his hand for his six-shooter; but the Ranger

who was behind him was expecting this, and he caught the outlaw's arm and hung on to it.

Hardin's companion drew his six-shooter, however, and Armstrong immediately put a bullet in his head. Then a fight with Hardin began all over the car. He kicked and bit like a wildcat, trying his best all the while to get at his revolver. It took five minutes to handcuff and disarm him.

Without waiting for requisition papers or even to notify the Florida officers of the capture, Armstrong and his party started for Texas. They actually kidnapped Hardin and were going through Alabama before they were stopped. Then an officious lawyer got an order from an Alabama court, which delayed the party twenty-four hours. The news that John Wesley Hardin was on the train drew great crowds to stations all through Louisiana and eastern Texas. As the party approached Austin, the crowds grew larger and larger. In Austin itself, the streets near the railroad station were filled with a great crowd and it was whispered that a lot of DeWitt County desperadoes were there to rescue Hardin.

This rumor reached the ears of the Rangers who had gathered in Austin, and they telegraphed to Armstrong. The consequence was that Hardin was taken off the train on the outskirts of Austin and conveyed to the jail by the Rangers on horseback long before the crowd at the depot knew what had happened.

Hardin was tried on one of the many indictments

against him, and found guilty of murder in the second degree! The Governor said he would pardon Hardin if he was not sentenced to be hanged, and to have him tried on the other eighteen murder indictments until some jury would find him guilty of murder in the first degree. Unfortunately this was not done. Hardin was sentenced to the state penitentiary at Huntsville for twenty-five years. When he went to jail he swore that if he outlived his sentence, he would hunt down every man who took part in his capture and kill them all.

John Armstrong and his four companions received $800 each from the state for bringing in Hardin. They regretted, later, that they had not turned him over to the Louisiana authorities, for there was a reward of $12,000 for him in Louisiana, for murders committed there.

Strange as it may seem, Hardin was pardoned by Governor Hogg of Texas in 1893. What possible reason there could be for granting a pardon to such an unspeakable villain, it is difficult to conceive; but certain it is that by the governor's action the man was set free. He studied law while being held in the penitentiary, and when he was set at liberty he soon announced his intention of starting a practice at the bar.

For awhile after his release, he was on his good behavior, but soon he showed signs of going back to his old life. He went to El Paso on the night of May 2, 1895, and held up the Gem gambling house there in a most sensational manner. He played faro until he lost several hundred dollars. Then he suddenly drew his six-shooter and, pointing it at the head of the faro dealer, said:

"You are too cute for me, —— you! Now just hand over the money I paid for my chips and all the rest you have in the drawer."

The dealer, a man named Baker, handed over the money without a word and Hardin walked out of the place. Hardin left town, but returned in August to see a woman who lived there. He found, on his arrival, that the woman had been arrested a few days before by a policeman named Selman. Hardin threatened to run Selman out of the town.

Two nights later — August 19, 1895 — Constable Selman, the father of the policeman, walked into a barroom where Hardin was shaking dice. As soon as Hardin saw Selman, he whirled around and put his hand to his hip to draw his six-shooter. Selman was quicker than he, however, and sent a bullet crashing through his head. As Hardin was falling, Selman sent two more bullets through his heart.

The worst of all of the bad men of Texas thus died "with his boots on," as he had often sworn he would die.

I should like to go on and tell, in detail, all the exploits of the Rangers, but, interesting as it is to recall those exciting days, I feel that the reader has already supped a plate too full of action. I would enjoy recounting how Captain Hall and his men rounded up a great band of Mexican bandits, who, in 1878, arranged to invade Texas under General Escobedo,[1] the man who shot Maximilian; how we came near taking retaliatory measures and invading Mexico in force when Governor Hubbard threatened to issue a proclamation that called for fifty thousand men; how we made a forced march of 250 miles in three and a half days from El Paso to the stronghold of Escobedo's men, and succeeded in arresting him and his followers.

All these matters have much reminiscent interest to me, however, to give them with proper detail would make too long a story. The killing of Sam Bass[2] and his notorious gang in August, 1878, by Lee

[1]General Mariano Escobedo, an ex-muleteer, was one of General Porfirio Diaz's most capable officers in the fight to wrest Mexico from Hapsburg Archduke Maximilian. Escobedo was surely responsible for capturing Maximilian, but Jennings statement that Escobedo was "the man who shot Maximilian" is unfounded. On June 19, 1867, on a hill overlooking the city of Queretaro, a firing squad of unnamed soldiers executed Maximilian. See Alfred Jackson Hanna and Kathryn Abbey Hanna, *Napoleon III and Mexico: American Triumph over Monarchy* (Chapel Hill: University of North Carolina Press, 1971), pp. 299–300; Carleton Beals, *Porfirio Diaz: Dictator of Mexico* (Philadelphia: J. B. Lippincott Company, 1932), pp. 159–60.

[2]Sam Bass (1851–78) died on July 21, 1878, at Round Rock, Texas, approximately fifteen miles north of Austin. Although Lee Hall and John Armstrong were part of the Ranger force that captured the Bass gang and killed Sam Bass in an attempted bank robbery in Round Rock on July 19, Major John B. Jones was the leader. See Webb, *The Texas Rangers*, pp. 371–91; Raymond, *Captain Lee Hall of Texas*, pp. 147–65.

Hall and others of the Rangers; the final breaking up of every band of desperadoes in Texas; the establishment of law and order where formerly outlaws governed; the making of the great state into an orderly, prosperous country, where life and property is as safe as in New York is the record of the Rangers. It is a record of which the survivors of the old troop have good reason to be proud.

I say "the survivors," for the great majority of the old comrades I loved are dead. Charley McKinney, as I have told, was murdered by a man whom he tried to arrest. The murderer was afterward hanged in San Antonio. Every little while, I hear of another of the Rangers passing away. McNelly died of consumption in September, 1877.

King Fisher and Ben Thompson, the latter having a "killing" record of some thirty odd men, were both killed in one night by William H. Simms, a gambler of San Antonio.[3] They entered a variety theatre owned by Simms with the expressed purpose of "cleaning it out." Simms, who was mild-mannered and gentlemanly, went to the box where the two "man-killers" were, and expostulated with them. Eventually, Thompson called him an obscene name and "reached" for his revolver.

In an instant, Simms shot him through the head.

[3] On the night of March 11, 1884, at the Vaudeville Theatre in San Antonio, King Fisher and Ben Thompson were killed instantly. Stories differ in regard to the individual assassins. See Askins, *Texans, Guns & History*, pp. 76–86; Raymond, *Captain Lee Hall of Texas*, pp. 215–17.

Thompson, as he fell, managed to fire his pistol twice into the floor, although a bullet had passed through his brain. Fisher had his hand on his pistol, but before he could use it, Simms shot him through the heart. Simms was tried and acquitted, the plea being self-defense. I saw Simms on my last visit to Texas. Never have I met a more entertaining man. He dislikes greatly to talk of the killing of Fisher and Thompson. It made him for a time the "mark" for every aspiring "bad man" who went to San Antonio. After getting drunk, they would straightaway make up their minds that they would kill Simms, the man who killed two men in a night. Simms was forced to shoot three of these brash cowboys who came to kill him.

"I got very tired of it," he said to me. "I wanted to live in peace, but they wouldn't let me. Sometimes I would go up to New England and hunt out some quiet, retired village where I might be at rest, but, although I went under an assumed name at such times, my identity was sure to be discovered and then I was looked upon with suspicion.

"I was in one of these little New England towns, one summer, and was enjoying myself greatly in a quiet way, when one day the barber who was shaving me said:

'You don't seem to me to be such a bad man, Mr. Simms.'

"Well, I jumped so that the barber almost cut my throat with his razor.

"Who told you my name was Simms and that I was a bad man?" Simms demanded.

The barber replied that an agent for a laundry company who was once a county clerk in San Antonio told him that Simms had killed twenty-four men. Simms knew that part of the story was a lie and set out to find the laundryman. Soon he noticed that men had gathered in small groups and were eyeing him as though he were some sort of wild animal. Presently, a young man stepped up to him and said:

"I should very much like to have you patronize our laundry, sir."

Simms jumped for him and grabbed him by the collar. The young man grew as white as one of the shirts his laundry did up.

"So you're the man who has told everyone that I killed twenty-four men," Simms shouted. "Who are you anyway? I know you were never the county clerk at San Antonio."

"I-I worked in the county clerk's office," he stammered, "and I really did hear that you had killed twenty-four men."

"Young man," Simms replied, "you and I are going to take a little walk out into that cornfield over there. Only one of us is coming back, and I think I'll be the one to come back."

The laundryman begged for his life, and Simms told him he'd let him off if he'd promise to go to everyone he had talked to and tell them he had lied. The young man did so, but in a few days Simms left town. As he said, "The place had lost all of its charm for me."

The old company of Rangers was at an end when Captain Hall resigned in 1880. I resigned late in 1877,[4] and returned to Philadelphia. I thought I had seen enough adventure for a man of twenty-two. I tried to live a quiet, civilized life, but the tameness of an existence in the city was more than I could stand and, in 1881, I started West again, this time for Colorado. I became a prospector and miner in the Rockies, and put in nearly three more years of wild living in the mining camps and the mountains. Someday I may tell about those days, for they were filled with adventure.

It is a relief to put on paper the record of the free, outdoor existence of bygone years. I am glad I have done it, for it is fitting that the history of Captain McNelly's and Captain Hall's Texas Rangers should live after we who made up that body have passed away.

[4]Jennings was honorably discharged from the Rangers on February 1, 1877. See Ingmire, *Texas Ranger Service Records, 1847–1900*, III, 72.

EPILOGUE

In 1878 Napoleon Augustus "Al" Jennings—soon after serving an eight-month "hitch" with the McNelly Rangers—returned to Philadelphia because of the death of his father. Only twenty-two years old, he would not stay at home for long—"the city seemed literally to smother him." Besides, his adventures in Texas had inoculated him with a kind of restlessness—an infatuation with the West and a desire to be part of the fast-changing American scene. And so over the next several years, he worked in a variety of jobs across the western United States, herding cattle on the open range, driving a mountain stagecoach, prospecting and placer mining in out-of-the-way locales, and doing odd jobs whenever necessary for food and warmth.

But eventually Jennings decided that his life's work should be the field of journalism where he could demonstrate his passion for writing, his ability to verbalize his experiences. Yet he still could not submerge within himself a certain wanderlust, an urge to meet new challenges. In 1884 he returned home and hired on as a reporter for the *Philadelphia News*, then had short tenures with its two city rivals, the *Times* and *Tribune*. By 1887 his experience and reputation were great enough to warrant a job with Charles Dana's prestigious *New York Sun*. Five years later, however, he accepted a position with the *San Antonio Express*, during which time he interviewed former Rangers and gathered material for the story you have just read.

By 1894 Jennings returned to New York City and found new excitement in becoming a reporter for Joseph Pulitzer's *New York Evening World*. From 1895 to 1897, he delighted in lampooning New York City Police Commissioner Theodore Roosevelt by ridiculing his efforts with such sarcastic epithets as "Teddy Toddlekins, Boy Detective." Then, in 1898, came the Spanish-American War which gave vent both to his versatility and creativity. He claimed to have supplied Americans with the fighting slogan "Remember the Maine." His newspaper columns featured innumerable "fiery verses" that epitomized the valor and patriotism of Americans, thereby winning him the appellation of "the automatic poet." And, although at his desk in New York City, he wrote in first person—as would be his customary literary technique—about the exploits and daring of the Rough Riders in Cuba; in fact, he acquired a new respect for their courageous leader, Colonel Roosevelt, and soon thereafter became an ardent admirer and close friend.

Jennings found a wide audience for his writings. For *Town Topics* he contributed, one author observed, "sophisticated articles." But, in the main, his forte had to do with adventure and heroism. For the *Saturday Evening Post*, for example, he wrote articles entitled "A Dash for the Border," "La Ley de Fuga," and "Lee Hall, Fighting Man." And, of course, Charles Scribner's Sons published in 1898 his memorable *A Texas Ranger*[1]

After 1900, Jennings' career was difficult to trace. He married operatic and vaudeville singer Madam Edith Helena, served both as her manager and press agent, and accompanied her on tours in Europe and the United States. Then, in 1910, with Francisco Madero leading a revolution against the government of Porfirio Diaz, he covered those memorable events in Mexico City for the *New York Herald*. And at times, during and after World War I, he would contribute short essays and stories until his death in New York City on December 15, 1919.

But how did it come about that a Philadelphia-born lad, who eventually settled in New York City, wrote this epic piece about that faraway frontier land of Texas in the 1870s and its fabled law enforcement organization, the Texas Rangers? On one occasion, Jennings provided the answer: "I am a writing man; I needed money; I had a story to tell; I told it."[2] As you, the reader, now realize, Jennings successfully accomplished his purpose.

[1] See Dobie, *Prefaces*, pp. 15–18; Raymond, *Captain Lee Hall of Texas*, pp. 324–25; N. A. Jennings, "Lee Hall, Fighting Man," *Saturday Evening Post*, January 6, 1900.
[2] Dobie, *Prefaces*, p. 17.

Index

INDEX

Abilene, Kansas, xxviii

Adams, S. J.: Texas Ranger, 121, 278–79

Alabama, 125

Alamo: battle of, xxxi

Albuquerque, New Mexico, 114n

Alexander, Major A. J., lxi, 175, 176n, 179, 181, 195–96

Allen, "Black": Texas Ranger, 121

Allen, Warren: outlaw, 236

Armoy, Ireland, 4n

Armstrong, John B.: Texas Ranger, lxv, 121, 173, 180, 183–84, 190, 200, 203, 205, 267–68, 271–80, 284–85, 320–23, 325n; biographical information, 255n; leads Ranger scouting expedition, 255–66; physical description, 128, 131.

Atascosa County, Texas, 13n, 39n, 67, 78–79, 243

Atascosa Creek, 20

Augur, General C. C., lii

Augustine, Dave: outlaw, 294

Austin, Stephen F.: colony of, xxxvii

Austin, Texas, xxvi, 4n, 6, 33, 322, 325n

Baker: hotel proprietor, 9–10

Baker House: hotel in San Antonio, 6

Balcones Escarpment, xxiv

Banks, Major General Nathaniel P., 118, 119n

Bass, Sam: outlaw, xxxi, lxvi; death of, 325

Baton Rouge, Louisiana, 119n

Beeville, Texas, 307

Belknap, Secretary of War W. W., lii, lv, 176, 196, 199

Benavides: Mexican bandit, 58n

Black codes, xxv

Bonham, Texas, 309n

Boyd, George: Texas Ranger, 121, 126, 155–57, 255n, 258, 260, 263, 268, 272–74

Branding, 15

Brashear City, Louisiana, xliv, 118

Brazzell, Dr. Philip, 286, 289, 293–94; biographical information, 290n; death of, 286

Brenham, Texas, xliv

Brownsville, Texas, xxxii, xxxiv, xlv, li, lvi, lx, lxi, 85, 139, 146, 152, 155, 158, 160, 165, 169, 174, 218, 223

Bruton, Bill: outlaw, 236, 252

Bruton, Wes: outlaw, 236, 252

Buffalo: hides, 24–25; hunting, 23–24

Burbank: customs inspector, 90–91

Burton, H. W. See White, Ham

Burton, T. J., xliii, 113

337

California, 126–27, 306

Callicott, William: Texas Ranger, xlix

Camargo, Mexico, 193, 209

Cameron County, Texas, xxxvi, 135

Campbell, Captain George W., 113

Camp Ringgold. *See* Ringgold Barracks

Cap Rock, 102n

Cardwell, Crockett, 78n. *See also* Kelly, Crockett

Carleton, Lieutenant Henry Guy, 195–96

Carrizo Springs, Texas, 234, 239–40, 257, 258n, 272

Castroville, Texas, 228n

"Catclaws": thorny bushes, 280

Cattle: illegal trade in hides, 134; market, xxviii, 16; numbers lost in raids, xxxiii, 17n, 139n; roundup, 15, 17; rustling, xxxiii–xxxvi, 17–18, 102, 105–06, 134–36, 139, 146, 149, 169–90ff, 208, 210, 228, 233, 237, 281; stolen returned to King, 208–11. *See also* Longhorns and Mavericks

Cattle Kingdom, xxviii

Chaparral, 69, 193, 220, 234, 249, 273

Chisholm Trail, xxviii

Clark, T. Hynes: cattleman, 135

Clendenin, Major D. R.: command of Eighth Cavalry, 176; forbids crossing of Rio Grande, lxi, 176n; letter to Steele, 199

Clinton, Texas, 285, 290, 296–97

Coahuila: Mexican state of, lv

Coke, Governor Richard, xxxvii, xlv, lvi, 101n, 106n, 246n, 303n

Collin County, Texas, 228n

Collins, Michael: historian, lxvii

Colorado River, 109

Comanche County, Texas, 309n

Comanche Indians, xxviii, lxv

Concord, New Hampshire. *See* St. Paul's School

Confederate Army, 113

Coranto: dance, 304. *See also courante*

Corpus Christi, Texas, xxxi, xxxv, xlv, lvi, 21, 133–35, 264

Corsicana, Texas, 101n

Cortina, Juan N.: outlaw, xxxii–xxxiii, xxxv, xxxvi, lvi, lix, lxii, lxv, 145–46, 149–51, 175

Cox, William: outlaw, 294

Courante: dance, 304n. *See also coranto*

Criss, Lawrence Christopher, 23

Cuba, 132

Cuero, Texas, 290n, 294, 313, 315

Ciudad Porfirio Diaz. *See* Piedras Negras

Culver, M. S.: cattleman, 135

David's Landing, 159n

Davis, Governor E. J., xxvi–xxvii, xxxvi, xxxvii, lvi,

82n, 106, 119–20; as Union general, xliv, 82n

Deggs, J. W.: Texas Ranger, 284–85

Deggs, Thomas: Texas Ranger, 121

Del Rio, Texas, xxxiv

Derringers: carried by women, 244

Devine, T. N.: Texas Ranger, 121, 258, 261, 278–80

DeWitt County, Texas, xxxi, xliv, lxv, 78n, 285–86, 290, 293, 299, 301, 303, 319, 322

Diaz, General Porfirio, lxii, lxv, 54, 66, 325n

Dimmit County, Texas, 231–32, 252, 258n

Dobie, J. Frank: Texas folklorist, l

Duncan, John: private detective, 309n, 319–23

Durham, George (L. P.): Texas Ranger, xlix, l, 121, 126, 189, 225n, 251, 258, 278–79

Duval County, Texas, 122

Dwyer, Joseph E.: state senator, xlvi

Eagle Pass, Texas, xxxi, lii, lxv, 228n, 231, 237–40, 264–68, 272, 275

Edinburg, Texas, xlv, 136, 174n

El Paso, Texas, 309n, 323

Encinal, Texas, 113

Escobedo, General Mariano, 325; biographical information, 325n

Espinoso, Guadaloupe, 144–45

Evans, Tom "Lumber": Texas Ranger, 92–94, 121, 125, 258, 261; tenure as Ranger, 93n

Falconer, Thomas: member of Santa Fe Expedition, 102n

Fandango: dance, 152, 155–57, 276

Fannin County, Texas, 309n

Farnsworth, Lieutenant H. J., 174

Farragut, Admiral David G., 119n

Fehrenbach, T. R.: historian, xxxii

Fiesta, 26, 29, 277

Fish, U.S. Secretary of State Hamilton, lii, lx–lxi

Fisher, (John) King: outlaw, xxviii, xxxi, lxvi, 33, 228, 252, 255, 257, 276–77, 326–27; atrocities of, 231–33, 240–41; biographical information, 228n; captured by Rangers, 234–36, 238–40; physical appearance, 237–38

Flores, Juan: alcalde of Camargo, 193; general, xxxiii

Ford, John Salmon "Rip": Texas Ranger, xxxviii, xlii

Fort Brown, xxxii, lix, lxi, 146, 169, 196, 199

Fort Clark, 236

Fort Ewell, 277

Fort McIntosh, 34, 43, 58

Fort Ringgold. *See* Ringgold Barracks

Fort Worth, lxv

Fourteenth Amendment, xxvi

Fourteenth Texas Legislature, xxxvii, xlii

Fredericksburg, Texas, 281

Frio County, Texas, 243

Frontier Battalion, xlii, lxv–lxvi, 101

Galveston, Battle of, xliii, 82n, 117

Galveston News, 47–48

Galveston, Texas, xxiii, 29n

Gatling gun, 193

Georgia, 289n

Germans, 282–83

Gillespie County, Texas, 281

Glendenning, Lieutenant, 62–63, 66

Goff, Secretary of Navy, 306

Goliad: massacre, xxxi

Goliad, Texas, 232

Gonzales, Gregorio: City Marshal of Laredo, 39–47, 75–77, 228, biographical information, 39n

Goodnight-Loving Trail, xxviii

Gorman, B.: Texas Ranger, 121

Gourley, Andy: Texas Ranger, 121

Granger, General Gordon, xxiii

Grant, U. S.: as President, l, lii, lv, lvii, 139n, 149n, 175–76, 203; as General of the Army, li

Grayson County, Texas, xxv, 245

Green, Colonel Thomas, 82n, 114, 117–19

Gregory, Nelson: Texas Ranger, 121

Griffen, M. Fleming: Texas Ranger, 121

Griffin, W. H.: Texas Ranger, 278–79, 302

Gringo: origin of word, 51

Gulf of Mexico, 133

Hall, George: Texas Ranger, 121, 149, 183–84, 189–90

Hall, (Jesse) Lee "Red": Texas Ranger, lxv, 283, 285–86, 289n, 290, 293–99, 301–10, 313–17, 319–24, 325–26; biographical information, 245–46; first scouting expedition, 252–53; joins up, 249; letter to Steele, 289; resigns, 329; succeeds McNelly, 122

Hall's Rangers, 245–329ff; camp life of, 249–53, 257; arrests and trial of feud participates, 286, 289–90, 293–99

Hamilton, Andrew Jackson: governor of Texas, xxv

Hardin, John Wesley: outlaw activities, xxxi, lxvi, 309–10, 313–17, 319–24; parents of, 309n, 315; biographical information, 309n

Hardy, S. N.: Texas Ranger, 121

Harriet Lane: capture of in Battle of Galveston, 117

Hayes, President Rutherford B.: 306

Haynes, John J.: customs collector, lix, 58n

Hays, Ranger Captain John Coffee "Jack," xli

Headly, Dr.: American leader of Mexicans, 204, 206–08

Heidrichs, Charles: outlaw, 294

Heister, Frank: outlaw, 294

Hidalgo County, Texas, 136, 170

Hogg, Governor James Stephen, 323

Honeycutt, Jim: outlaw, 236

Hubbard, Governor Richard B.: appoints Lee Hall to Texas Rangers, 246; biographical information, 246n; lieutenant governor of Texas, xxxvii

Indian Territory, 16, 245

Jacal, 267; definition of, 267n

Jennings, N. A. "Al": arrives in Texas, xlviii, 3, 5–6; arrested, 39; chief of police in Laredo, 50–54; clerk at Fort McIntosh, 36–37; cowboy, 10; death, 333; Diaz revolutionist, 68–72; discharged from Rangers, 329; education, xlvii, 3–4; family, xlvi–xlviii; first horseback ride in Texas, 12, 14; first trip to Laredo, xlviii, 21, 26; gambling, 6; with Hall Rangers, 245–329ff; later years, 329, 331–33; marriage to Madam Edith Helena, 333; meets McNelly, xlix, 87–88; with McNelly Rangers, xlix–l, 88–245ff, 331; newspaper reporter, 331–32; publication, disputes, and explanations of *A Texas Ranger*, xlix–lxvii; publications, 332–33; ranch hand, 20; return to Philadelphia, 329; in San Antonio, 6–11; special deputy U.S. Marshal, 40–50; trip to Texas, xlviii, 3, 5; visits Nueva Laredo, 29–31

Jennings, N. A., Sr., xlvi–xlvii, 4–5

Johnson, Andrew: U.S. President, li

Johnson, J. B.: outlaw, 281–83

Jones, Ranger Major John B.: biographical information, 101n; command of Frontier Battalion, xlii, 101; involved in death of Sam Bass, 325n

Juarez, Mexican President Benito, li, lxii

Kansas, 16, 33n, 236

Karnes County, Texas, 283

Kells, Lieutenant Commander DeWitt C., lix–lxi, 176n

Kelly, Crockett, 78–81. *See also* Cardwell, Crockett

Kenedy, Mifflin: cattleman, xxviii

Kentucky, 228n

Kerr, W. A.: friend of McNelly, 113

Key, Noley: outlaw, 257–58, 261

Kickapoo Indians, lii, lv

King Ranch, xxxiii

King, Richard: cattleman, xxviii, lxvi, 17n, 211

Kiowa Indians, xxviii, lxv

Knox, Colonel John Armoy: articles in the *Texas New Yorker*, 4–5

Laguna Madre, 140

Lake Espantoso, 258, 267

La ley de fuga, 238; definition of, 239n

Lamar, Texas President Mirabeau B., 102n

La Parra, Texas, 135, 139

Laredo, Texas, xxxi, xlviii, lii, lvi, 20–21, 35–36, 39n, 45, 47, 49, 61, 68, 75, 87, 228; in *Galveston News*, 48; Jennings first trip, 25–26, 29; Jennings last visit, 80; population in 1870, 20n; population in 1874, 29

La Salle County, Texas, 125, 243

Las Cuevas, Rancho de: lx, 172, 174n, 176, 185, 199, 214–15; McNelly orders raid on, 181–83; Rangers attack, xlix, lxi–lxii, lxvi, 186, 189–90, 193, 195–96, 200, 203–08; results of raid, 217

Las Rucias: Ranger encampment, 139

Leadville, Colorado, 33n

Lerdists, 57, 64, 66, 70

Lerdo, Mexican President Sebastian, lix, lxii, 54

Live Oak County, Texas, 232, 243–44

Llano Estacado, 102n. *See* also Staked Plains of Texas

Longhorns, 15n. *See* also Cattle and Mavericks

Longley, Bill: outlaw, xxxi

Maben, Horace: Texas Ranger, 121

Mackenzie, Colonel Ranald S., lv

Mackey, A. S.: Texas Ranger, 121

Magruder, Major General John B., xxiii, 117n

Mansfield, Battle of, xliv, 82n

Martin, "One-Eyed John": outlaw, 260

Mason, Texas, 289n

Matamoros, Mexico, xxxii–xxxiii, 146, 164, 166, 212, 214–15; Cortina places under martial rule, 151; Jennings visits, 152

Maverick County, Texas, 231–32, 239–40

Maverick, Samuel A.: cattleman, 15n

Mavericks, 15; derivation of word, 15n. *See* also Cattle and Longhorns

Maximilian, Emperor: death of, xxiii, li, 325n; rise to power, l–li

Mayers, Edward: Texas Ranger, 121, 272–74

Mayfield, John: killed by Rangers, 284–85

McAlister: outlaw, 260–62

McCarty, George: Rangers arrest, 252

McCoy, Joseph G.: cattle buyer and railroad builder, xxvii–xxviii

McCulloch, Ranger Captain Ben, xli

McGovern, Thomas: Texas Ranger, 121, 125

McIntosh, Colonel J. B., 35

McIntyre: Laredo restaurant owner, 75, 77, 81

McKay, "Cow": Texas Ranger, 121, 125–26

McKinney, Charley: Texas Ranger, 92, 94, 96, 100, 121, 320; death of, 122, 125, 326; tenure as Ranger, 92n

McKinney, W. W.: Texas Ranger, 121, 125, 276

McMullen County, Texas, 243

McNelly, John: Texas Ranger, 121

McNelly, Leander H.: Texas Ranger, lix, lxi, lxv, lxvi–lxvii, 86–227ff, 245, 267, 319; biographical information, xliii–xliv, 82n; death of, 245, 326; family of, xliv, 86, 127–28; illness, 255; in Civil War, xliii–xliv, 106, 113–14, 117–20; in Texas State Police, xliv, 106, 119–20; letters to General William Steele, 212–15, 231–33; physical appearance, xlii–xliii, 82, 85; raises Ranger company, 125; resigns, 301

McNelly's Rangers, xlii, xlvi, lxi, lxv, 85–163ff, 169–245ff, 283; camplife, 218–26; creation of, 106, 109; diet, 99–100; dress and manner, 131–32; equipment and pay, 110–11; Jennings describes, 81–82

Mead, J. J.: commissioner, xxxiv

Meadows, William: outlaw marshal of Cuero, 294

Melvin, Thomas: Texas Ranger, 121

Merriam, Major Henry C., 58, 61, 64–65

Merritt, Lieutenant, 193

Mestizo, lxii

Mexico City, xli, lvi, lxv

Mexican War: fighting, xxxi, xxxviii; Nueva Laredo established as a result, 26n

Mississippi, 125

Mississippi River, 119n

Missouri, 266

Monte: card game, 11, 29–30, 69

Monterrey, Mexico, 175, 214

Mullin, George: outlaw, 260

Murrah, Pendleton: Texas governor, xxiii

Navarro County, Texas, 19n, 101n

Navarro, Jose Antonio: descendants, 19–20, 39n; biographical information, 19n

Navarro, Sixto: Laredo magistrate, 39–41, 44–47; biographical information, 39n

New Orleans, Louisiana, 118

New York, 4n

Nichols, S. M.: Texas Ranger, 121

Norther: Jennings experiences weather in Texas, 22–24

Nueces County, Texas, 134–35

Nueces River, xxviii, 49, 228n, 262; criminal activities along, 231–32, 277; Rangers patrol, 255–57; Ranger swims, 280

Nueces Strip, xxxiii–xxxiv, xlv–xlvi, lvi, lxii, lxv–lxvi

Nueva Laredo, Mexico, 29–33; established, 26n; fiesta, 26; fighting in, 54, 57, 64–66, 68, 70–72, 277

Oakland, Texas, 245n

Oakville, Texas, 231, 244–45, 251, 253, 277

Obenchain, Burd. *See* Porter, Frank

Ogilsbie, Captain, 122

Ohio, 306

Olguine, Mario "Aboja": outlaw, 145–46

Ord, General E. O. C., xlv, lvi, lxi

Orrell, T. J.: Texas Ranger, 121, 128, 253; arrests J. B. Johnson, 281–83; tenure as Ranger, 128n

Owasco: at Battle of Galveston, 117n

Palo Alto, Battle of, 159n

Parker County, Texas, 284

Parrott, A. L.: Texas Ranger, 121, 126, 179, 258, 278–79

Pease, Elisha M.: ex-governor of Texas, xxv

Pendencia Creek, 231, 234

Pensacola, Florida, 320–22

Peterson, Hamilton C.: U.S. Commissioner, xlviii, 37–50, 58, 61–62, 67, 75–80, 228; biographical information, 38n; death of, 80

Philadelphia, Pennsylvania, 4, 9, 87, 95, 329

Piedras Negras, xxxii, lv, 212, 214, 239, 267

Pierce, Shanghai: cattleman, xxviii

Pleasants, Judge Henry Clay: district judge in DeWitt County, 290, 297–99, 307; biographical information, 290n

Pleasanton, Texas, 13–14, 20, 39n

Point Isabel, Texas, xxxiv, 17n

Port Hudson, Louisiana, 118–19; battle of, 119n

Porter, Frank (alias of Burd Obenchain): outlaw, 235–37

Posse comitatus, 109; definition of, 109n

Potter, Colonel J. H., lxi, 176, 196, 199–200

Queensberry, T. M.: Texas Ranger, 121

Queretaro, Mexico, 325n

Racy, Jack: Texas Ranger, 121

Rancho Davis, 169

Randlett, Captain James F., lxi, 174, 179

Ranger "Fugitive List," 303n

Ratama Ranch, 170

Rattlesnakes, 49, 223–24, 278, 314

Rector, H. J. : Texas Ranger, 121, 219–22, 252, 301–02

Red River, xlii

Red River Campaign, 82n, 118–19

Reichel, W. O.: Texas Ranger, 121

Remey, George C.: captain of *Rio Bravo*, lxi, 139n, 176n

Reynolds: rancher, 10–14

Ringgold Barracks, 159, 211–12

Ringgold, Major David, 159n

Rio Grande, xxviii, xxxi–xxxii, xxxiv–xxxv, xli–xlii, xlv, xlviii, lii, lv, lix–lx, lxv–lxvii

Rio Grande City, Texas, 17n, 159n, 208–09, 211

Robb Commission, xxxiv–xxxvi, xlvi, li–lii

Robb, Thomas P.: commissioner, xxxiv

Roberts, Al: outlaw, 236

Roberts, "Jim": outlaw, 260

Robeson, George M.: Secretary of Navy, 139n

Robinson, Lieutenant T. J.: Texas Ranger, 121, 140, 170–72, 185, 203, 205; death of, 122

Rock, J. S.: Ranger scout, 149n

Roosevelt, Theodore, 132, 332

Ross, John: founder of Rossville, 19n; friend to Jennings, 19–21, 31, 35, 67, 78

Ross, William F.: brother of John Ross, 21–22, 67; founder of Rossville, 19n

Rossville, Texas, 19n

"Rough Riders," 132, 195

Round Rock, Texas, 325n

Rowe, Horace: Texas Ranger, 121, 126, 251, 256

Rudd, W. L.: Texas Ranger, 121, 125–26, 128, 264, 275, 279; tenure as Ranger, 264n

Ruiz, Pancho: outlaw, 264

Rurales: Mexican rural constabulary, 189, 210; description, 189n

Ryan: Irish friend of Jennings, 68, 72–75, 78, 81

Ryan, Jake: outlaw, 294

Salinas, Rafael: captured by Texas Rangers, 140

San Antonio *Express*, 267

San Antonio, Texas, xlv, 6, 10, 13n, 15, 19, 34, 64, 82n, 114, 125, 255, 261, 267, 281, 283, 305, 320, 326, 328

San Diego, Texas, 122

Sandobal, Jesus "Ole Casoose": Texas Ranger, 121, 163–68, 171–73, 183; background and appearance, 158–60; tenure as Ranger, 157n

Santa Fe Expedition: Jose Antonio Navarro as participant, 19n; Thomas Falconer as participant, 102n

Santa Maria, Texas, 169

Savage, Richard H., xxxiv

Sayers, Captain Joe, 114

Schofield, General John M., li

Scott, G. M.: Texas Ranger, 121

Selman, Constable John, 309n, 324

"Seven up"; gambling game, 308

Seward, U.S. Secretary of State William H., li

Shears, Robert: Brownsville marshal, xxxii

Shelby, General Joseph, xxiii; 120

Sheridan, General Philip H., li

Sherman, General William Tecumseh, lv

Sibley, General Henry H.: McNelly serves with, xliii, 82n; in Battle of Val Verde, 114n

Siebert, F.: Texas Ranger, 121

Sierra Madres: mountains in Mexico, xxxvi, li

Simms, William H., 33–34, 326–29

Singleton, Frank: criminal, 307–08; executed, 309

Sitterlee, Joseph: outlaw, 293–94, 296

Smith, D. R.: Texas Ranger, 121

Smith, General Kirby, xxiii

Smith, L. B. "Sonny": Texas Ranger, xlix, 121; death of, 143–44; funeral, 146

St. Clair: friend to Jennings, 41–42, 61–63, 73–74, 88

Steele, Adjutant General William, xlvi, 145n, 176n; Clendenin letter to, 199; Hall letter to, 289; McNelly letters to, 212–15, 231–33; reports to, 146n, 303

St. Louis, Missouri, 320

St. Paul's School: Jennings educated at, xlvii–xlviii, 4n

Staked Plains of Texas, 102. *See* also Llano Estacado

Stanley, S. W.: Texas Ranger, 121

Starr County, Texas, xlv

Stegall, N. R.: Texas Ranger, 121

Stevens, Speaker of the House Thaddeus, xxv

Stock meeting, 13, 15

Sullivan, T. J.: Texas Ranger, 121

Sumner, Senate Majority Leader Charles, xxvi

Sutton, Deputy Sheriff William, 289n

Sutton-Taylor Feud: arrests and trial, xxvi, xliv, lxv, 293–99; background, 285–86, 289n; Hall letter concerning, 289

Sweet, George H.: publisher of the *Texas New Yorker*, 4n

Talley, G. W.: Texas Ranger, 121

Tamaulipas: Mexican state of, xxxiii, xxxv

Taylor, Charles, 289n

Taylor, Creed, 289n

Taylor, Doboy, 289n

Taylor, Hays, 289n

Taylor, Jim, 289n

Taylor, General Zachary, xli

Tejanos, xxxii, xlvi

Templeton, Bill: outlaw, 236

Terry's Texas Rangers, 101n

Texas New Yorker, xlvii, 4–5

Texas Panhandle, xlii

Texas Rangers: inception and history, xxxvii–xlii, lxvi

Texas Revolution, xxxi

Texas Siftings, 4–5

Texas State Police: background, xxvi–xxvii, 106n; McNelly appointed, 119–20; McNelly service in, 106

Thirteenth Texas Legislature, xxxvi

Thompson, Ben: outlaw, xxxi, 33–34; death of, 326–27

Thompson, Bill: outlaw, 32–34; biographical information, 33n

Throckmorton, James W.: governor of Texas, xxv

"Twisted Charley": story told by L. C. Criss, 23–26

Union Pacific Railroad, xxvii–xxviii

United States Commission to Texas: investigates cattle rustling, 17n

U.S.S. *Plymouth*, lix

U.S.S. *Rio Bravo*: Grant dispatches to Rio Grande, 139n; DeWitt C. Kells as captain of, lix–lx, 176n

Val Verde, Battle of, xliii, 114, 117

Valdez, Juan: ranch hand, 160

Vaquero, 160, 237

Vera Cruz, xxxiii

Vicksburg, Mississippi, 119n

Victoria, Texas, 301–02

Vigilance committees, 134–36, 236

Virginia, 82, 122, 125, 290

Wainwright, Will: outlaw, 236

Walker, Alfred: Texas Ranger, 121

Walker, Ranger Captain Samuel, xli

Walton, Buck: advises McNelly, 120

Washington County, Texas, xliii, 82n, 113

Watson, David: Texas Ranger, 121

Webb, Deputy Sheriff Charles, 309n

Webb, Walter Prescott: historian, xli, lxvii

Wells, Fargo Express, 304

Wells, R. H.: Texas Ranger, 121

Welsh, W. T.: Texas Ranger, 121

Western Trail, xxviii

White, Ham (alias H. W. Burton): arrested, 306; outlaw activities, 303–07

Williams, F. J.: Texas Ranger, 121

Williams, James: Texas Ranger, 121

Williams, M. C. "Polly": Texas Ranger, 121, 126

Wilson, Thomas: U.S. consul at Matamoros, lx

Wright, L. B.: Texas Ranger, 121–22, 127–28, 140, 144, 285

Wright, Linton L.: Texas Ranger, 121–22, 151, 185

Young, Captain S. B. M., 195

List of The Lakeside Classics

The Lakeside Classics

Number	Title	Year
1.	The Autobiography of Benjamin Franklin . . .	1903
2.	Inaugural Addresses of the Presidents of the United States from Washington to Lincoln . .	1904
3.	Inaugural Addresses of the Presidents of the United States from A. Johnson to T. Roosevelt	1905
4.	Fruits of Solitude by William Penn	1906
5.	Memorable American Speeches I. The Colonial Period	1907
6.	Memorable American Speeches II. Democracy and Nationality	1908
7.	Memorable American Speeches III. Slavery	1909
8.	Memorable American Speeches IV. Secession, War, Reconstruction	1910
9.	The Autobiography of Gurdon Saltonstall Hubbard	1911
10.	Reminiscences of Early Chicago	1912
11.	Reminiscences of Chicago During the Forties and Fifties	1913
12.	Reminiscences of Chicago During the Civil War .	1914
13.	Reminiscences of Chicago During the Great Fire	1915
14.	Life of Black Hawk	1916
15.	The Indian Captivity of O. M. Spencer	1917
16.	Pictures of Illinois One Hundred Years Ago . .	1918
17.	A Woman's Story of Pioneer Illinois by Christiana Holmes Tillson	1919
18.	The Conquest of the Illinois by George Rogers Clark	1920

Number	Title	Year
19.	Alexander Henry's Travels and Adventures in the Years 1760-1776	1921
20.	John Long's Voyages and Travels in the Years 1768-1788	1922
21.	Adventures of the First Settlers on the Oregon or Columbia River by Alexander Ross	1923
22.	The Fur Hunters of the Far West by Alexander Ross	1924
23.	The Southwestern Expedition of Zebulon M. Pike	1925
24.	Commerce of the Prairies by Josiah Gregg	1926
25.	Death Valley in '49 by William L. Manly	1927
26.	Bidwell's Echoes of the Past—Steele's In Camp and Cabin	1928
27.	Kendall's Texan Santa Fe Expedition	1929
28.	Pattie's Personal Narrative	1930
29.	Alexander Mackenzie's Voyage to the Pacific Ocean in 1793	1931
30.	Wau-Bun, The "Early Day" in the North-West by Mrs. John H. Kinzie	1932
31.	Forty Years a Fur Trader by Charles Larpenteur	1933
32.	Narrative of the Adventures of Zenas Leonard	1934
33.	Kit Carson's Autobiography	1935
34.	A True Picture of Emigration by Rebecca Burlend	1936
35.	The Bark Covered House by William Nowlin	1937
36.	The Border and the Buffalo by John R. Cook	1938
37.	Vanished Arizona by Martha Summerhayes	1939
38.	War on the Detroit by Thomas Verchères de Boucherville and James Foster	1940
39.	Army Life in Dakota by De Trobriand	1941

Number	*Title*	*Year*
40.	The Early Day of Rock Island and Davenport by J. W. Spencer and J. M. D. Burrows	1942
41.	Six Years with the Texas Rangers by James B. Gillett.	1943
42.	Growing Up with Southern Illinois by Daniel Harmon Brush	1944
43.	A History of Illinois, I, by Gov. Thomas Ford . .	1945
44.	A History of Illinois, II, by Gov. Thomas Ford	1946
45.	The Western Country in the 17th Century by Lamothe Cadillac and Pierre Liette	1947
46.	Across the Plains in Forty-nine by Reuben Cole Shaw	1948
47.	Pictures of Gold Rush California	1949
48.	Absaraka, Home of the Crows by Mrs. Margaret I. Carrington	1950
49.	The Truth about Geronimo by Britton Davis . .	1951
50.	My Life on the Plains by General George A. Custer	1952
51.	Three Years Among the Indians and Mexicans by General Thomas James	1953
52.	A Voyage to the Northwest Coast of America by Gabriel Franchère	1954
53.	War-Path and Bivouac by John F. Finerty	1955
54.	Milford's Memoir by Louis Leclerc de Milford	1956
55.	Uncle Dick Wootton by Howard Louis Conard .	1957
56.	The Siege of Detroit in 1763	1958
57.	Among the Indians by Henry A. Boller	1959
58.	Hardtack and Coffee by John D. Billings	1960
59.	Outlines from the Outpost by John Esten Cooke .	1961

Number	Title	Year
60.	Colorado Volunteers in New Mexico, 1862 by Ovando J. Hollister	1962
61.	Private Smith's Journal	1963
62.	Two Views of Gettysburg by Sir A. J. L. Fremantle and Frank Haskell	1964
63.	Dakota War Whoop by Harriet E. Bishop McConkey	1965
64.	Honolulu by Laura Fish Judd	1966
65.	Three Years in the Klondike by Jeremiah Lynch	1967
66.	Two Years' Residence on the English Prairie of Illinois by John Woods	1968
67.	John D. Young and the Colorado Gold Rush	1969
68.	My Experiences in the West by John S. Collins	1970
69.	Narratives of Colonial America, 1704-1765	1971
70.	Pioneers by Noah Harris Letts and Thomas Allen Banning, 1825-1865	1972
71.	Excursion Through America by Nicolaus Mohr	1973
72.	A Frenchman in Lincoln's America, Volume I, by Ernest Duvergier de Hauranne	1974
73.	A Frenchman in Lincoln's America, Volume II, by Ernest Duvergier de Hauranne	1975
74.	Narratives of the American Revolution	1976
75.	Advocates and Adversaries by Robert R. Rose	1977
76.	Hell among the Yearlings by Edmund Randolph	1978
77.	A Frontier Doctor by Henry F. Hoyt	1979
78.	Mrs. Hill's Journal – Civil War Reminiscences by Sarah Jane Full Hill	1980
79.	Skyward by Rear Admiral Richard E. Byrd	1981

Number	*Title*	*Year*
80.	Helldorado by William M. Breakenridge	1982
81.	Mark Twain's West	1983
82.	Frontier Fighter by George W. Coe	1984
83.	Buckskin and Blanket Days by Thomas Henry Tibbles	1985
84.	Autobiography of an English Soldier in the United States Army by George Ballentine	1986
85.	Life of Tom Horn	1987
86.	Children of Ol' Man River by Billy Bryant	1988
87.	Westward Journeys by Jesse A. Applegate and Lavinia Honeyman Porter	1989
88.	Narrative of My Captivity among the Sioux Indians by Fanny Kelly	1990
89.	We Pointed Them North by E. C. "Teddy Blue" Abbott and Helena Huntington Smith	1991
90.	A Texas Ranger by N. A. Jennings	1992